Nan D. Hunter is a professor of law at Brooklyn Law School. She is the coauthor with William Eskridge of the casebook, *Sexuality, Gender, and the Law.* In 1986, she founded and became the first director of the ACLU Lesbian and Gay Rights Project and the ACLU AIDS Project. She is the author of numerous articles in the fields of constitutional law, health law, and sexuality and gender law.

Courtney G. Joslin is a staff attorney at the National Center for Lesbian Rights, where she works primarily on family law and youth issues. After graduating from Harvard Law School, she clerked on the Rhode Island Supreme Court and the U.S. District Court for the Northern District of California. Joslin is the author of several articles and publications on LGBT rights.

Sharon M. McGowan currently works at the National Legal Department of the ACLU in New York as the William J. Brennan First Amendment Fellow. Prior to joining the ACLU, she was an associate at Jenner & Block in Washington, D.C., where she served as co-counsel with Lambda Legal Defense & Education Fund on the groundbreaking case of *Lawrence v. Texas.* She is also a contributing author to *Lesbian and Gay Law Notes.* McGowan graduated from Harvard Law School cum laude and clerked on the U.S. Court of Appeals for the First Circuit and the U.S. District Court for the Eastern District of Louisiana.

THE RIGHTS OF LESBIANS, GAY MEN, BISEXUALS, AND TRANSGENDER PEOPLE

The Authoritative ACLU Guide to
a Lesbian, Gay, Bisexual, or Transgender Person's Rights

Fourth Edition

Nan D. Hunter
Courtney G. Joslin
Sharon M. McGowan

General Editor of the Handbook Series
Eve Cary

SOUTHERN ILLINOIS UNIVERSITY PRESS
CARBONDALE

Library of Congress Cataloging-in-Publication Data

Hunter, Nan D.
The rights of lesbians, gay men, bisexuals, and transgender people : the authoritative ACLU guide
to a lesbian, gay, bisexual, or transgender person's rights / Nan D. Hunter, Courtney G. Joslin,
Sharon M. McGowan.— 4th ed.
p. cm. — (An American Civil Liberties Union handbook.)
Includes bibliographical references and index.
1. Gay rights—United States. 2. Homosexuality—Law and legislation—United States.
3. Bisexuals—Legal status, laws, etc.—United States. 4. Transsexuals—Legal status, laws, etc.—
United States. I. Joslin, Courtney G., date. II. McGowan, Sharon M., date.
III. Title. IV. Series.

KF4754.5.Z9 H86 2004
342.73′087—dc21
ISBN 0-8093-2518-7 (pbk. : alk. paper)   2003010471

Contents

Introduction to the ACLU Handbook Series
Eve Cary, General Editor

This book is one of a series published in cooperation with the American Civil Liberties Union (ACLU), which are designed to inform individuals about their rights in particular areas of law. A guiding principle of the ACLU is that an informed citizenry is the best guarantee that the government will respect individual civil liberties. These publications carry the hope that individuals informed of their rights will be encouraged to exercise them. In this way, rights are given life. If rights are rarely used, however, they may be forgotten and violations may become routine.

In order to understand and exercise individual rights, it is important to know something about how our legal system works. The basic document that sets up our legal system is the United States Constitution. The Constitution explains how we elect the government of the United States and provides the government with the specific powers it needs to run the country. These include the power to pass laws that are "necessary and proper" for carrying out the other powers. The government does not have the authority to do anything that the Constitution does not permit it to do. Therefore, a better question to ask than "Do I have the right to do this?" is "Does the government have the right to stop me from doing this?"

Although the government may not deny a citizen the right to do something unless the Constitution gives it the power to do so, the framers of the Constitution thought certain rights are so critical they should be specifically guaranteed. Therefore, the framers added ten amendments, known as the Bill of Rights, that are among the most important rights the government may never deny to its citizens. Four of the amendments to the Constitution are particularly important for individuals seeking to understand their rights in relation to the government.

The First Amendment contains two important statements. The first is that "Congress shall make no law . . . abridging freedom of speech, or of the press; or the right of the people peaceably to assemble, and to petition the government for a redress of grievances." This means that a person cannot be forbidden from or punished for expressing opinions out loud or in print, either individually or with a group of people, as long as he or she does it at a reasonable time and in a reasonable place and manner.

The second statement of the First Amendment is that "Congress shall make no law respecting an establishment of religion, or prohibiting the free exercise thereof." This means that the government may neither prohibit nor encourage the practice of a particular religion; indeed, government may not encourage the practice of religion at all. In short, religion is none of the government's business.

The Fourth Amendment says, "The right of the people to be secure in their persons, houses, papers, and effects, against unreasonable searches and seizures, shall not be violated, and no Warrants shall issue, but upon probable cause, supported by Oath or affirmation, and particularly describing the place to be searched, and the persons or things to be seized." This means that the police may neither search a person nor anything he or she is carrying, nor may they make an arrest, unless they have a very good reason for believing that the person has committed a crime. Moreover, they may not search a house or other private place without a warrant signed by a judge who has decided it is reasonable to believe that the person involved has committed a crime. (Note that the police have more leeway in searching automobiles.)

The Fifth Amendment says, "No person shall . . . be deprived of life, liberty, or property without due process of law." This means that the government may not punish individuals without giving them a fair chance to defend themselves.

In addition to the rights guaranteed by the Bill of Rights, the Fourteenth Amendment says, "No State shall deprive any person of life, liberty or property without due process of law; nor deny to any person within its jurisdiction the equal protection of the laws." This amendment means that, just as the federal government may not punish individuals without giving them a fair chance to defend themselves, the government of a state may not do so either. Moreover, all laws must apply equally to all citizens who are in the same situation as one another. For example, the government may not pass a law saying that people of one race or sex or religion are allowed to do something that people of another race or sex or religion are not allowed to do. (It may, however, pass laws that apply to children but not to adults, since children are not always in the same situation as adults. For example, laws requiring children but not adults to go to school are constitutional, as are laws prohibiting children from buying alcohol and cigarettes.)

Before going any further, it is important to understand two things. First, when we talk about "the government" in this book, we mean not only elected officials but also the people who are hired to work for the government, such as police officers and public school principals. All of these people must obey the Constitution when they are performing their jobs.

Second, the Constitution applies *only* to the people who work for the government. It does not apply to private individuals or people who work in the private sector. This means, for example, that while the principal of a public school may not make students say prayers in class because that would violate the First Amendment guarantee of freedom of religion, students in parochial or other private schools may be required to pray.

In addition to the United States Constitution, each state also has its own constitution. Many of the provisions of these state constitutions are the same as those in the United States Constitution, but they apply only to the actions of state officials. Thus, a public school principal in New York is prohibited from holding religious services in school, not just by the federal Constitution but also by the New York State Constitution. While a state may not deny its citizens rights guaranteed by the United States Constitution, it may, and often does, provide more rights. For example, while the Supreme Court has held that the death penalty does not violate the federal constitution, the Massachusetts Supreme Court has held that it does violate the Massachusetts Constitution.

Although federal and state constitutions do not oversee the actions of the private sector, limitations on personal behavior do exist. Both Congress and all of the state legislatures pass laws that apply to the private sector. The laws enacted by Congress are for the entire country. Those passed by the state legislatures are just for the people of that state. Thus, for example, people in New York may have more or fewer or different rights and obligations than do the people in Louisiana. In fact, in Louisiana anyone over the age of eighteen can buy alcohol, while in other states the legal drinking age is twenty-one.

Just as we have separate federal and state governments, we also have separate systems of federal courts and state courts. The job of the federal courts is to interpret laws passed by Congress; the job of the state courts is to interpret laws passed by their own state legislatures. Both courts have the power to interpret the United States Constitution. State courts may, in addition, interpret their own state constitutions.

In this book, you will read about lawsuits that individuals have brought in both federal and state courts asking the courts to declare that certain actions by state officials are illegal or unconstitutional. In the federal system, these suits are filed in a district court, which is a trial court that decides cases in a particular district. The district court hears the evidence and reaches a decision. The losing party may then appeal to one of the thirteen circuit courts of appeals, which hear appeals from several districts. The loser in the Circuit court may ask the Supreme Court of the United States to decide the case. Because the Supreme Court agrees to hear only a small fraction of the cases that litigants wish to bring before it, as a practical matter, the circuit court is usually the court of last resort. Each state also has its own court system. All are a little different from one another, but each works in basically the same way as the federal court system, beginning with a trial court, which hears evidence, followed by two levels of appellate courts.

In such a complicated system, it is inevitable that courts may disagree about how to interpret a particular law. When this occurs, the answer to the question "What are my rights?" may be "It depends where you live." Moreover, the law may change; in some areas of law, it is changing very rapidly. An effort has been made in this book to indicate areas of the law in which movement is taking place, but it is not always possible to predict precisely when this will happen or what the changes will be.

If you believe that your rights have been violated, you should, of course, seek legal assistance. The ACLU affiliate office in your state may be able to guide you to the available legal resources. If you consult a lawyer, take this book with you as he or she may not be familiar with the law applicable to your particular situation. You should be aware, however, that litigation is usually expensive, takes a long time, and carries with it no guarantee of success. Fortunately, litigation is not always necessary to vindicate legal rights. On occasion, government officials themselves are not aware of their legal obligations to respect the rights of individuals and may change their practices or policies when confronted by an individual who is well informed about the law. We hope that this book will help provide the basic information about the legal principles applicable to this area of law and will, as well, suggest arguments that you might make on your own behalf to secure your rights.

This introduction is being written in the aftermath of the terrorist attacks on the World Trade Center and on the Pentagon. It is precisely at times of national stress like these that civil liberties come under attack. It is therefore crucial in such times that Americans rededicate themselves to protecting the precious liberties that our Constitution and laws guarantee us. This book is part of that effort.

PREFACE

This book offers a map for navigating the turbulent and constantly changing waters of the law of sexual orientation and gender identity. It is the fourth edition of a work first published in 1975, and the changes that have occurred in the structure and perspective of this book reflect the changes in the law that it discusses.

The authors of the first edition began their introduction as follows: "Upon hearing that we were undertaking to write a book on the rights of gays, a wit remarked: 'it must be a very short book.'" Although much change is reflected in the simple fact that the book has gotten longer, the most significant changes have been in its content rather than in its volume. In some instances, the deletions are as notable as the additions.

For example, the first edition contained chapters on discrimination related to occupational licenses and security clearances, topics that no longer merit a chapter's worth of attention because those legal problems have so greatly diminished. Other fields have expanded, and for positive reasons. Instead of one chapter each on employment and family issues, as in prior editions, we now have separate chapters on employment in the public sector and employment in the private sector and separate chapters on relationships and parenting issues. The expanded coverage signals not more problems but the creation of entirely new fields of employment and family law generated by the demands of growing numbers of people for equality and respect.

Most obviously, the title has changed, for the second time. In the third edition, the title used for the first two editions—*The Rights of Gay People* —was changed to *The Rights of Lesbians and Gay Men*. For this edition, we changed it again, to *The Rights of Lesbians, Gay Men, Bisexuals, and Transgender People*. Although this phrase is somewhat unwieldy, we used it because of the importance of recognizing specificity and difference within our own community and especially because of the strong link between sexual orientation and transgender issues. Thus, you will see the abbreviation LGBT throughout the book.

Some developments in the realm of LGBT civil rights law occurred so close to the publication of this book that their full impact could not be known. For example, in June 2003, the United States Supreme Court struck down consensual sodomy laws as unconstitutional. This decision, *Lawrence v. Texas* (discussed in chap. 2), will likely have a positive impact not only on criminal law but also in all other areas where liberty, equality, and human dignity are governing principles. Likewise, in November 2003, the Massachusetts Supreme Judicial Court (the highest court in that state) ruled that the state could not deny same-sex couples access to the civil institution of marriage. The court postponed the implementation of its decision in *Goodridge v. Department of Public Health* (discussed in chap. 9) for 180 days, meaning that as this book goes to press, same-sex couples could not yet marry in Massachusetts. Just as with *Lawrence*, the full impact of the *Goodridge* decision will not be known for years to come, and certainly will not be limited to the realm of family law.

In fact, both of these decisions will likely influence all areas of the law that impact the lives of LGBT people (discussed in the other eleven chapters of this book). Although it is impossible to make any concrete predictions, we believe that one thing is clear—the tide has turned with regard to the treatment of lesbian, gay, bisexual, and transgender people under the law.

Ultimately, this is a book about the value of diversity and the right to dissent. It is remarkable how often courts have ignored these fundamental constitutional principles when cases involve some aspect of human sexuality or gender identity. The antidiscrimination efforts chronicled herein reflect nothing so much as the fight to force the government and other institutions to adhere to these elementary precepts when dealing with issues of sexual orientation and gender identity. How society treats LGBT people serves as a social barometer for the degree to which the nation will honor its promise to respect those who dissent from any set of political or cultural conventions.

We offer this book as a tool to help readers who encounter unjust treatment. It is not, however, a substitute for legal advice. Indeed, one warning that recurs frequently in these pages is the need to secure competent and sympathetic counsel. But the book provides an overview for understanding general themes in legal doctrine and for starting the process of asserting rights provided by the law.

Toward that end, we have included two appendices in addition to the main text. The first contains contact information for national and regional LGBT legal groups. The second provides an overview of the legal system to help explain some of the terms and concepts that appear throughout the book.

Most importantly, we invite each of you to become part of the process of changing the law—by claiming those rights that the law has already recognized, by seeking to establish the next frontier of rights, and by supporting those brave individuals who refuse to be treated as second-class citizens. When one strips away the jargon and the formalities, the bedrock truth is that people make the law. We invite you to join the fight for justice.

ACKNOWLEDGMENTS

This book has benefited from the labors of many people. We especially note our thanks to the following individuals:

To those of our colleagues who read and commented on drafts—Michael Adams, Mary Bonauto, Matthew Coles, Sheryl Harris, Jennifer Levi, Martha Matthews, Jennifer Middleton, Shannon Minter, Judy Rabinowitz, Jennifer Richard, and Stacey Sobel
To the law students who worked many hours to provide research assistance— Tony Brown, Robin Fukuyama, Melissa Gable, Emily Kern, George Thomas Kochilas, Theone Luong, Jodie Marksamer, Lisa Mottet, Simon Stern, and John Sweeney
To the clerical and support staff who make all such projects possible—Tim Altmeyer, Gaynor Cunningham, Kai Byuhl Jo, and Golda Lawrence

We also want to acknowledge the authors of previous editions of this book upon whose work we have built—E. Carrington Boggan, Marilyn G. Haft, Charles Lister, Sherryl E. Michaelson, John P. Rupp, and Thomas B. Stoddard.

Finally, there are those to whom we owe special thanks, for their many and diverse forms of support:

To all those who have been family to me, from Nan
To my family and, in particular, Carolyn Gramstorff, from Courtney
To Ginger Berrigan, Gerald Frug, the McGowans, and above all, Kerry Quinn, from Sharon

PART 1
Sexual Orientation and the State

1

Expression: The Right *Not* to Be Silent

The rights that are perhaps most commonly associated with our freedoms as Americans are our freedoms of speech and expression. For lesbian, gay, bisexual, and transgender people, these rights are especially important, as they directly influence our ability to come out and enjoy an open and proud existence in our day-to-day lives. The contours of our constitutional freedoms, however, are more complicated than the absolute language contained in the First Amendment might suggest. This section explains the extent to which the Constitution protects the speech and expression of LGBT people, as well as the scenarios in which it may be wise to exercise those rights with a heightened sense of caution.

Do I have the right to join a lesbian, gay, bisexual, or transgender (LGBT) organization?

Yes. The First Amendment's guarantees of freedom of speech and association and the Fifth and Fourteenth Amendments' protection of liberty mean that you have the right to join a lesbian, gay, bisexual, or transgender organization or to start your own organization. This is true whether the organization is intended to foster the discussion of LGBT issues, to promote social interaction, or to engage in political advocacy.[1] Unfortunately, however, even though you have the right to join an LGBT organization, the First Amendment does not prohibit people—including private employers—from discriminating against you because of your membership. Nevertheless, no one can prevent you from joining.

May I keep my membership secret from the government?

Under most circumstances, you cannot be required to disclose your membership in an LGBT organization. Cases from the era of the African American civil rights movement protect the rights of organizations to keep the names of their members confidential.[2] The courts have recognized that many individuals would not join organizations that support unpopular positions if they could not do so anonymously.[3] In some instances, however, voluntary organizations may be required to provide certain information to government-reporting agencies—namely, when the government has a "compelling interest" in the information. This means that the government's need for the information must be so important or urgent that it outweighs your interest in association.[4] For example, organizations with tax-exempt status may have to reveal information to the Internal Revenue Service (IRS) about the sources of their income.[5] Organizations that participate in electoral politics through lobbying or campaign contributions may also be required under state and federal election laws to report information about major donors.[6] But in general, the Supreme Court has recognized that forced disclosure of the names of people who contribute to organizations that espouse unpopular views can undermine the associational rights of members, and it has ruled that those organizations cannot be forced to divulge names of contributors. The same principle that has been applied to contributors is also true of membership lists.[7]

Could I ever be forced to tell my employer that I am a member?

If you are an employee of a governmental agency, the First Amendment generally protects you from being required to disclose your membership in organizations. For public schoolteachers, however, the situation is more complex. The Supreme Court has held that teachers have "obligations of frankness, candor and cooperation in answering inquiries" from the school board about their fitness to teach.[8] In 1974, for instance, a federal court of appeals decided the case of a teacher who did not reveal the fact that he was involved in a gay student organization in college when he was asked on a questionnaire about extracurricular activities.[9] The court upheld the school's decision to transfer him to an administrative position on the grounds that he had misrepresented himself. As schools and courts become more comfortable with the idea that homosexuality is not incompatible with teaching children,[10] these cases may be relegated to the past. Some school systems now recruit LGBT teachers, and others that have fired gay teachers have had those decisions overturned in court.[11] (See chapter 3 for more details.)

If you are ever asked to disclose this information, it is important for you to realize that the Constitution does not protect any "right" to lie. In order to protect your constitutional rights, you should consult with a lawyer and decide whether to answer the question. Refusing to answer is one thing; offering false information, on the other hand, is something entirely different. You may face criminal prosecution, civil penalties, or both when, for example, you sign an affidavit and swear under penalty of perjury that the statements contained in the form or application are true. You may even forfeit your ability to challenge the policy under which you were asked the question in the first place.[12]

As a general matter, the Constitution does not apply to the actions of private individuals or organizations; it applies only to actions *by the government*. Therefore, private employers may ask you to disclose your group affiliations, but it is up to you to decide whether or not to disclose them. While other antidiscrimination laws might prevent an employer from asking questions that are completely irrelevant to job qualifications and are being used merely as pretexts for discrimination, the First Amendment only prevents action by the state that censors, compels, or otherwise chills free speech. A dishonest answer on a job application, if discovered, might have negative consequences, including termination. An honest answer might prevent you from being hired. For a more detailed discussion of what to do in the employment context, see chapters 3 and 6.

Do I have the right to go to an LGBT rights parade or be an LGBT rights activist and not lose my job?

In states or cities with no laws prohibiting discrimination against LGBT employees, coming-out speech or political activity could lead to your termination. There is no absolute right to be involved in political activity without risk of losing your job. Private employers generally have broad rights to fire employees for activities with which they disagree, even if the activity happens in the workers' off-duty time. For instance, in a 1995 Pennsylvania case, the court found no violation of state or federal law when an employer fired an employee who appeared on a local television program, identified himself as a gay man, and spoke out against homophobic violence.[13] Some states, including those that lack antidiscrimination laws, may have specific laws protecting employees who engage in political activity or other types of off-work conduct from retaliation by their public- or private-sector employers.[14]

Although most states do not have laws that forbid employers from firing an employee because of political activism, public employees do have some protection. Public employees are shielded by the First Amendment, and though the protection is limited, it does mean that in many cases, government employers may not retaliate against you for your political activity or speech so long as the speech is not disruptive to the workplace. Although some early cases allowed public employers to fire employees for "flaunting" their homosexuality by, for example, becoming a plaintiff in same-sex marriage litigation or by simply talking openly about their lives,[15] other decisions have protected the right of LGBT people to be involved in a range of political advocacy, including making public speeches in support of LGBT rights[16] and talking to the media.[17]

If I choose not to come out, will the law protect me against disclosures of my sexual orientation?

The constitutional right to privacy encompasses an individual's right to avoid the involuntary disclosure of personal matters.[18] A federal court of appeals has recognized that sexual orientation is "an intimate aspect" of one's personality and is therefore "entitled to privacy protection."[19] In *Sterling v. Borough of Minersville,* an eighteen-year-old killed himself after the police officer who arrested him and his male friend threatened to disclose his sexuality to his grandfather. After learning about the events leading up to her son's death, the deceased's mother sued the borough and the officers involved. The court acknowledged that the state may in some circumstances be entitled to disclose such highly personal information, but only when the government interest in doing so is "genuine, legitimate and compelling."[20] Even though the police officer never actually disclosed the information, the court found the threat to disclose sufficient to violate the deceased's constitutional rights because the "security of [his] privacy ha[d] been compromised by the threat of disclosure."[21]

When the disclosing party is a private individual rather than a government agent, recourse may be had through civil litigation. A party who publicly discloses private facts about an individual may be held liable if the information is of the kind that would be "highly offensive to a reasonable person" and "is not of legitimate concern to the public."[22] The First Amendment, however, significantly restricts the ability of an individual to recover damages for the disclosure of such information,[23] and some states have rejected this cause of action entirely.[24] Therefore, any victim of "outing" would need to examine what claims are available in a particular jurisdiction before filing suit.

May the police prohibit peaceful demonstrations by LGBT rights groups?

No. The state may only regulate the "time, place and manner" of public demonstrations. Moreover, such regulations must do so in a way that leaves open ample alternatives for communication.[25] Courts have specifically upheld the right of LGBT people to march, to demonstrate, or to have a parade without regard to the state's approval or disapproval of their message.[26]

May the police require a permit for LGBT demonstrations?

Yes, but it cannot be conditioned on the government's approval of the demonstrators' message.[27] The state may take into account considerations such as traffic flow[28] or the desire of multiple groups to protest in a particular area,[29] but agencies must narrowly tailor such regulations so that any restriction on speech is minimal.[30] The state also may not give officials so much discretion that they have the authority to deny permit applications based on "broad criteria unrelated to proper regulation of public places."[31]

May the organizers of a parade prohibit my LGBT group from marching in their event?

Yes. Parade organizers have the right to control the message being conveyed by their parade, and that includes the decision about who may participate in their event. The Supreme Court, in *Hurley v. Irish-American Gay, Lesbian and Bisexual Group of Boston*,[32] upheld the right of the South Boston Allied War Veterans Council to exclude GLIB, an LGBT Irish group, from a St. Patrick's Day parade. The parade organizers were allowed to exclude GLIB even though they had included a wide range of other organizations in their celebration. If, however, a parade is a citywide celebration sponsored by a governmental entity rather than by a private group, the right to access to public places guaranteed by the First Amendment will apply. In general, it will be much easier to sponsor your own event than to force other private organizations to include your group in their events.

Does my LGBT rights group have the right to advertise in public spaces such as buses or subways?

A public transit system is not required to make spaces available for advertising,[33] but once it opens the space to some political groups, it may not discriminate against LGBT organizations.[34] This includes advertising spaces on subways,[35] the exterior of buses,[36] and bus shelters that are publicly owned, as well as those owned and maintained by a private entity acting in conjunction with the state.[37] (If the bus shelter is found to be truly private property, however, the First Amendment would permit its owner to select which advertisements to accept.)

May we show our video on public television or buy a television or radio ad?

No one has a "right" of access to air time.[38] Congress has decided to adopt a system whereby private individuals hold broadcast licenses, and those license holders are "trustees" for the general public. Although the license holders have a duty to present "representative community views and voices on controversial issues which are of importance to [their] listeners," they ultimately have the editorial discretion to decide how best to fulfill their obligation.[39] According to the Supreme Court, this scheme adequately protects individuals because broadcasters who abuse their discretion may be penalized by having their license awarded to someone else. Even though many broadcasters in fact only provide a forum for the expression of others' views (rather than their own), the Supreme Court has made clear that the First Amendment's protections regarding speech also incorporate broadcasters' choices about what to air.[40] As a result, no individual can force a broadcaster to air a particular program or advertisement.

Previously, under a series of Federal Communications Commission (FCC) rulings known collectively as the *fairness doctrine,* radio and television broadcasters were required to discuss public issues and give all sides of an issue fair coverage.[41] As part of this policy, broadcasters had to give individuals or groups time to reply to personal attacks or political statements.[42] In 1987, the FCC announced that it was abandoning the fairness doctrine because it was "no longer constitutional or in the public interest."[43] The Court of Appeals for the D.C. Circuit affirmed the FCC's decision to renounce the policy but reserved judgment on the issue of the constitutionality of the fairness doctrine in general.[44] In 2000, the D.C. Circuit ordered the FCC to repeal the regulations regarding mandatory response time for personal attacks and political statements in light of the fact that the agency had failed to issue any kind of decision in a First Amendment challenge to these provisions that had been pending for over two decades.[45] Although the court issued its ruling primarily as a rebuke of the agency's inaction, the opinion also expressed grave concerns about the constitutionality of any policy that imposed a duty on private broadcasters to provide response time to a party on demand.

The rules granting broad discretion to programmers may not always apply in the context of public-broadcasting channels. In *CBS v. Democratic National Committee,* one Supreme Court justice argued that the Corporation for Public Broadcasting, the congressional agency responsible for public-television programming, should not have the same discretion as private license holders. He suggested that the government "as owner and manager would not . . . be free to pick and choose such news items as it desired" and could not let "politics, ideological slants [or] rightist or leftists tendencies" influence its programming decisions.[46] This view has not been adopted in a majority opinion, however, and as yet, the Supreme Court has not clearly ruled on whether public broadcasters must be neutral in deciding what to broadcast.

May the government censor publications or artistic materials on the grounds that LGBT material is obscene?

To censor written or visual material as obscene, the government must satisfy the test laid out in *Miller v. California,* which asks (a) whether the "average person, applying contemporary community standards" would find that the work, taken as a whole, appeals to the prurient interest; (b) whether the work depicts or describes, in a patently offensive way, sexual conduct specifically defined by the applicable state law; and (c) whether the work, taken as a whole, lacks serious literary, artistic, political, or scientific value.[47] Unless all three parts of this test are met, a work cannot be censored as obscene. The simple fact that a work is homoerotic is not enough. For example, when the city of Cincinnati prosecuted a museum director for displaying the controversial works of Robert Mapplethorpe, most famous for his photographs of male nudes and men engaging in sexual activities, the jury refused to find that the exhibit lacked "serious artistic value," meaning that it could not be classified as obscene.[48]

Some states offer greater protection to sexual speech under their state constitutions than the federal constitution provides. For example, Oregon does not allow obscenity prosecutions; it protects this speech to the same degree that all other speech is protected.[49]

May the government deny funding for LGBT art?

Sometimes it may. In *National Endowment for the Arts v. Finley*, the Supreme Court announced that the government may make its decisions regarding which artists to fund with state money by taking into consideration general standards of "decency" and "respect."[50] Specifically, the Court held that when the government is acting as a patron of the arts, it may selectively choose to underwrite some activities and not others based on its subjective belief that particular projects promote the public interest.[51] Therefore, LGBT artists, along with those who, through their artistic expression, do not satisfy the ostensibly "neutral" criteria of promoting decency and respect for traditional American values, cannot compel the government to fund their work on an equal basis.

As a general matter, however, the state may not attempt to suppress disfavored viewpoints by wielding its spending power in a discriminatory fashion.[52] The Court's ruling in *Finley* was contingent on its view that "decency" did not constitute a viewpoint; therefore, it was not impermissible viewpoint discrimination to require that art be "decent" in order to be eligible for funding from the National Endowment of the Arts. The Supreme Court has further recognized that even when the state uses viewpoint-neutral factors to make its funding decisions, an individual may be able to prove that the First Amendment has been violated if he or she can demonstrate that the criteria are being applied in a manner that is designed to drive certain disfavored points of view from the marketplace of ideas.[53]

In general, are LGBT groups eligible for government funding and tax-exempt status?

Yes. Many LGBT organizations receive government grants for a variety of reasons, often for social and health services. A federal appeals court ruled that a gay and lesbian student organization that had already won official recognition from a public university could not later be denied funding on the basis of the viewpoints that the organization espoused.[54] Likewise, if an LGBT group otherwise qualifies for tax-exempt, tax-deductible status, the IRS's own rules make clear that the group should be treated no differently than any other charitable or educational organization.[55] Since issuing this rule in 1978, the IRS has approved the applications of numerous LGBT groups for tax-exempt status.

May our Web site be censored in any way?

Private Internet servers such as America Online are not the government and therefore can censor the content of a Web site without violating any First Amendment rights.[56] The government, on the other hand, may not censor a Web site unless it does so in a manner that is narrowly tailored to further a compelling state interest.[57] Nevertheless, the federal government has sought to impose liability for the publication of certain material over the Internet, and LGBT Web sites are frequently swept up in the hysteria.[58] Congress's first attempt to censor the Internet, the Communications Decency Act, was struck down by the Supreme Court as a violation of the First Amendment in *ACLU v. Reno.*[59] Undeterred, Congress passed a second law called the Child Online Protection Act (COPA), which prohibits Internet users from using the Internet to communicate material that would be deemed "patently offensive as measured by contemporary community standards" to minors under the age of eighteen.[60] The ACLU once again challenged the constitutionality of this Internet regulation, and the U.S. Court of Appeals for the Third Circuit struck down the law on the grounds that it was overbroad and penalized constitutionally protected activity.[61] The Supreme Court agreed that this law raised significant constitutional doubts and could not be enforced until such doubts were resolved but remanded the case so that the lower court could consider a wider range of First Amendment issues.[62] After receiving additional briefing from the parties, the Third Circuit reaffirmed its decision that COPA ran afoul of the First Amendment.[63] In October 2003, the Supreme Court agreed to review the Third Circuit's second decision,[64] with oral argument scheduled to occur after publication of this book.

Do I have the right to access LGBT Web sites from computers in public libraries?

In most cases, adult library patrons should be able to access these Web sites.[65] While librarians have the discretion to decide what books to stock on their shelves, a library may not prevent its patrons from accessing a particular Web site based on the viewpoint expressed there.

A library may, however, be able to prevent patrons from using its library computers to access sexually explicit sites, but the Supreme Court has not yet considered that particular issue. In a 2003 decision regarding libraries and the Internet, the Supreme Court upheld a federal law called the Children's Internet Protection Act (CIPA), which requires public libraries to install so-called technology protection measures—that is, filtering software—on their computers as a condition of receiving federal government funds.[66] Justice Anthony Kennedy and Justice Stephen Breyer, who provided the necessary votes to uphold the law against a facial constitutional challenge, noted that CIPA allows adult patrons to ask librarians to disable the filtering software, thus preserving full access to the Internet for adults. Their opinions left open the possibility, however, that practical difficulties with disabling the software or a lack of cooperation by librarians might render this law unconstitutional as applied in a particular case. The rights of minors to access particular Web sites on public library computers is also highly uncertain. The ACLU and other critics of filtering software have repeatedly demonstrated that not only are these programs ineffective in screening out obscene material but they are also invalid under the First Amendment because they inadvertently block vast amounts of constitutionally protected information.[67] Challenges to these and other Internet censorship laws are ongoing, and so the law in this area will continue to evolve rapidly.

If we want to send our publication into prisons, may the prison officials censor our materials?

In most circumstances, they may. Prison officials may censor materials that they believe will have an adverse effect on the prison environment without violating the First Amendment so long as the regulation is "reasonably related to legitimate penological interests."[68] Mere disagreement with or distaste for the message in the publication does not justify censorship, but the courts are extremely unwilling to second-guess prison officials regarding their evaluation of the types of material that may undermine the security or stability of a penal facility.[69] For example, in some cases, prison officials have been permitted to censor gay-related materials by arguing that they can promote sex among the inmates in violation of prison regulations.[70] Other rationales that courts have approved for censorship of sexually explicit material include the prevention of harassment of female prison guards and the rehabilitation of inmates.[71]

Although courts previously offered greater protection to the First Amendment interests of short-term detainees who had not yet been convicted of any crime, there may no longer be a distinction between pretrial detention centers (i.e., jails) and long-term prison facilities.[71] Some prison censorship policies, however, have been struck down as so broad that they were not rationally related to the asserted penological interest at stake. For example, the Court of Appeals for the Ninth Circuit invalidated one prison's ban on the receipt of all subscription nonprofit-organization mail.[72] Other prison regulations have been successfully challenged on the grounds that they were unconstitutionally vague as to the type of information that would be censored.[73]

NOTES

1. *See Gay Students Org. v. Bonner,* 367 F. Supp. 1088 (D.N.H.), *modified,* 509 F.2d 652 (1st Cir. 1974); *Owles v. Lomenzo,* 329 N.Y.S.2d 181, 38 A.D.2d 981 (App. Div. 1972), *aff'd sub nom, Gay Activists Alliance v. Lomenzo,* 341 N.Y.S.2d 108, 293 N.E.2d 255 (1973).

2. *See NAACP v. Alabama ex rel. Patterson,* 357 U.S. 449, 465 (1958); *NAACP v. Alabama ex rel. Flowers,* 377 U.S. 288 (1964).

3. *See Bates v. City of Little Rock,* 361 U.S. 516, 527 (1960); *Shelton v. Tucker,* 364 U.S. 479 (1960).

4. *See California Bankers Ass'n v. Shultz,* 416 U.S. 21 (1974); *NAACP v. Committee on Offenses Against Admin. of Justice,* 204 Va. 693, 133 S.E.2d 540 (1963).

5. *See* 26 U.S.C. § 501.

6. *See Buckley v. Valeo,* 424 U.S. 1 (1976).

7. *See Ex parte Lowe,* 887 S.W.2d 1 (Tex. 1994) (Ku Klux Klan (KKK) membership list protected); *but see Marshall v. Bramer,* 828 F.2d 355 (6th Cir. 1987) (requiring disclosure, under seal, of KKK membership list after firebombing attack).

8. *Beilan v. Board of Pub. Educ., Sch. Dist. of Phila.,* 357 U.S. 399, 406 (1958).

9. *See Acanfora v. Board of Educ. of Montgomery County,* 491 F.2d 498 (4th Cir. 1974).

10. *See, e.g., Irizarry v. Board of Educ. of Chicago,* 251 F.3d 604 (7th Cir. 2001) (affirming the right of school board to offer domestic-partner benefits only to same-sex rather than to all unmarried partners). Other school boards that have demonstrated their support of gay and lesbian teachers include Hartford, Connecticut, and Madison, Wisconsin, both of which offer same-sex partner benefits to teachers in their school systems, and Anchorage, Alaska, where official school-board policy prohibits harassment of students and employees on the basis of sexual orientation.

11. For an example that may represent a new trend in cases regarding gay teachers, see *Weaver v. Nebo Sch. Dist.,* 29 F. Supp. 2d 1279 (D. Utah 1998).

12. *See Acanfora, supra* note 9.

13. *See DeMuth v. Miller,* 438 Pa. Super. Ct. 437, 652 A.2d 891 (1995).

14. *See Cal. Labor Code* § 1101; Col. Rev. Stat. Ann. § 8-2-102.

15. *McConnell v. Anderson,* 451 F.2d 193 (8th Cir. 1971); *Gish v. Board of Educ. of Paramus,* 145 N.J. Super. 96, 366 A.2d 1337 (App. Div. 1976); *Singer v. United States Civil Serv. Comm'n,* 530 F.2d 247 (9th Cir. 1976), *vacated,* 429 U.S. 1034 (1977).

16. *National Gay Task Force v. Board of Educ. of Oklahoma City,* 729 F.2d 1270 (10th Cir. 1984), *aff'd by an equally divided court,* 470 U.S. 903 (1985).

17. *Acanfora, supra* note 9; *Aumiller v. University of Del.,* 434 F. Supp. 1273 (D. Del. 1977).

18. *Whalen v. Roe,* 429 U.S. 589, 599 (1977); *Nixon v. Administrator of Gen. Servs.,* 433 U.S. 425, 457 (1977) (accord).

19. *Sterling v. Borough of Minersville,* 232 F.3d 190, 196 (3d Cir. 2000).

20. *Id.* at 195–96 (quoting *Doe v. Southeastern Pa. Transp. Auth.,* 72 F.3d 1133, 1141 (3d Cir. 1995)).

21. *Id.* at 197.

22. Restatement (2d) of Torts, § 652D. *See also* Barbara Moretti, "Outing: Justifiable or Unwarranted Invasion of Privacy? The Private Facts Tort as a Remedy for Disclosures of Sexual Orientation," 11 *Cardozo Arts & Ent. L.J.* 857 (1993).

23. *See New York Times Co. v. Sullivan,* 376 U.S. 254 (1964).

24. *See, e.g., Hall v. Post,* 323 N.C. 259, 372 S.E.2d 711 (1988).

25. *Forsyth County, Ga. v. Nationalist Movement,* 505 U.S. 123, 130 (1992) (citing *United States v. Grace,* 461 U.S. 171, 177 (1983)).

26. *See Irish Lesbian and Gay Org. v. Giuliani,* 143 F.3d 638, 649 (2d Cir. 1998) ("If ILGO proves this to be the case [i.e., that the permit denial stemmed from disapproval of ILGO's message], then it will be entitled to an injunction to prevent denials based on prejudice in future years.").

27. *See Consolidated Edison Co. v. Public Serv. Comm'n,* 447 U.S. 530, 534 (1980).

28. *See Clark v. Community for Creative Non-Violence,* 468 U.S. 288, 293 (1984); *Grayned v. City of Rockford,* 408 U.S. 104, 115 (1972).

29. *See Cox v. New Hampshire,* 312 U.S. 569, 576 (1941).

30. *See Oliveri v. Ward,* 801 F.2d 602 (2d Cir. 1986) (invalidating an order of the New York City Police Department (NYPD) preventing Dignity, an organization of gay Catholics, from standing on the steps of St. Patrick's Cathedral during the Pride parade, and requiring the NYPD to grant equal time in front of St. Patrick's to both Dignity and antigay demonstrators)

31. *Shuttlesworth v. Birmingham,* 394 U.S. 147, 153 (1969).

32. *Hurley v. Irish-American Gay, Lesbian and Bisexual Group of Boston,* 515 U.S. 557 (1995).

33. *See Lehman v. City of Shaker Heights,* 418 U.S. 298 (1974).

34. *See Gay Activists Alliance v. Washington Metro. Area Transit Auth.,* 48 U.S.L.W. 2053 (D.D.C. 1979); *Alaska Gay Coalition v. Sullivan,* 578 P.2d 951 (Alaska 1978).

35. *See AIDS Action Comm. of Mass. v. Massachusetts Bay Transp. Auth.*, 42 F.3d 1 (1st Cir. 1994).

36. *See United Food & Commercial Workers Union, Local 1099 v. Southwest Ohio Reg. Transit Auth.*, 163 F.3d 341 (6th Cir. 1998); *New York Magazine v. Metropolitan Transit Auth.*, 987 F. Supp. 254 (S.D.N.Y. 1997), *aff'd in part, vacated in part*, 136 F.3d 123 (2d Cir. 1998).

37. *See Metro Display Advertising, Inc. v. City of Victorville*, 143 F.3d 1191 (9th Cir. 1998).

38. *See Arkansas Educ. Television Comm'n v. Forbes*, 523 U.S. 666, 674-75 (1998).

39. *CBS v. Democratic Nat'l Comm.*, 412 U.S. 94, 112 (1973).

40. *See Forbes, supra* note 38, at 674.

41. *See Red Lion Broad. Co. v. FCC*, 395 U.S. 367 (1969).

42. *See Amendment of Part 73 of the Rules to Provide Procedures in the Event of a Personal Attack or Where a Station Editorializes as to Political Candidates*, 8 F.C.C.2d 721 (1967).

43. *In re Syracuse Peace Council*, 3 F.C.C.R. 2035 (1988), *denying reconsideration of* 2 F.C.C.R. 5043 (1987).

44. *Syracuse Peace Council v. FCC*, 867 F.2d 654, 656 (D.C. Cir. 1989).

45. *Radio-Television News Dirs. Ass'n v. FCC*, 229 F.3d 269 (D.C. Cir. 2000).

46. *CBS, supra* note 39, at 149 (Douglas, J., concurring). Justice Stewart agreed with Justice Douglas's analysis about public television. *See id.* at 143 (Stewart, J., concurring).

47. *Miller v. California*, 413 U.S. 15, 24 (1973).

48. *See* Terry Kinney, "Art Gallery, Director Acquitted in Mapplethorpe Photo Exhibit Obscenity: Jury Rejects the Prosecution's Contention that Sexually Graphic Works Lack Artistic Value," *L.A. Times*, Oct. 7, 1990, at 1.

49. *See State v. Henry*, 732 P.2d 9 (Or. 1987).

50. *National Endowment for the Arts v. Finley*, 524 U.S. 569 (1998).

51. *See id.* at 588.

52. *See id.* at 587; *see also Simon & Schuster, Inc. v. Members of N.Y. State Crime Victims Bd.*, 502 U.S. 105, 116 (1991); *Regan v. Taxation with Representation of Wash.*, 461 U.S. 540, 550 (1983).

53. *See Finley, supra* note 50, at 587.

54. *See Gay and Lesbian Students Ass'n v. Gohn*, 850 F.2d 361 (8th Cir. 1988).

55. *See* Rev. Rule 78-305, 1978-33 I.R.B.

56. *See Howard v. America Online Inc.*, 208 F.3d 741, 754 (9th Cir. 2000); *CompuServe Inc. v. Cyber Promotions, Inc.*, 962 F. Supp. 1015, 1025–26 (S.D. Ohio 1997); *Cyber Promotions, Inc. v. American Online, Inc.*, 948 F. Supp. 436 (E.D. Pa. 1996).

57. *See ACLU v. Reno*, 521 U.S. 844 (1997).

58. *See, e.g.,* Edward Stein, "Queers Anonymous: Lesbians, Gay Men, Free Speech, and Cyberspace," 38 *Harv. C.R.-C.L. L. Rev.* 159 (2003).

59. *See ACLU v. Reno, supra* note 57.

60. 47 U.S.C. § 223(d).

61. *See ACLU v. Reno*, 217 F.3d 162 (3d Cir. 2000), *aff'g* 31 F. Supp. 2d 473 (E.D. Pa. 1999).

62. *Ashcroft v. ACLU,* 535 U.S. 564 (2002).

63. *ACLU v. Ashcroft,* 322 F.3d 240 (3d Cir. 2003).

64. Ashcroft v. ACLU, 72 U.S.L.W. 3130 (Oct. 14, 2003) (No. 03-218).

65. *See Mainstream Loudoun v. Board of Trustees of Loudoun County Library,* 24 F. Supp. 2d 552 (E.D. Va. 1998).

66. *United States v. American Library Ass'n,* 123 S. Ct. 2297 (2003).

67. Additional information regarding the flaws of Internet-blocking software, including three expert reports analyzing these programs, can be found on the ACLU's Web site at <http://www.aclu.org/Cyber-Liberties/Cyber-Liberties.cfm?ID=12017&c=55>.

68. *See Turner v. Safley,* 428 U.S. 78, 89 (1987).

69. *See Mauro v. Arpaio,* 188 F.3d 1054, 1059 (9th Cir. 1999) (en banc).

70. *See Amatel v. Reno,* 156 F.3d 192 (D.C. Cir. 1998); *see also Thompson v. Patterson,* 985 F.2d 202 (5th Cir. 1993) (pornographic magazines); *Espinoza v. Wilson,* 814 F.2d 1093 (6th Cir. 1987) (materials that "advocated or legitimized a homosexual lifestyle," including the *Advocate* and *Gay Community News*).

71. *See Mauro, supra* note 69, at 1059.

72. *See id.* Under prior Ninth Circuit jurisprudence, the First Amendment interests of pretrial detainees, who are "presumed to be innocent of crime and whose detention is based solely upon inability to make bail," were entitled to greater protection than those of convicted criminals. *See Martino v. Carey,* 563 F. Supp. 984, 1004 (D. Ore. 1983) (citing *Inmates of San Diego County Jail v. Duffy,* 528 F.2d 954, 956 (9th Cir. 1975)). Judge Kleinfeld, dissenting in *Mauro,* insisted that the *Turner* standard was inappropriate for assessing the claims of pretrial detainees because the state has no "penological interests" to assert against individuals not yet convicted of a crime. *See Mauro, supra* note 68, at 1067 (Kleinfeld, J., dissenting). The Second Circuit indicated its agreement with Judge Kleinfeld that the distinction remains relevant for the purposes of assessing the appropriate level of protection for constitutional rights in the context of correctional facilities. *See Benjamin v. Fraser,* 264 F.3d 175, 187 n.10 (2d Cir. 2001).

73. *See Prison Legal News v. Cook,* 238 F.3d 1145 (9th Cir. 2001).

74. *See Amatel, supra* note 70 (rejecting First Amendment challenge but remanding case for determination of whether regulation was unconstitutionally vague); *Aiello v. Litscher,* 104 F. Supp. 2d 1068 (W.D. Wis. 2000) (accord). *See also Wolf v. Ashcroft,* 297 F.3d 305, 309 (3d Cir. 2002) (reversing grant of judgment for government in challenge to policy banning prisoners from viewing movies rated R or NC-17).

11

Criminal Law

I n 2003, the Supreme Court announced in the clearest possible terms that all citizens, regardless of sexual orientation, have a constitutionally protected right of privacy that prevents the government from intruding on noncommercial sexual relationships between consenting adults. Consequently, after decades of living under the threat of criminal prosecution, LGBT people are now free to establish intimate relationships with those of the same sex.

The Supreme Court did not, however, always hold this view. In a notorious and mean-spirited opinion from 1986, *Bowers v. Hardwick,* the Court stated that there was no "fundamental right [of] homosexuals to engage in acts of consensual sodomy."[1] Justice Byron White, writing for the Court, mocked the notion that LGBT people had a constitutionally protected right of privacy with regard to their sexual relationships, describing such claim as "facetious."[2]

Seventeen years later, in *Lawrence v. Texas,* the Supreme Court was faced with a case in which the state of Texas criminally prosecuted two men who were having sex at home. In an inspiring opinion written by Justice Anthony Kennedy, the Court found that "adults may choose to enter into [a homosexual] relationship in the confines of their home and their own private lives . . . and still retain their dignity as free persons."[3] Even though some citizens may wish to express moral disapproval of homosexuality, the Court insisted that "the State cannot demean [homosexuals'] existence or control their destiny by making their private sexual conduct a crime."[4] Finding no legitimate state interest to justify such a profound intrusion into an individual's personal and private life, the Court overturned the convictions and, in doing so, explicitly overruled *Bowers,* noting that the case "was not correct when it was decided, and it is not correct today."[5]

Many states had already recognized the importance of this fundamental liberty interest and had invalidated their sodomy laws prior to the decision in *Lawrence* by interpreting comparable provisions under their state constitutions. But as the Supreme Court noted in *Lawrence*, *Bowers* had been used in various ways to brand LGBT people as presumptive criminals and relegate them to second-class citizenship. Therefore, the importance of *Lawrence* extends far beyond the thirteen states whose sodomy laws were invalidated by the Supreme Court's ruling.

In addition, numerous jurisdictions have gone further than mere decriminalization of private sexual conduct and have recognized that LGBT people need protection against senseless acts of violence motivated by prejudice and ignorance. By including sexual orientation as a protected category in their hate-crime laws, some states have raised the penalties for those who target victims simply because they are (or are perceived to be) gay. The laws in a handful of states also cover gender identity. Finally, states have begun to recognize the existence of gay and lesbian couples by extending the protections of domestic violence laws to people in same-sex relationships.

SEX CRIMES

What is a sodomy law?

Sodomy laws generally prohibit oral and anal sex and other "deviate" sexual practices, regardless of the sex of the participants. Some states criminalized these activities under the terms *deviate sexual intercourse, buggery,* or *crimes against nature.* While some states' laws (either through legislative action or judicial interpretation) prohibited specific acts only when performed by individuals of the same sex, the majority of states prohibited acts known as sodomy irrespective of the sex of the participants. Even in these states, however, sodomy laws were often selectively enforced and used to persecute LGBT people.

Not to be confused with consensual sodomy laws are the laws in all states prohibiting sex in public, coercive or nonconsensual sex, and sex with minors under a certain age, as well as the exchange of sex for money.[6]

How have these laws been used outside of the criminal context?

Sodomy laws have been indirectly, and in many cases harshly, applied outside of the bounds of criminal law. One of the most significant effects of sodomy laws is that they have been used to justify discrimination against LGBT people in other kinds of cases, even if they have never been arrested for or convicted of sodomy.[7] In child custody and some employment cases, for example, LGBT people frequently faced the argument that they are intrinsically criminal because they could be assumed to be violating a state's sodomy law.[8] Even though an overwhelming majority of heterosexual persons also engage in the same sexual acts,[9] they were not made the target of presumptions of criminality.

May the government make it illegal for me to have sex with another adult in the privacy of my home?

No, it may not. The Supreme Court's decision in *Lawrence v. Texas* leaves no doubt that a state may not criminalize private, noncommercial sexual relations between consenting adults. Therefore, state laws purporting to criminalize such conduct (i.e., sodomy and fornication laws) are no longer valid.

Prior to the *Lawrence* decision, which states had sodomy laws?

At the time *Lawrence* was decided, thirteen states and Puerto Rico had sodomy laws. These states were Alabama, Florida, Idaho, Kansas, Louisiana, Mississippi, Missouri,[10] North Carolina, Oklahoma, South Carolina, Texas, Utah, and Virginia. In three other states, the laws were still in place but were probably unenforceable. In Michigan, a state trial court judge declared the sodomy and gross indecency statutes unconstitutional, and the state did not appeal.[11] A Minnesota trial judge struck down that state's sodomy statute and certified the case as a class action to ensure that her ruling applied to all Minnesota citizens, and not merely those named in the lawsuit.[12] The Minnesota attorney general's office declined to appeal the ruling.[13] Likewise, in Maryland, a state trial court struck down the sodomy statute, and no appeal was taken.[14]

Which states had repealed/invalidated their sodomy laws in the years leading up to the *Lawrence* decision?

Between 1990 and 2003, ten states eliminated their sodomy laws. Courts in Arkansas, Georgia, Kentucky, Maryland, Montana, and Tennessee found those states' sodomy laws to be unconstitutional.[15] Four states repealed their sodomy laws: Arizona and New York[16] in 2001, Rhode Island in 1998, and Nevada in 1993. The District of Columbia also repealed its sodomy law in 1993. Finally, although many had considered the Massachusetts sodomy law unenforceable against private consensual conduct since the 1970s, the Massachusetts Supreme Judicial Court explicitly confirmed this understanding in 2002.[17]

What is a *solicitation* statute?

Solicitation statutes criminalize the invitation, request, or offer to perform an illegal act. Any state that had a sodomy law could also prosecute people for soliciting, whether or not there was a specific solicitation law on the books, because in every state, soliciting another person to engage in any criminal activity is a crime. Now that consensual sodomy can no longer be criminalized, states may not prosecute someone for soliciting another to engage in a private, consensual, noncommercial act.

Most state that had decriminalized consensual sodomy prior to *Lawrence* have also legalized the solicitation of sodomy—again, because solicitation statutes usually apply only to offers to commit a crime. In some of those states, however, the courts have also narrowed the reach of the solicitation statute[18] or have gone so far as to overturn the statutes as unconstitutional.[19] Soliciting sex for money, however, is still prohibited under prostitution laws. Solicitation of sex in public can also still be prosecuted in jurisdictions that have public lewdness or other comparable statutes.

What is a *loitering* statute?

Loitering statutes, also known as *vagrancy* or *disorderly conduct* statutes, make it a crime to be in a public place for no apparent purpose or for an illegal or improper purpose. Some states have general loitering laws, which are typically very vague or ambiguous about what behavior is actually illegal. If the law is so unclear that one could not figure out from reading it what would be legal behavior and what illegal, the law may be unconstitutionally vague. For instance, the Supreme Court struck down a Chicago "anti-gang" loitering law because it gave law enforcement officers too much discretion in deciding how to enforce its broad prohibitions.[20] Other states have laws that specifically target sexual activities. Delaware's law, for example, criminalizes lingering in a public place "for the purpose of engaging in or soliciting another person to engage in sexual intercourse or deviate sexual intercourse."[21]

What are *lewd conduct* laws?

Lewd conduct laws are catch-all provisions that extend beyond oral and anal sex to prohibit any "deviate" sexual conduct. For example, Arizona prohibits "lewd and lascivious acts" that are aimed at "appealing to or gratifying the lust, passion or sexual desires of either of such persons."[22] Oklahoma has criminalized acts "openly outraging public decency."[23] In most cases, the statute is meant to cover acts committed in public, such as the exposure of one's genitalia to another in a manner "likely to cause affront or alarm."[24] The same conduct is also prohibited in many states under the label of "public indecency" laws.[25] Some states, such as Massachusetts, have limited their laws prohibiting "open and gross lewdness" to specific acts performed in front of children.[26]

How are solicitation, loitering, and lewd conduct statutes used to target LGBT people?

In many cities and states, the police use loitering and solicitation laws to harass LGBT people, most often men, by patrolling gay bars, cruising spots, and other places where LGBT people congregate and then arresting men who are there apparently seeking sex, or by assigning male police officers to pose as gay and then to come on to gay men in that locale. Though some lawyers have tried to challenge these practices, it is often difficult to prove a pattern of discriminatory enforcement if the law carries the same penalties for heterosexual solicitation. The Ohio Supreme Court, however, struck down a state solicitation law that had different penalties for same-sex and opposite-sex solicitation, ruling that it violated the equal protection clauses of the U.S. and the Ohio constitutions.[27]

A challenge may also be successful if a specific individual is targeted by the police. In October 1999, a Boston-area judge prohibited the Massachusetts State Police from harassing a particular gay man with a prior record who frequented a public rest area. The judge ruled, "It is without dispute that [a gay man] is entitled to use public roads and rest areas without having to fear harassment by the police."[28] In settling this case, the head of the Massachusetts State Police issued an order in 2001 clarifying that "[o]fficers should not order someone to leave a public area in the absence of unlawful conduct."[29]

Community pressure may also prove effective. The Detroit City Council ordered the Detroit Police Department to end a decoy program aimed at arresting gay men after the Triangle Foundation, a local gay rights group, publicized the police activity. Finally, after *Lawrence,* the police will not be able to sustain a prosecution when the underlying conduct was private, consensual, and noncommercial.

If the police are undercover trying to arrest gay men, isn't that entrapment?

It probably is not, legally speaking. Although it may feel as though you were lured into committing a crime, the Supreme Court has severely limited the defense of entrapment. If you claim entrapment, you must prove not only that the police set a trap but also that you had no "predisposition" to commit the kind of crime charged.[30] In other words, courts may be unsympathetic to the claim that a gay man was "duped" into doing something that he was not otherwise willing to do, because courts may assume that being gay already predisposes a person to engage in the prohibited act. Therefore, entrapment claims rarely succeed. After *Lawrence,* however, merely engaging in private, consensual, noncommercial sexual activity is not a crime.

What should I do if I am arrested for solicitation, loitering, lewd conduct, or public indecency?

First of all, you should not resist arrest in any way, as doing so may result in a separate charge for the crime of resisting arrest. But you should also not volunteer any information or admit to any conduct to the arresting officer or any other police official. You are not required to give anything other than your name and address and should refuse to discuss anything else before talking to a lawyer. Once you have asked to speak to an attorney, the police are required to stop their questioning. Do not be goaded or tricked into a conversation by comments by or between the officers. Once you start speaking and offering information, many courts will consider that to be a waiver of your rights.

Should I plead to lesser charges?

You should always consult with an attorney when deciding whether or not to accept the offer of a plea bargain. On the one hand, accepting a plea offer may result in receiving a lesser charge and avoiding the financial and nonmonetary costs of a trial, including embarrassment and other negative effects on personal relationships or professional opportunities (such as losing your job or professional license).[31] If you plead guilty to a criminal offense, however, you have relieved the state from having to prove its case beyond a reasonable doubt. Anyone faced with this decision should also consider the impact that any past criminal record may have on the case, either at trial or during sentencing.

If the crime to which you plead guilty is a sex offense, your plea may also mean that you have to register with the government as a sex offender on a public registry. (See next question for additional details on sex-offender registration.) A California court of appeals has ruled, however, that when a defendant pleads guilty to a specific lesser charge to avoid the sex-offender registration requirement, the judge may not unilaterally include a registration requirement because of the nature of the conduct that led to the arrest.[32]

If I was once convicted of solicitation, loitering, or sodomy, do I now have to register as a sex offender?

You might. It depends on the registration laws in your state and the criminal offenses for which your state requires ongoing registration.

Laws requiring registration for sex offenders are under attack in some states. The Massachusetts Supreme Court struck down portions of its sexual-offender registration laws because they violated the due process rights of people convicted of certain sexual crimes.[33] In that case, the individual had been convicted of consensual sex in public. He argued that he should be able to have a hearing to prove that he did not pose a threat to society and should not be required to register. The Massachusetts Supreme Court agreed. The New Jersey courts have also limited registration to cases in which there is "clear and convincing evidence" of the need for community notification.[34] In one case, the New Jersey Supreme Court invalidated the automatic lifetime registration requirement for individuals who were convicted of their offense as juveniles (under fourteen years old), finding it to be inconsistent with the rehabilitative purposes of the state's juvenile justice system.[35] In another, a New Jersey appellate court refused to uphold a registration requirement for a defendant who, at age twenty-one, had consensual sex with a fifteen-year-old, finding that this type of case did not come within the "heartland" of the cases requiring community notification.[36] Sex-offender registration laws vary significantly from state to state but at a minimum must provide a potential registrant with the opportunity to be heard and the right to the assistance of counsel. It is also not yet clear what (if any) impact the *Lawrence* decision will have on registration requirements. Therefore, if you have been convicted of a crime for which registration is required, you should confer with an attorney to determine what rights you may have either to challenge the registration in your particular case or to change your "offender level," which determines how widely information about your criminal history may be distributed.

Is there any way to have an arrest taken off my permanent record?

Many states have laws that permit arrest records to be wiped clean *(expunged)* or sealed for a party whose arrest does not result in conviction.[37] Even if a state does not have a specific statute laying out the procedure for cleansing one's record, an individual may petition the court to have the record expunged or sealed.

May the fact that I am gay be raised in a criminal trial?

It may only be raised if it is relevant to the case. For example, a defendant's sexual orientation would be relevant to the issue of motive in a case in which the accused was on trial for allegedly murdering the new lover of his ex-boyfriend out of jealousy.[38] But a prosecutor may not inflame the jury by playing to homophobia and prejudice.[39] The judge is charged with ensuring that a criminal defendant receives a fair trial, and invocations of racism, sexism, or homophobia should not be allowed. Counsel must object to questionable behavior during a trial at the time that it occurs; otherwise, any argument that the conduct undermined the integrity of the proceedings may be waived.

I am having mutually consensual sex with someone who is under-age. Can I get in trouble?

Yes. Minors under a certain age cannot legally consent to sex, so sex with someone who is underage is considered *statutory rape.* The age at which persons are considered old enough to consent to engage in sexual activity varies from state to state. Statutory rape charges may be brought against anyone having sex with a minor, even if the state does not have a consensual sodomy law in place. You should find out the age of consent in your jurisdiction to determine the risk involved in continuing the sexual relationship.

What is the law about accessing sexually explicit Internet sites?
What about escort services on the Internet?

The First Amendment guarantees your right to access sexually explicit adult information on the Internet. In *Stanley v. Georgia,* the Supreme Court held that a state may not make the mere possession of obscene material a crime and upheld the right to be free from government interference in "the privacy of a person's own home."[40]

Although Internet conversation is generally legal, courts may allow criminal prosecutions for conversations that resemble traditional solicitation of prostitution. The North Carolina Supreme Court has remarked: "The terms 'escort bureau' and 'escort service' are often regarded as euphemisms for prostitution."[41] If that is true of the escort service a person is using and it is covered under state prostitution laws, he or she may risk criminal prosecution.[42] One may also face criminal liability for "luring" a minor to engage in sexual activity, even when the invitation is offered over the Internet (e.g., chat rooms).[43] These prohibitions encompass both homosexual and heterosexual conduct (see also chapter 1).

HATE CRIMES, HARASSMENT, AND VIOLENCE

According to the *FBI Uniform Crime Reports,* there were 1,393 reported incidents of hate crimes motivated by sexual-orientation bias in 2001. Heightened reporting by state and local law enforcement agencies has started to reveal the magnitude of hate-related violence across the country. Specifically, the data demonstrate an increased number of hate crimes targeted against gay men and lesbians throughout the 1990s—from 8.9 percent in 1991 to 16.7 percent in 1999.[44] The vast majority of the victims of homophobic hate crimes were gay men (two out of every three).

Federal law currently does not require reporting of hate crimes based on gender or gender expression; therefore, the data are far less comprehensive for gender-related crimes. (As this book goes to press, legislation is pending before Congress that would add *gender* as a reporting category.) According to the National Coalition of Anti-Violence Programs, however, hate crimes against transgender people increased by almost 15 percent between 2000 and 2002, with 242 incidents of violence reported in 2002.[45]

What is a hate crime?

A hate crime is conduct that already violates a criminal law but is also specifically motivated by the victim's race, religion, sexual orientation, or ethnicity.[46] Physical or sexual assaults, including rape, assault, and murder, that are driven by bias against the victim on the basis of one of these traits may qualify as a hate crime. An action that is not otherwise a criminal violation cannot be considered a hate crime merely because the person who did it was motivated by bias. For instance, it is not a hate crime to make racist statements or to refuse to associate with certain groups of people. As a preliminary matter, the conduct must break the law. Only then may the question of motivation come into play.

If someone calls me "dyke" or "faggot" but doesn't actually touch me, is that a hate crime?

No. It is rude, ignorant, and homophobic, but such comments, no matter how offensive or discomfiting, are constitutionally protected under the First Amendment in most circumstances and do not rise to the level of a crime.

What is a hate-crimes law?

There are different types of hate-crimes laws. Some enhance the penalties for crimes motivated by hate or bias (i.e., longer sentences or higher fines).[47] Others allow victims to sue their attackers in civil court for a monetary award (to compensate for pain, suffering, and other harm the victim has experienced) or for a restraining order from the court that would prevent the attacker from harassing or coming near the victim again in the future. The third class of laws require government agencies to gather statistics to monitor the frequency and severity of hate crimes within a particular area. These laws usually do not bestow any independent rights onto the victims of hate crimes, but they can be useful tools for law enforcement trying to prevent future violations.

There are two federal hate-crimes laws that include sexual orientation. The Hate Crimes Statistics Act encourages, but does not require, states and localities to report all hate crimes to the Federal Bureau of Investigation (FBI), which compiles statistics and issues an annual report.[48] The Hate Crimes Sentencing Enhancement Act, passed in 1994, authorizes harsher sentences (increasing the penalties by up to three sentencing levels) for crimes that are proven to be hate motivated.[49] This law did not, however, create a new federal law prohibiting hate crimes; instead, it simply increased the penalty for conduct already prohibited by federal law (e.g., crimes involving interstate commerce and those committed on federal land) when the actions were motivated by bias. In both 2001 and 2003, a bipartisan coalition of Senators introduced the Local Law Enforcement Enhancement Act,[50] which would, among other things, expand federal jurisdiction to cover serious crimes of violence motivated because of a person's actual or perceived gender, sexual orientation, or disability.[51] An earlier version of this bill, titled the Hate Crimes Prevention Act, passed in the Senate in 2000 but was not approved by the House of Representatives.

Which states have hate-crimes laws that cover sexual orientation?

Twenty-nine states and the District of Columbia currently include sexual orientation in their hate-crimes legislation: Arizona, California, Connecticut, Delaware, Florida, Hawaii, Illinois, Iowa, Kansas, Kentucky, Louisiana, Maine, Massachusetts, Minnesota, Missouri, Nebraska, Nevada, New Hampshire, New Jersey, New Mexico, New York, Oregon, Pennsylvania, Rhode Island, Tennessee, Texas, Vermont, Washington, and Wisconsin. Fifteen other states' laws do not include sexual orientation,[52] two states have hate-crimes laws that do not specifically list particular protected categories,[53] and the remaining four have no hate-crimes legislation whatsoever.[54]

Which states have hate-crimes laws that cover gender identity?

California, Minnesota, Missouri, New Mexico, Pennsylvania, Vermont, and the District of Columbia specifically protect transgender people from hate crimes.

If I am ever the victim of a crime because I am lesbian or gay, what should I do?

You should report the crime to the police and seek out a victim assistance agency in your area. Every state and city has such services available, and the police department should refer you to a program if you request information. Other cities also have nonprofit organizations, such as New York's Anti-Violence Project or Boston's Violence Recovery Program, which assist LGBT victims of crime. The crime should also be reported to the National Hate Crimes Hotline at 1-800-347-HATE.

Do I have to come out to the police to report a hate crime? Will my complaint be available to the public?

A victim is not required to disclose his or her sexual orientation to the police. For a crime to be classified as motivated by hate or bias, it only matters *what the perpetrator thought* at the time of the crime. At some level, it is irrelevant whether or not the victim was in fact an LGBT individual. The prosecutor will have to prove beyond reasonable doubt that the crime was motivated by homophobic or transphobic bias in order to obtain enhanced hate-crimes penalties, but there are many ways to prove that without having the victim testify about his or her sexual orientation. Therefore, although in some cases it may be helpful, it is not necessary for a victim of a hate crime to self-identify his or her sexual orientation or gender identity to the police.

In general, judicial proceedings are open to the public. But exceptions do exist, such as when records or parts of records are sealed for the protection of state secrets, trade secrets, or informers. False names can also be used to protect the privacy of children, rape victims, or other particularly vulnerable parties or witnesses.[55] Usually, information is kept confidential to guarantee a criminal defendant a fair trial rather than to protect the victim from unwanted publicity. In cases of sexualized or particularly humiliating types of violence, however, courts may be more willing to consider sealing the files.

What are my rights as the victim of a hate crime?

Depending on where you live, you may have a range of options. In some states, victims of crimes are given the opportunity to participate in the criminal prosecution of their offender by, for example, testifying at the sentencing hearing. Many states have passed a victim's bill of rights, which specifies the level of involvement a victim is entitled to have in a criminal proceeding.

A victim of a crime, including a hate crime, may have a number of other remedies against his or her attacker, such as filing a civil case to seek damages for lost wages and physical and emotional pain and suffering. You may want to consult with an attorney to explore your legal options.

What is the *gay panic* defense?

The *gay panic* defense is a claim that a criminal should be excused for a violent crime because he or she "panicked" in a belief that the victim was gay or lesbian, or in response to the victim's "advances." Most judges, including the trial judge in the Matthew Shepard murder case, have rejected this excuse as a nondefense.[56] There are still courts, however, willing to let defendants make this argument to a jury. A federal judge in Tennessee even suggested that the failure of an attorney to explain away his client's past murders through the "homosexual panic" defense might qualify as "ineffective assistance of counsel."[57]

What can I do if the police harass me because I am gay or ignore my complaints?

Every citizen is entitled to the equal protection of the laws. Therefore, police officers must pursue complaints of criminal conduct perpetrated against LGBT people the same way they would for any other citizen. If the police do not take your complaint seriously, you should consider a number of options. If the officer at the precinct treats you disrespectfully, or worse, begins to treat you as though *you* were to blame, consider taking your claim to another officer who may be more receptive. Many police departments in major cities have an officer who serves as a liaison to the LGBT community. There are often civilian complaint boards or internal-affairs units within the police department, whose purpose is to prevent police abuse. If the police begin to harass you or continue to ignore your complaints, you should consider contacting a lawyer to pursue some form of legal action.[58]

Do the laws against domestic violence cover same-sex couples?

Under the general criminal law, the couple's relationship makes no difference. In criminal court, a batterer can be prosecuted for assault or another crime regardless of his or her relationship to the victim. In addition, some states have passed additional statutes specifically prohibiting physical abuse between intimate partners or other family members (e.g., elder abuse). Depending on their wording and how the courts have interpreted them, these laws might apply to same-sex couples as well. For example, the Ohio courts have interpreted that state's domestic-violence law, which targets violence between cohabitants, to include homosexual partners,[59] noting that to do otherwise would immunize perpetrators of violence simply because of the sex of their victim.[60]

May I go to family court and get a restraining order against an abusive partner?

It varies depending on the state. In New York, family court only has jurisdiction to hear disputes between individuals who are married or who have a child in common.[61] South Carolina's domestic-violence law covers "household members," defined as spouses, ex-spouses, parents and children, those related by blood, those who have a child in common, and "a male and female who are cohabiting or formerly have cohabited," thereby excluding same-sex couples.[62] California family courts, however, have jurisdiction to issue restraining orders to prevent violence between current or former cohabitants and those who are or were in a "dating or engagement relationship," which would include gay and lesbian couples.[63] Massachusetts law makes clear that "[u]nmarried persons who live together, or who did so in the past, are also within the court's jurisdiction under [the domestic-violence statute], regardless of whether the relationship between them is homosexual, heterosexual, or not sexual."[64]

For some people, it may be preferable to proceed in family court, where the petitioner can usually exercise significant control over his or her case and can choose from a wide variety of options, ranging from a court order excluding the abusive partner from the home to a judicial mandate simply to "stay away." In an area that does not allow same-sex partners to use the family court system in these circumstances, however, an abused individual only has the option of pursuing a complaint through the criminal justice system. Criminal complaints are handled by an assistant district attorney, who usually consults with the victim but is not bound by his or her wishes when determining what action to pursue. Each case is unique, and anyone in an abusive situation should seek legal advice to explore which options make the most sense under the circumstances.

Notes

1. *Bowers v. Hardwick,* 478 U.S. 186, 192, 194 (1986).
2. *Id.* at 194.
3. *Lawrence v. Texas,* 123 S. Ct. 2472, 2478 (2003).
4. *Id.* at 2484.
5. *Id.*
6. Nevada gives its counties the option to legalize prostitution, but no jurisdiction has chosen to do so.
7. *See generally* Diana Hassel, "The Use of Criminal Sodomy Laws in Civil Litigation," 79 *Tex L. Rev.* 813 (2001); Christopher Leslie, "Creating Criminals: The Injuries Inflicted by 'Unenforced' Sodomy Laws," 35 *Harv. C.R.-C.L. L. Rev.* 103 (2000).
8. *See, e.g., Ex parte D.W.W.,* 717 So. 2d 793, 796 (Ala. 1998) (affirming trial court's

decision to limit lesbian mother's visitation rights because she "is continually engaging in conduct that violates the criminal law of this state" and would therefore be "[e]xposing her children to such a lifestyle, one that is illegal under the laws of this state and immoral in the eyes of most of its citizens"); *Shahar v. Bowers,* 114 F.3d 1097, 1105 & n.17 (11th Cir. 1997) (en banc), *reh'g denied,* 120 F.3d 211 (1997), *cert. denied,* 522 U.S. 1049 (1998) (finding that Georgia's attorney general was justified in revoking job offer made to Shahar, based on concerns that her lesbianism would "interfere with the Department's efforts to enforce Georgia's laws against homosexual sodomy" and "harm the public perception of the Department").

9. *See* Robert T. Michael, et al., *Sex in America* 139–41 (1994) (finding that 73 percent of women had engaged in passive and 68 percent in active oral sex at some time in their lives, that 79 percent of men had engaged in passive and 77 percent in active oral sex at some time in their lives, and that about a quarter of American men had engaged in anal sex); P. Blumenstein & P. Schwartz, *American Couples* 236, 242 (1981), *cited in United States v. Able,* 968 F. Supp. 850, 864 (E.D.N.Y. 1997), *overruled by* 155 F.3d 628 (2d Cir. 1998). *See also W.N.J. v. Yocom,* 257 F.3d 1171 (10th Cir. 2001).

10. In Missouri, an intermediate court of appeals held that the sodomy statute could not be used to prosecute consensual sexual relations, a ruling that had the effect of decriminalization in that part of the state. *State v. Cogshell,* 997 S.W.2d 534 (Mo. Ct. App. 1999).

11. *Michigan Org. for Human Rights v. Kelley,* No. 88-815820 (Wayne Cnty. Cir. Ct. 1990) (unpublished).

12. *Doe v. Ventura,* 2001 WL 543734 (Hennepin Cnty. Dist. Ct. 2001).

13. See "State Won't Appeal Sodomy Law Decision," *St. Paul Pioneer Press,* Sept. 5, 2001, at B2.

14. *Williams v. State,* No. 98036031 / CL-1059, 1998 Extra LEXIS 260 (Md. Cir. Ct. Balt. City Oct. 15, 1998).

15. *See Jegley v. Picado,* 349 Ark. 600, 80 S.W.2d 332 (2002); *Powell v. State,* 510 S.E.2d 18 (Ga. 1998); *Williams v. State,* 1998 Extra Lexis 260 (Balt. City Cir. Ct. 1999) (state entered into agreement not to appeal or enforce the statute); *Gryczan v. State,* 283 Mont. 433, 942 P.2d 112 (1997); *Campbell v. Sundquist,* 926 S.W.2d 250 (Tenn. Ct. App. 1996); *Commonwealth v. Wasson,* 842 S.W.2d 487 (Ky. 1992).

16. New York's consensual sodomy law had already been struck down as unconstitutional. *See People v. Onofre,* 72 A.D.2d 268 (4th Dept. 1980), *aff'd,* 51 N.Y.2d 476 (1980).

17. *See Gay & Lesbian Advocates & Defenders v. Attorney General,* 436 Mass. 132, 763 N.E.2d 38 (2002) (reaffirming *Commonwealth v. Balthazar,* 366 Mass. 298, 318 N.E.2d 478 (1974)).

18. *See, e.g., Pryor v. Municipal Court,* 158 Cal. Rptr. 330, 599 P.2d 636 (1979) (California's "disorderly conduct" statute must be limited to acts or solicitations in public involving "touching of the genitals, buttocks, or female breast, for purposes of sexual arousal, gratification, annoyance or offense").

19. The Ohio Supreme Court struck down that state's solicitation statute as a facially invalid content-based restriction on speech and a violation of federal and state equal protection guarantees. *State v. Thompson,* 95 Ohio St. 3d 264, 767 N.E.2d 251 (2002). *See also State v. Tusek,* 52 Or. App. 997, 630 P.2d 892 (Or. App. 1981) (Oregon statute out-

lawing solicitation to engage in "deviate sexual intercourse" violates the First Amendment); *People v. Uplinger,* 460 N.Y.S.2d 514, 447 N.E.2d 62 (1983), *cert. denied,* 467 U.S. 246 (1984) (New York statute outlawing loitering for the purpose of engaging in "deviate sexual intercourse" is unenforceable in light of earlier judicial decision invalidating the state's consensual sodomy statute).

20. *See City of Chicago v. Morales,* 527 U.S. 41 (1999).

21. Del Code. Ann. tit. 11, § 1321(5) (2000).

22. Ariz Rev. Stat. Ann. § 13-1412 (2001).

23. Okla Stat. Ann. § 22 (2001).

24. *See, e.g.* Ala. Code § 13A-12-130 (2001).

25. *See, e.g.,* Mich. Comp. Laws § 750.338 (2001).

26. *See Commonwealth v. Fitta,* 390 Mass. 394, 461 N.E.2d 820 (1984) (limiting scope of Massachusetts's "open and gross lewdness" law).

27. *Thompson, supra* note 19.

28. *See* Press Release, Gay & Lesbian Advocates & Defenders, "Massachusetts Superior Court Judge Issues Preliminary Injunction Against State Police in Case of Gay Man Who Claimed Harassment," October 29, 1999, at <www.glad.org>.

29. *See* Press Release, Gay & Lesbian Advocates & Defenders, "GLAD Settles Harassment Case with Massachusetts State Police," March 1, 2001, at <www.glad.org>.

30. *See Mathews v. United States,* 485 U.S. 58, 63 (1988).

31. This threat is especially grave for those who teach or deal with children (*see* chapters 3 and 6).

32. *See People v. Olea,* 69 Cal. Rptr. 2d 722, 59 Cal. App. 4th 1289 (1997).

33. *See Doe v. Attorney General,* 430 Mass. 155, 715 N.E.2d 37 (1999) *[Doe IV]; Doe v. Attorney General,* 426 Mass. 136, 686 N.E.2d 1007 (1997) *[Doe III]; Doe v. Attorney General,* 425 Mass. 217, 680 N.E.2d 97 (1997) *[Doe II]; Doe v. Attorney General,* 425 Mass. 210, 680 N.E.2d 92 (1997) *[Doe I].*

34. *See, e.g., In re: R.F.,* 317 N.J. Super. 379, 722 A.2d 538 (App. Div. 1998).

35. *See In the Matter of Registrant J.G.,* 169 N.J. 304, 777 A.2d 891 (2001). For a list of the registration requirements for those convicted of sex offenses as juveniles, *see id.* at nn.5–14 and accompanying text.

36. *See In re: E.I.,* 300 N.J. Super. 519, 526, 693 A.2d 505, 509 (App. Div. 1997).

37. *See* Andrew D. Leipold, "The Problem of the Innocent, Acquitted Defendant," 94 *Nw. U. L. Rev.* 1297, 1315 n.64 (2000) (offering examples of state expungement statutes).

38. *See People v. Rozo,* 303 Ill. App. 3d 787, 708 N.E.2d 1229 (1999); *but see State v. Woodard,* 769 A.2d 379, 383 (N.H. 2001) (finding disclosure of evidence to jury about defendant's consensual homosexual relationship to be prejudicial error in case accusing her of sexual assault of young girl); *State v. Ellis,* 820 S.W.2d 699, 702 (Mo. Ct. App. 1991) (ruling that evidence regarding defendant's homosexuality was inadmissible to establish propensity to engage in sexual activities with minors). For a case dealing with the admissibility of testimony about a witness's sexual orientation in the context of a civil suit, *see United States v. Santos,* 201 F.3d 953, 964 (7th Cir. 2000) (holding that trial court erred in preventing cross-examination regarding witness's lesbianism because in that particular case it was relevant to issue of witness's motivations for testifying against defendant).

39. *See, e.g., State v. Young,* 1998 WL 258466 at *35 (Tenn. Crim. App.) ("The prosecutor's comments regarding the defendant's lifestyle were completely irrelevant to those issues [before the jury]."); *Chumbler v. Commonwealth,* 905 S.W.2d 488, 493 (Ky. 1995) (evidence regarding defendants' sexual habits was irrelevant and only served to inflame the jury, thus "poisoning the atmosphere of the trial").

40. *Stanley v. Georgia,* 394 U.S. 557, 564 (1969).

41. *Treants Enters, Inc. v. Onslow County,* 360 S.E.2d 783, 786 (N.C. 1987).

42. *Cf. Alliance for Community Media v. FCC,* 56 F.3d 105, 117 (D.C. Cir. 1995) (commenting that many public-access channels "basically solicit prostitution through easily discernible shams such as escort services").

43. *See, e.g., People v. Foley,* 709 N.Y.S.2d 467, 731 N.E.2d 123 (2000) (upholding McKinney's Penal Law § 235.22, which criminalizes "computerized dissemination of indecent material to minors").

44. The FBI's *Uniform Crime Reports* can be found on-line at <www.fbi.gov/ucr/ucr.htm>.

45. According to the NCAVP's report, 194 male-to-females (MTFs) and 18 female-to-males (FTMs) were victims of hate violence in 2000, and in 2002, 220 MTFs and 22 FTMs were targeted. The report can be found on-line at <www.avp.org>.

46. There have been mixed opinions about including sex or gender as a hate-crime category because of the complications that would result from classifying all rapes or acts of domestic violence as hate crimes. For one discussion of the issue of crime against women, *see Brzonkala v. Virginia Polytechnic Inst.,* 169 F.3d 820 (4th Cir. 1999), *aff'd sub nom. United States v. Morrison,* 529 U.S. 598 (2000), and its analysis of the Violence Against Women Act.

47. The prosecutor must prove specifically and beyond a reasonable doubt that the crime was motivated by hate or bias to trigger any sentence-enhancement provisions. *See Apprendi v. New Jersey,* 530 U.S. 466 (2000).

48. *See* Pub L. No. 101-275, 104 Stat. 140 (1990).

49. *See* Pub L. No. 103-322 § 280003, 108 Stat. 1796, 2096 (1994).

50. Text of pending federal legislation is available at <http://thomas.loc.gov>.

51. Federal law currently only covers hate crimes motivated by bias based on race, religion, national origin, or color, and only when the perpetrator acted with the purpose of preventing the victim from exercising a "federally protected right," such as voting. *See* 18 U.S.C. § 245 (2001).

52. Those states are Alabama, Alaska, Colorado, Idaho, Maryland, Michigan, Mississippi, Montana, North Carolina, North Dakota, Ohio, Oklahoma, South Dakota, Virginia, and West Virginia.

53. Georgia and Utah have laws addressing bias crime, but they do not delineate specific categories for protection. In a 2001 case, however, the appellate court in Utah reversed the imposition of heightened penalties under that state's statute. *See J. W. v. State,* 30 P.3d 1232 (Utah Ct. App. 2001).

54. They are Arkansas, Indiana, South Carolina, and Wyoming.

55. *See, e.g., Doe v. Blue Cross & Blue Shield United of Wisc.,* 112 F.3d 869, 872 (7th Cir. 1997).

56. "Jury Finds Roofer Guilty in Gay Student's Slaying: Wyoming Panel to Recom-

mend Life or Execution," *Ft. Lauderdale Sun-Sentinel*, Nov. 4, 1999, at 1A (noting Judge Barton Voigt's refusal to allow defendant to argue gay panic as defense). *See also People v. Page*, 193 Ill.2d 120, 139, 737 N.E.2d 264, 275 (2000).

57. *Cf. Abdur'Rahman v. Bell*, 999 F. Supp. 1073, 1100–01 (M.D. Tenn. 1998) (finding that although homosexual panic defense "does not provide a justification for the murder, it does provide the jury with some information upon which to evaluate it"). On review, however, the Sixth Circuit rejected the trial court's suggestion that counsel's failure to pursue this defense qualified as ineffective assistance of counsel. *See* 226 F.3d 696, 707–09 (6th Cir. 2000) (upholding defendant's death penalty sentence).

58. For example, the Sixth Circuit has held that selective prosecution on the basis of sexual orientation violates an individual's constitutional guarantee of equal protection of the laws. *See Stemler v. City of Florence*, 126 F.3d 856 (6th Cir. 1997).

59. *See State v. Yaden*, 118 Ohio App. 3d 410, 416–17, 692 N.E.2d 1097, 1100–1 (1997).

60. *See State v. Linner*, 77 Ohio Misc. 2d 22, 27 & n.2, 665 N.E.2d 1180, 1184 (Hamilton Cnty. Mun. Ct. 1996).

61. *See, e.g.,* New York Const., art. 6, § 3 (explaining limited scope of family court jurisdiction).

62. S.C. Code Ann. § 20-4-20 (b) (2000).

63. West's Ann. Cal. Fam. Code § 6211 (2000).

64. See Abuse Prevention Guidelines, No 3:02 (Commentary) (interpreting Mass. Gen. Laws 209A, sec. 1). In a noteworthy 2001 case concerning domestic violence in a gay male relationship, a Massachusetts appellate court ruled that rather than simply accepting allegations of reciprocal abuse, the judge must make specific written findings before issuing "mutual restraining orders." *See Sommi v. Ayer* and *Keller v. Ayer*, Mass. Appeals Court, No. 99-P-432 (March 28, 2001).

III

Government Employees

LGBT people working in the civilian public sector have the strongest set of employment protections under law, because, in addition to whatever statutes protect private-sector employees, public-sector employees are also able to invoke the protections of the Constitution. The Constitution is framed to protect the rights of individuals from abuses of governmental power, and those protections apply when the government is acting as an employer as well as when it is functioning to regulate or prohibit various activities. In other words, a public employer may not act arbitrarily in the way that a private employer can. Thus, those who work for federal, state, and local government agencies have a powerful weapon at their disposal if they are fired or otherwise suffer from discriminatory treatment.

In addition to these constitutional protections, executive orders issued by governors and mayors offer an added layer of protections and benefits to many public-sector employees, even in states that lack antidiscrimination laws. Likewise, an increasing number of cities have begun to make domestic-partner benefits available to municipal employees. Although there have been challenges to such benefit plans, most challenges have failed. Similarly, in many areas of the country, local governments have struggled against conservative elements within their states that were determined to nullify their efforts to promote equality. Consequently, concerned citizens need to monitor the developments at every level of government—state, county, and city—to determine how broad the protections and benefits available to LGBT public employees actually are.

May the government discriminate against employees because of sexual orientation?

As a general principle, no, unless they are in the military (see chapter 4).

In *Romer v. Evans*,[1] the Supreme Court stated that any time the government treats a person differently because of sexual orientation, it must have a rational reason for doing so. The Supreme Court has not yet said that sexual orientation has the legal status of a "suspect category"—which would mean that government discrimination against gay men and women would be presumptively unconstitutional in the same way that discrimination on the basis of sex or race is. Nevertheless, government discrimination based on sexual orientation must be justified by *some* legitimate purpose.[2] The fact that some individuals—whether coworkers, supervisors, employers, or the public at large—dislike LGBT people or have stereotypes and fears about them is not a good enough reason to allow discrimination.[3] In light of this pronouncement by the Supreme Court, an increasing number of courts have recognized that public employers have a duty to treat all of their employees fairly, regardless of sexual orientation.[4] As discussed below, however, this protection has been enforced less well in some job categories—such as law enforcement—than in others.

How long have government workers had this protection?

While *Romer* has now directly addressed government discrimination on the basis of sexual orientation, it did not involve an employment case. Even before *Romer*, however, legal advocates had been winning cases on behalf of LGBT public employees. These cases, litigated over a thirty-year period, cumulatively created the body of precedent that offers solid legal protection for government workers.

The watershed moment occurred in 1969, in *Norton v. Macy*,[5] a case involving a National Aeronautics and Space Administration employee. There, a federal appeals court ruled that an employee could not be fired solely because of allegations of "immoral conduct." Norton was fired after he received a citation for a traffic violation, which was issued when the police saw him meeting another man in Lafayette Square, directly across from the White House. To justify firing Norton, the court held, the government had to show "some reasonably foreseeable, specific connection between [the] employee's potentially embarrassing conduct and the efficiency of the service."[6] Mere assertions of "immorality" would not suffice. The court invoked the "elementary concepts of liberty, privacy and diversity" to reject the idea that it was "an appropriate function of the federal bureaucracy to enforce the majority's conventional codes of conduct in the private lives of its employees."[7] The *Norton* case did not end discrimination, but it did set the stage for the protections that followed.

Are there any specific protections for lesbian, gay, and bisexual federal employees other than in case law?

Yes. President Clinton issued an executive order in 1998 protecting federal civilian employees from discrimination on the basis of sexual orientation.[8] The Clinton executive order added sexual orientation to the list of protected characteristics in the already existing order that prohibited other forms of discrimination in federal government employment, and this order has remained in effect under President George W. Bush.

Because executive orders are not statutes (i.e., laws passed by Congress), however, they can be changed or withdrawn by subsequent presidents. In addition, the remedies that one can seek pursuant to an executive order are much less than those available if there is a statutory violation. For example, employees lack the right to bring a claim of sexual-orientation discrimination before the federal agency that enforces antidiscrimination laws, the Equal Employment Opportunity Commission (EEOC). Only the passage of a statute outlawing all sexual-orientation-based discrimination in employment could authorize those lawsuits.[9] The leading proposal for such a statute now before Congress is the Employment Non-Discrimination Act (ENDA).[10]

Are there any statutory provisions that protect federal employees?

Yes. Triggered by the *Norton* decision, the federal Civil Service Commission in 1973 issued revised regulations barring discrimination based on characteristics unrelated to job performance. Specifically, the policy stated:

You may not find a person unsuitable for Federal employment merely because that person is a homosexual or has engaged in homosexual acts, nor may such exclusion be based on a conclusion that a homosexual person might bring the public service into public contempt. You are, however, permitted to dismiss a person or find him or her unsuitable for Federal employment where the evidence establishes that such person's homosexual conduct affects job fitness—excluding from such consideration, however, unsubstantiated conclusions concerning possible embarrassment to the Federal Service.[11]

In 1978, the statute governing the Civil Service was amended to prohibit discrimination "against any employee or applicant for employment on the basis of conduct which does not adversely affect the performance of the employee or applicant or the performance of others."[12] Federal employees who believe they have been discriminated against may file a complaint under this law with the Office of Special Counsel (OSC).[13]

In addition to the pertinent statutes and regulations, there have also been formal interpretations issued by the federal Office of Personnel Management (OPM). An OPM policy letter first stated during the Carter administration that the Civil Service statute and regulation should be interpreted as prohibiting discrimination on the basis of sexual orientation. Despite a lack of support for this position during the intervening administrations,[14] the Carter OPM policy letter became the precursor to President Clinton's executive order.

Do federal law enforcement or military agencies have policies against hiring LGBT employees?

Those policies have been changed. Under civil service regulations, lesbians, gay men, and bisexuals may work at the Department of Defense in civilian positions. Technically, the military cannot refuse to accept closeted gay men and lesbians in the armed services under the "Don't Ask, Don't Tell" (DADT) policy, but openly gay people may not serve.[15] (For further information, see chapter 4.)

In the past, the Federal Bureau of Investigations (FBI) and the Central Intelligence Agency (CIA) refused to hire lesbians or gay men by claiming that they were security risks.[16] In particular, the agencies claimed that gay or lesbian people were particularly susceptible to blackmail, an argument that clearly loses its footing when applied to people who are out and accordingly have nothing to fear from disclosure of their sexual orientation. This practice ended when President Clinton amended the security-clearance regulations by an executive order in 1995. The order prohibited discrimination on the basis of sexual orientation and stated, "No inference concerning the standards in this section may be raised solely on the basis of the sexual orientation of the employee."[17] Like the 1998 Clinton executive order, however, this one can be changed by a subsequent president or by Congress. As of 2003, however, neither President Bush nor Congress has rescinded these protections.

What about state and local governments?

The legal principles announced in *Romer v. Evans, Norton v. Macy,* and other court opinions prohibiting sexual-orientation discrimination in federal employment[18] extend to all government employers, including state and local governments. State and city laws that prohibit sexual-orientation discrimination in employment apply to public employees. Some governors have issued their own executive orders prohibiting sexual-orientation discrimination against state employees.[19]

Are the rules any different for teachers or for people who work with children?

They should not be, but courts have only recently started to enforce the mandate against sexual-orientation discrimination in these settings. Although the first court decision in favor of a gay teacher came in 1969 in *Morrison v. State Board of Education,*[20] there were numerous defeats in the 1970s and 1980s: a federal appeals court allowed an Ohio school system to fire a guidance counselor after she told a secretary and several other teachers that she was bisexual;[21] the Supreme Court of Washington allowed a "known homosexual" to be fired from his teaching position at a high school in Tacoma in 1977;[22] and the Wisconsin Supreme Court allowed the administrators of a state-run home for mentally retarded boys to fire a gay man who had served as houseparent, on the ground that he failed to project "the orthodoxy of male heterosexuality."[23] In other states, executive orders pronounced openly gay people "immoral" and unfit to teach.[24]

A strong proequality trend has begun to take hold in more recent teacher cases, however, especially since the Supreme Court's decision in *Romer.* Three federal trial court decisions illustrate this development. In *Glover v. Williamsburg Local School District Board of Education,*[25] decided in 1998, an Ohio federal district court ordered that the school reinstate a gay teacher who had been fired because of "animus toward [the teacher] as a homosexual."[26] Also in 1998, a federal court in Utah vindicated the rights of Wendy Weaver, a high school teacher who had lost her assignment as volleyball coach after the school learned that she was a lesbian.[27] In a sweeping decision, the court held that the school district could not prevent the teacher from discussing her sexual orientation on the same terms that heterosexual teachers were permitted to do so. Nor could it prevent her from being out to students without violating her First Amendment rights. The court also held that bias against Weaver because she was a lesbian was not a rational reason to bar her from coaching the volleyball team. Finally, in 2002, a federal district court in New York ruled that a lesbian high school teacher who had sued school officials for failing to take measures to prevent students from harassing her based on her sexual orientation stated a valid equal protection claim.[28]

Antidiscrimination laws protecting teachers exist at the state, local, and individual school system level.[29] Some school systems actively recruit openly LGBT teachers, in part to serve as role models for LGBT youth.[30] As more LGBT teachers come out, school officials and parents will undoubtedly become more comfortable with the idea of LGBT people teaching and working with children. All states, however, will revoke a teaching license after a criminal conviction for certain crimes, including crimes of sexual misconduct, whether homosexual or heterosexual.[31]

What about police or other "sensitive" positions?

Police and prosecutors are in a positions of "public trust," a fact that has led some agencies to refuse to hire or to fire gay men and lesbians in those jobs. This is probably the area of public employment in which it has been the most difficult for LGBT advocates to prevail.

In *Shahar v. Bowers*,[32] Robin Shahar was denied the opportunity to work in the Georgia Attorney General's Office after the state attorney general, Michael Bowers (the same Bowers from *Bowers v. Hardwick*), learned that she had engaged in a private commitment ceremony with her female partner. Bowers had insisted that the public would be confused if an open lesbian worked at an office that was charged with the mission of upholding Georgia's laws, including the sodomy law that was still in force at the time. The Eleventh Circuit Court of Appeals allowed Bowers to revoke his job offer. It agreed that there could be a loss of morale or cohesiveness from allowing an open lesbian to work in the attorney general's office, enforcing the state's criminal laws.[33] In upholding Bowers's decision, the court stressed "the sensitive nature of the pertinent professional employment."[34]

There are also still states where LGBT police officers are at risk. For example, in a 1992 case, a South Carolina police officer was fired for inappropriate sexual conduct with another man.[35] The police officer had insisted that he was not homosexual and that the men had only been masturbating together in the same room. Nevertheless, the court ruled against him on the basis that, regardless of whether or not he was gay, the firing was permissible because the Supreme Court had held in *Bowers v. Hardwick* that there was no fundamental right of privacy to engage in homosexual sex. Cases like this demonstrate how the existence of sodomy laws, which made some consensual sexual activity a crime, created an especially difficult obstacle for LGBT people who wanted to serve in law enforcement. With the Supreme Court's decision in *Lawrence v. Texas*, which invalidated consensual sodomy laws as a violation of the constitutional right to privacy, this barrier to equality has been removed. (See chapter 2 for a fuller discussion of sodomy laws and the *Lawrence* decision.)

Even prior to the *Lawrence* decision, however, a positive trend similar to the teacher cases had begun to emerge in the law enforcement context. For instance, in *Quinn v. Nassau County Police Department*,[36] a federal district court in New York agreed with a gay police officer who alleged that the police department violated his constitutional right to equal protection when it looked the other way and allowed officers to harass and abuse him on the job. Although the police department insisted that it was legal to discriminate because of sexual orientation, the judge strongly disagreed: "[G]overnment action . . . cannot survive a rational basis review when it is motivated by irrational fear and prejudice towards homosexuals."[37]

The Dallas Police Department, in particular, has been the subject of repeated lawsuits. In 1981, the department refused to hire Steven Childers, an openly gay man, in its property room.[38] When Childers sued, a federal district court held that because many people openly despise and fear homosexuals, the police department could refuse to hire him. The court found, "There [were] also legitimate doubts about a homosexual's ability to gain the trust and respect of the personnel with whom he works."[39] The Texas Court of Appeals reversed course in 1993, however, by ruling that Dallas could not prevent lesbians and gay men from serving as police officers based solely on disapproval of their private, consensual sexual activities.[40] In fact, police departments in many cities are now actively recruiting LGBT people so that their police forces will more adequately reflect the communities they serve.

Do public employees have the right to come out at work or to speak out about LGBT issues and keep their jobs?

In most cases, they do. In an important case called *Pickering v.*

Board of Education,[41] the Supreme Court established the rule that the First Amendment applies to public-employee speech. A public employee has a constitutional right to speak out on matters of public concern, unless his or her employer can demonstrate a stronger, countervailing interest in promoting the effective functioning of the workplace by limiting the employee's speech. If a public employer tries to discipline an employee for saying something controversial, it may be violating the employee's rights. A court must consider the actual effect of the employee's speech and determine whether it impaired discipline, had a negative impact on staff interaction, or affected the employee's job performance.[42]

Applying this test to employees who have come out publicly has produced different results in different cases, but most recent cases support a worker's right to come out. In 1979, the California Supreme Court ruled that "coming out" speech is protected as political speech.[43] Because that state's labor law prohibits all employers, including private employers, from interfering in employees' political activities, employers in California are barred from firing employees for coming out. Likewise, a federal appeals court struck down an Oklahoma law that required all teachers who "advocated" homosexuality to be fired.[44] In 1980, a county employee in Texas was fired when he told his boss that he was gay and planned on speaking to the county commissioner about gay and lesbian civil rights. The federal appeals court reviewing his case required that he be rehired because the county violated his First Amendment rights.[45]

Although courts have become increasingly vigilant about protecting the free speech and expression rights of public employees,[46] public employees in certain areas of the country are still at risk of termination from their job simply for being out.[47] For the most part, however, the First Amendment and the *Pickering* rule should protect an employee who decides to come out on the job or engage in political activity outside of the workplace.[48] In almost every job, coming out or advocating for LGBT rights should not have an adverse impact on how an employee performs or on how the agency functions. Perhaps most importantly, government employers should not be able to rely on the negative reactions of coworkers to justify disciplining employees who speak out.

May a public employer offer benefits to married employees, such as insurance coverage for their spouses, and refuse to extend that coverage to partners of lesbian and gay employees?

A growing number of state and local governments are extending partner benefits to their lesbian and gay employees, but almost all of these gains have resulted from legislative or administrative actions, rather than from lawsuits. Most courts have upheld the practice of favoring married workers in the distribution of benefits, on the ground that it is marital-status discrimination rather than sexual-orientation discrimination and thus is permitted by law, even though lesbians and gay men have no option of marrying their partners.[49] The lawsuits, however, have not been a waste. In Denver, for example, advocates were able to persuade local lawmakers to vote to extend partner benefits, even though they had lost a challenge in court, by virtue of the public education and political mobilization that lawsuits can help generate.[50]

Over 150 governmental employment systems have added domestic-partner coverage to the list of benefits that they offer to their employees. The state governments include California, Connecticut, Iowa, Maine, New Mexico, New York, Oregon, Rhode Island, Vermont, and Washington. Massachusetts state government employees have limited partner benefits.[51] Large cities that have adopted such policies include Atlanta, Baltimore, Chicago, Denver, Detroit, New Orleans, New York, Philadelphia, Seattle, and Tucson.

Even in litigation, there are a few hopeful signs. In 1998, the Oregon Court of Appeals ordered the Oregon Health Sciences University to provide the same health and life insurance benefits to the same-sex partners of its employees.[52] In a groundbreaking ruling, the court held that refusing to provide these benefits violated the state constitution's equal protection clause. Likewise, the decision of the Vermont Supreme Court regarding same-sex marriage[53] led to legislation requiring state and local employers to provide equal benefits to gay and lesbian employees and their partners. In 2001, New York's highest court recognized that offering special benefits to married couples (e.g., priority for subsidized student housing) can have an impermissibly disparate impact on gay men and lesbians who cannot marry their partners.[54]

One problem that local government employees face is that in some states, the issue of public-employee benefits must be determined by state, rather than municipal, law. Boston and Minneapolis passed domestic-partnership legislation that was later overturned because of state laws preventing cities from changing the terms of insurance coverage.[55] In other places, however, local provisions have been upheld;[56] the outcome will depend on the structure of each state's insurance and benefits law. LGBT employees in Austin, Texas, encountered a different problem: they won domestic-partner benefits only to have those benefits rescinded through a referendum amendment to the city charter.[57] Consequently, activists must be prepared to fight on a variety of fronts, first to win, then to defend, equal treatment under law.

Prior to commencing any action (litigation or otherwise) designed to challenge the distribution of employee benefits, individuals should consult with an LGBT rights attorney. Insurance law is filled with complex legal issues (e.g., most plans offered to private-sector employees are governed by federal, not state, law). Proceeding without careful consideration of all the ramifications could be wasteful or even counterproductive.

NOTES

1. *Romer v. Evans,* 517 U.S. 620 (1996).

2. *See id.* at 634; *see also Lawrence v. Texas,* 123 S.Ct. 2472, 2484 (2003) (O'Connor, J., concurring).

3. *See City of Cleburne v. Cleburne Living Ctr.,* 473 U.S. 432, 448 (1985); *U.S. Dep't of Agric. v. Moreno,* 413 U.S. 528, 534–35 (1974).

4. *See, e.g., Quinn v. Nassau County Police Dep't,* 53 F. Supp. 2d 347, 356 (E.D.N.Y. 1999) ("The Romer Court established that government discrimination against homosexuals, in and of itself, violates the Equal Protection Clause.") (citing *Romer, supra* note 1, at 633–34); *Miguel v. Guess,* 112 Wash. App. 536, 554, 51 P.3d 89, 97 (2002), *review denied,* 148 Wash.2d 1019, 64 P.3d 650 (2003).

5. *Norton v. Macy,* 417 F.2d 1161 (D.C. Cir. 1969).

6. *Id.* at 1167.

7. *Id.* at 1165.

8. Exec. Order No. 13,087 (May 29, 1998), amending Exec. Order No. 11,478 (August 8, 1969).

9. *See* William J. Clinton, "Statement on Signing an Executive Order on Equal Employment Opportunity in the Federal Government," *Weekly Compilation of Presidential Documents,* Vol. 34, No. 22, June 1, 1998, available at 1998 WL 14393521.

10. Text of pending federal legislation is available at <http://thomas.loc.gov>.

11. *Civil Service Bulletin,* Dec. 21, 1973, quoted in *Ashton v. Civiletti,* 613 F.2d 923, 927 (D.C. Cir. 1979).

12. 5 U.S.C. § 2302(b)(10).

13. For information about filing a complaint, go to the OSC's Web site <www.osc. gov/contacts.htm> or call the agency at (800) 872-9855 or (202) 653-7188.

14. *See* David Tuller, "Defeating Discrimination Step by Step: Gay Rights in the Federal Workplace," *S.F. Chronicle,* Feb. 10, 1994, at A1.

15. A gay man successfully argued that he could not be discharged from the army

because he had received explicit assurances that he would not be fired because of his sexuality. A federal appeals court refused to allow the military to renege on those promises. *See Watkins v. United States Army,* 875 F.2d 699 (9th Cir. 1989) (en banc), *cert. denied,* 498 U.S. 957 (1990). This case represents an unusual approach that would not be available to many men and women in the military. As a general matter, the courts have refused to invalidate the DADT policy on constitutional grounds. *See, e.g., Able v. United States,* 155 F.3d 628 (2d Cir. 1998).

16. *See, e.g., Dubbs v. CIA,* 866 F.2d 1114 (9th Cir. 1989); *Padula v. Webster,* 822 F.2d 97 (D.C. Cir. 1987) (FBI). These agencies had also relied on President Truman's Exec. Order No. 10,450 (1953), which specified "sexual perversion" as a basis for removal from federal service.

17. Exec. Order No. 12,968 (Aug. 7, 1995).

18. Another such case is *Swift v. United States,* 649 F. Supp. 596 (D.D.C. 1986).

19. As of this writing, Colorado, Delaware, Indiana, Kentucky, Montana, Pennsylvania, and Washington have such executive orders. Kentucky's executive order also prohibits discrimination against state employees based on gender identity. This is in addition to the fourteen states that have statutes prohibiting sexual-orientation (and in some cases gender identity) discrimination (see chapter 6).

20. *Morrison v. State Bd. of Educ.,* 1 Cal. 3d 214, 461 P.2d 375 (1969).

21. See *Rowland v. Mad River Local Sch. Dist.,* 730 F.2d 444, 446 (6th Cir. 1984), *cert. denied,* 470 U.S. 1009 (1985). Justices Brennan and Marshall had vigorously dissented from the decision of the Supreme Court not to hear Rowland's case, insisting that "discrimination against homosexuals or bisexuals based solely on their sexual preference raises significant constitutional questions under both prongs of our settled equal protection analysis." 470 U.S. at 1014 (Brennan, J., dissenting).

22. *See Gaylord v. Tacoma Sch. Dist. No. 10,* 88 Wash. 2d 286, 559 P.2d 1340 (en banc).

23. *Safransky v. State Pers. Bd.,* 62 Wis. 2d 464, 476, 215 N.W.2d 379, 385 (1974).

24. *See* 60 W. Va. Op. Atty. Gen. 46 (Feb. 24, 1983).

25. *Glover v. Williamsburg Local Sch. Dist. Bd. of Educ.,* 20 F. Supp. 2d 1160 (S.D. Ohio 1998).

26. *Id.* at 1174.

27. *See Weaver v. Nebo Sch. Dist.,* 29 F. Supp. 2d 1279 (D. Utah 1998); *see also Miller v. Weaver,* 66 P.3d 592 (Utah 2003) (rejecting attempt by citizens groups to force state board of education to fire Weaver).

28. *See Lovell v. Comsewogue Sch. Dist.,* 214 F. Supp. 2d 319 (E.D.N.Y. 2002). *But cf. Schroeder v. Hamilton Sch. Dist.,* 282 F.3d 946 (7th Cir. 2002) (rejecting comparable claim), *cert. denied,* 123 S.Ct. 435 (2002).

29. The New York City school board policy can be found on-line at <www.nycenet.edu/dhr/dhrmanua.htm>, and the District of Columbia's policy can be found on-line at <www.k12.dc.us/dcps/policies/policies_frame.html>. *See also* Rosemary Shinohara, "Board Widens Policy: New School Rule Passes Unanimously after Dozens Speak in Support," *Anchorage Daily News,* June 26, 2001, at A1 (expanding school board policy to protect students and employees from antigay harassment).

30. *See Irizarry v. Board of Educ. of Chicago,* 251 F.3d 604 (7th Cir. 2001).

31. *See, e.g.,* Cal. Educ. Code § 44425 (2000) (requiring automatic revocation

following conviction for unlawful intercourse with a female under eighteen, incest, sodomy with another person under eighteen, lewd and lascivious acts with a child under fourteen, oral copulation with another person under eighteen, and disorderly conduct involving the solicitation to engage in lewd or dissolute conduct in public); Va. Code 1950 § 22.1-296.1 (2000) (applicants for employment in public school must not have been convicted of a "crime of moral turpitude"). In *Shaw v. Minnesota*, 2001 WL 605096 (Minn. App.), the state suspended a teacher's license for two years after his arrest on such charges, even though the charges were ultimately dismissed.

32. *Shahar v. Bowers*, 114 F.3d 1097 (11th Cir. 1997) (en banc), *reh'g denied*, 120 F.3d 211 (1997), *cert. denied*, 522 U.S. 1049 (1998).

33. *See id.* at 1108.

34. *Id.* at 1110.

35. *See Dawson v. State Law Enforcement Div.*, 1992 WL 208967 (D.S.C. 1992).

36. *See Quinn, supra* note 4.

37. *Id.* at 357. *See also Emblen v. Port Auth. of New York/New Jersey*, 89 Fair Empl. Prac. Cas. (BNA) 233 (S.D.N.Y. 2002) (finding that plaintiff sufficiently proved equal protection violation due to antigay harassment).

38. *See Childers v. Dallas Police Dep't*, 513 F. Supp. 134 (N.D. Tx. 1981).

39. *Id.* at 147.

40. *See City of Dallas v. England*, 846 S.W.2d 957, 959 (Tex. App. 1993). *But cf. City of Sherman v. Henry*, 928 S.W.2d 464 (Tex. 1996) (holding that civil service commission could deny a promotion to a police officer because of his affair with the wife of another police officer).

41. *Pickering v. Board of Educ.*, 391 U.S. 563 (1968).

42. *See Rankin v. McPherson*, 483 U.S. 378, 338 (1987).

43. *Gay Law Students Ass'n v. Pacific Tel. & Tel.*, 595 P.2d 592, 610–11, 24 Cal. 3d 458, 488–89 (1979).

44. *See National Gay Task Force v. Board of Educ.*, 729 F.2d 1270 (10th Cir. 1984).

45. *See Van Ooteghem v. Gray*, 628 F.2d 488, 490 (5th Cir. 1980), *aff'd en banc*, 654 F.2d 304 (1981). *See also Ancanfora v. Board of Educ.*, 491 F.2d 498 (4th Cir. 1974) (holding that teacher could not be transferred to administrative position solely because he admitted in press interviews that he was gay); *Aumiller v. University of Del.*, 434 F. Supp. 1273 (D. Del. 1977) (invalidating discharge of college teacher who had been quoted in several newspapers about gay rights).

46. *See Weaver, supra* note 27, at 1279

47. *See Shahar, supra* note 32, at 1097.

48. *But see Melzer v. Board of Educ.*, 196 F. Supp. 2d 229 (E.D.N.Y. 2002) (rejecting First Amendment claim of teacher fired because of membership in North American Man-Boy Love Association (NAMBLA)); *Singer v. U.S. Civil Service Comm'n*, 530 F.2d 247 (9th Cir. 1976), *vacated and remanded*, 429 U.S. 1034 (1977) (federal employee fired after highly publicized attempt to reform the Washington state marriage laws); *McConnell v. Anderson*, 451 F.2d 193, 196 (8th Cir. 1971) (University of Minnesota employee fired for attempting to secure license to marry his same-sex partner).

49. *See Hinman v. Department of Pers. Admin.*, 167 Cal. App. 3d 516 (1985); *Rutgers Council of AAUP Chapters v. Rutgers Univ.*, 689 A.2d 828, 298 N.J. Super. 442 (App. Div.

1997); *Phillips v. Wisconsin Pers. Comm'n,* 482 N.W.2d 121, 167 Wis. 2d 205 (Ct. App. 1992).

50. *See* James Brooke, "Denver Extends Health Coverage to Partners of Gay Employees," *N.Y. Times,* Sept. 18, 1996, at A17; *Ross v. Denver Dep't of Health and Hospitals,* 883 P.2d 516 (Col. Ct. App. 1994). Even though the courts had found no basis on which the city could be ordered to provide the benefits, once the city decided to do so, the courts found that there was no barrier to that policy in state insurance law. *Schaefer v. City and County of Denver,* 973 P.2d 717 (Col. Ct. App. 1998).

51. In August 2001, acting governor Jane M. Swift announced that all state employees would get some same-sex partner benefits as their contracts were renegotiated over the next two years. These benefits would include leave to care for an ill partner, bereavement leave, and paid time off for court appearances or counseling for victims of domestic violence. The state would continue, however, not to offer health-care benefits to domestic partners of public employees. Yvonne Abraham, "Swift to Extend Same-Sex Benefits: Limited Rights Given to State Employees," *Boston Globe,* Aug. 16, 2001, at A1.

52. *See Tanner v. Oregon Health Sci. Univ.,* 157 Or. App. 502, 971 P.2d 435 (1998). This opinion also interpreted the state statute against sex discrimination to include a prohibition against sexual-orientation discrimination.

53. *See Baker v. State of Vermont,* 170 Vt. 194, 744 A.2d 864 (1999).

54. *See Levin v. Yeshiva Univ.,* 96 N.Y.2d 484 (2001).

55. *See Connors v. City of Boston,* 30 Mass. 31, 714 N.E.2d 335 (1999); *Lilly v. City of Minneapolis,* 527 N.W.2d 107 (Minn. 1995).

56. *See Heinsma v. City of Vancouver,* 29 P.3d 709 (Wash. 2001); *Lowe v. Broward County,* 766 So. 2d 1199 (Fla. App. 4th Dist. 2000); *Slattery v. City of New York,* 697 N.Y.S.2d 603, 266 A.D.2d 24 (App. Div. 1999); *Crawford v. City of Chicago,* 304 Ill. App. 3d 818, 710 N.E.2d 91 (1999); *City of Atlanta v. Morgan,* 492 S.E.2d 193 (Ga. 1997); *Schaefer, supra* note 50.

57. *See Bailey v. City of Austin,* 972 S.W.2d 180 (Tex. Ct. App. 1998), *reh'g overruled* (Aug. 13, 1998), *review denied* (Jan. 7, 1999).

IV

The Military

Countless lesbian, gay, and bisexual people have served honorably in the armed services. Nevertheless, the Department of Defense (DOD) persists in arguing that the presence of openly gay, lesbian, and bisexual service members is incompatible with military service. On July 19, 1993, the Clinton administration announced a new policy addressing gay people in the military, known as "Don't Ask, Don't Tell" (DADT).[1] Later that summer, Congress enacted a somewhat harsher version, and the president signed the bill into law.[2] While the government claims that the policy is meant to stop military officials from asking service members about their sexual orientation and to end harassment and witch hunts, even the Pentagon has admitted that antigay speech and harassment is common under the DADT policy.[3]

This chapter examines the current military policy regarding lesbian and gay service members. It draws substantially from information provided in the Servicemembers Legal Defense Network's (SLDN) *Survival Guide* (see appendix A).

What is the "Don't Ask, Don't Tell" policy regarding lesbian and gay service members?

The policy known as "Don't Ask, Don't Tell" was established in a law passed by Congress to protect the military from the supposed damaging effect on morale of having openly gay, lesbian, and bisexual service members.[4] It provides that a member of the armed forces shall be discharged if one or more of the following findings are made: (1) that the member has engaged in, attempted to engage in, or solicited another to engage in a homosexual act or acts; (2) that the member has stated that he or she is a homosexual or bisexual, or words to that effect; or (3) that the member has married or attempted to marry a person known to be of the same sex.[5] Prior to DADT, the military's policy on lesbian and gay service members required that gay people be discharged, but the policy was not set out in official federal regulations.[6]

The first explicit policy targeting all lesbians and gay men in the military arose out of the McCarthy-era anticommunist hysteria, during which gay people, like communists, were thought to be a threat to national security. In 1953, President Dwight D. Eisenhower issued an executive order that stated, "True, confirmed, or habitual homosexual personnel, irrespective of sex, will not be permitted to serve in the Army in any capacity and prompt separation of known homosexuals from the Army is mandatory."[7] Prior to that time, the military court-martialed and discharged soldiers discovered to have had engaged in same-sex acts, but it did not discharge individuals based on their sexual orientation alone.[8]

The military policy banning homosexuals grew more stringent in the decades that followed. The DOD issued a series of directives dealing with lesbian and gay enlisted personnel and officers, which made expulsion from the military mandatory. The DADT policy purported to loosen the restrictions on lesbian and gay service people. It was supposed to be an improvement over the old policy in two respects: (1) congressional and military leaders acknowledged for the first time that lesbians and gay men serve in military service and do so honorably, and (2) advocates claimed that it would end intrusive questions about members' sexual orientation and stop "witch hunts."

Unfortunately, however, in practice the policy has been a change for the worse in its impact on lesbian and gay service members. In 2000, the Pentagon discharged a record 1,231 service members pursuant to DADT.[9] The numbers reflect that the Pentagon is discharging service members under the policy at a rate of three to four each day.[10] By comparison, in 1994, just after the policy was implemented, 617 persons were discharged.[11]

In addition, reports of anti-LGBT harassment within the military have increased.[12] In response to the July 1999 antigay murder of Army Private First Class Barry Winchell, and because of pressure from SLDN, Secretary of Defense William Cohen ordered the Pentagon Inspector General (IG) to conduct a study of anti-LGBT harassment in the military.[13] The IG's report, released in March 2000, admitted for the first time that anti-LGBT harassment is widespread.[14] In particular, the survey found that 80 percent of the seventy-five thousand service members surveyed reported hearing anti-LGBT comments.[15] In addition, 37 percent said they had witnessed or experienced targeted incidents of such harassment, and 85 percent said their command tolerated anti-LGBT harassment.[16]

In addition to reporting on anti-LGBT incidents, the DOD's working group also made thirteen recommendations to improve the Pentagon's antiharassment efforts. Although the Pentagon adopted the recommendations, antigay harassment continues to be rampant.[17]

What can I do to protect myself if I am being harassed?

SLDN recommends that service members document any incidents of harassment, including what happened; the date, time and place of the incident; the name and description of the harasser; and the names of any witnesses.[18] If a service member receives a threatening note, he or she should handle the note as little as possible and place it in a sealed container. If a service member's property is destroyed or vandalized, he or she should take pictures of the property or have trustworthy witnesses view the property.

SLDN also advises that, for service members who are lesbian, gay, or bisexual, it is best if witnesses do not know their sexual orientation. This will reduce the possibility that the witness will have to testify against the service member.

Lesbian, gay, and bisexual service members who are harassed are in a precarious situation if they decide to report the harassment. If the service member's sexual orientation is revealed during the reporting or investigation process, the service member is likely to face discharge. Thus, SLDN advises service members who are harassed to contact an attorney or legal organization to assess their options before reporting the harassment.

Are there any exceptions to the policy?

If a service member is found to have committed, attempted, or solicited someone else for a "homosexual act," he or she can avoid discharge if he or she can prove the following five things: (1) the conduct was not that person's usual and customary behavior; (2) the conduct is unlikely to happen again; (3) the person did not use force, coercion, or intimidation; (4) the person's continued presence in the armed forces would be consistent with proper discipline, good order, and morale; *and* (5) the person does *not* have the "propensity" or intent to engage in homosexual acts.[19] This is sometimes referred to as the "gay for a day" defense. People who have also stated that they are lesbian, gay, or bisexual (rather than just claiming that they had a one-time encounter) can avoid discharge only by proving that they do not have sex or intend to have sex with military persons and that they do not engage in, attempt to engage in, have a propensity to engage in, or intend to engage in homosexual acts.[20]

Very few service members have been successful in retaining their jobs under these provisions. Gay, lesbian, and bisexual service members should be warned that they have very little chance of succeeding if they rely on these exceptions.

If a lesbian or gay service member wishes to speak with a doctor or clergy member about his or her sexual orientation while in the service, are those discussions confidential?

They probably are not. Conversations between service members and their military doctors or psychologists generally are not confidential, although there is a limited exception for disclosure to military doctors when the patient is being treated for HIV.[21] Moreover, as of 2003, some health-care providers continue to believe they have a duty to turn in lesbian, gay, or bisexual service members who sought their help. Service members have been discharged based on information disclosed in their private counseling sessions, and in other cases, inquiries have been made into members' medical records.

In 1999, after the murder of Private First Class Winchell, President Bill Clinton signed an executive order amending the *Manual for Courts-Martial* to provide for sentence enhancement in hate crimes based on race, gender, sexual orientation, and disability.[22] The executive order also provides, for the first time, a limited privilege for conversations with psychotherapists, preventing them from being used as incriminating evidence in criminal trials. But because service members facing discharge under DADT generally go through administrative rather than criminal proceedings, the privilege does not apply to them.[23]

All communications regarding spiritual guidance between service members and chaplains should be confidential.[24] While most chaplains respect this confidentiality, some do not. In addition, some chaplains continue to give service members bad advice, including directing service members to turn themselves in, rather than advising them to consult a military attorney for advice.[25]

Are people regularly discharged under the policy?

Yes. The numbers vary from year to year, but on average the Pentagon fires service members for being lesbian, gay, or bisexual every day. In 2000, 1,231 service members were discharged, the highest number of discharges since 1987.[26]

Is there a difference in the treatment of women and men under the policy?

Although the policy applies to both men and women, the military is particularly aggressive in enforcing the policy against women. Though women comprise only 15 percent of the active-duty force, 24 percent of discharges for homosexuality in 2000 were women.[27] These disproportionate numbers may reflect "lesbian-baiting"—some women in the military complain that they risk being accused of being lesbians if they rebuff or report sexual advances by men. In other cases, women may be harassed as being lesbians because they do not conform to gender stereotypes by, for example, performing as well as men in traditionally male activities or jobs.

What kind of discharge does one get if discharged for being lesbian or gay?

If a service member is discharged under DADT, the discharge should be characterized as Honorable or General Under Honorable Conditions (General).[28] There are, however, some major exceptions.

Despite the regulations, some commanders recommend General discharges for service members even though they have honorable records, particularly in cases involving "homosexual acts." In cases involving "aggravating circumstances," commanders and discharge boards can recommend an Other than Honorable (OTH) discharge characterization.

Aggravating circumstances under DADT include private, consensual adult sexual acts that occur on a military vessel or aircraft; superior-subordinate relationships that do not involve fraternization or abuse of authority; or public touching, even if it occurs off base.

How can an OTH discharge affect someone in civilian life?

Discharge characterizations affect a member's eligibility for veterans benefits and civilian employment opportunities. An Honorable discharge is required to guarantee that a service member is eligible for all veterans benefits and educational benefits under the Montgomery G.I. Bill program.[29]

Service members with a General discharge are eligible for most veterans benefits other than the G.I. Bill program, but a General discharge might lead to difficulties in gaining civilian employment. In addition to the problems mentioned with respect to General discharges, an OTH discharge bars collection of unemployment compensation related to military service in most states.[30]

May a person be court-martialed for being lesbian or gay?

No. He or she can, however, be court-martialed for conduct involving homosexuality. If the military claims that the service member engaged in sodomy or in "indecent acts" or that the person's lesbian or gay conduct violated military rules against fraternization between superiors and subordinates or somehow affected good order and discipline,[31] the military may subject the member to trial by court-martial.[32]

Typically, service members are charged with violating Article 125 (which prohibits sodomy, defined as oral or anal sex, whether heterosexual or homosexual) or Article 134 (which prohibits conduct unbecoming and indecent acts). Convictions under these articles can result in up to fifteen years' imprisonment for sodomy or five years for conduct unbecoming for each act, plus a punitive discharge and fines.

Service members have also been charged with making a false official statement for denying their sexual orientation on enlistment forms used under the old policy.

What besides discharge may the military do to someone who is lesbian or gay?

Service members who come out can face intrusive investigations into their private lives; criminal prosecution;[33] recoupment;[34] lower discharge characterizations;[35] and loss of educational, unemployment, and pension benefits.[36]

Has the DADT policy ever been challenged in court?

There have been about a dozen challenges to the current DADT policy.[37] Although gay and lesbian plaintiffs have won at the trial court level in some cases, no federal court of appeals has held that DADT is unconstitutional. Lawsuits addressing military policies regarding lesbians and gay men have been going on for more than forty years.[38]

The military policy may be more vulnerable to legal challenge in the wake of the Supreme Court's decision in *Lawrence v. Texas*,[39] striking down a Texas law banning same-sex sodomy. Scholars have argued that the DADT policy is vulnerable under *Lawrence* because the primary justification put forth by the military is the negative attitudes of heterosexual service members toward lesbian, gay, and bisexual members, and the Court in *Lawrence* said that moral disapproval is not a sufficient reason to uphold a law or policy. Other legal scholars have cautioned, however, that the DADT policy may survive a post-*Lawrence* challenge because of the great deference that is granted to the military.

What can trigger an investigation?

On rare occasions, the process begins because someone has been observed having sex with a person of the same sex. Sometimes, the person will be turned in by a military doctor or clergy member after the service member disclosed his or her sexual orientation. Most often, however, an investigation is triggered when the individual's name comes up in connection with another case or when he or she is turned in by someone who knows or suspects the person is gay. Even a claim that one member is gay often results in extensive investigations of everyone associated with that person.

An investigation can be started only by a service member's commanding officer, and only if the person has "credible information" that there is a reason for discharge. "Credible information exists where the information, considering its source and the surrounding circumstances, supports a reasonable belief that a service member has engaged in homosexual conduct. It requires a determination based on articulable facts, not just a belief or suspicion."[40]

How is the discharge decision made?

In some branches, discharge proceedings begin with a formal notification that tells the service member the basis of discharge.[41] Around the same time, service members are also given an election of rights form, on which they must demand any rights they wish in the discharge proceedings.[42] SLDN advises service members to consult an attorney before waiving any rights.[43]

In most circumstances, if requested, service members have the right to a hearing before an administrative discharge board.[44] In these hearings, service members have a right to a military attorney and may also bring a civilian attorney retained and paid for by them.[45] A discharge board is responsible for making recommendations to the discharge authority (the officer authorized to approve the discharge) on whether the service member should be discharged. The boards are usually three officers or senior enlisted members who hear evidence from the service member and from the military.[46] If a majority of the board members vote for discharge, they must also recommend what type of discharge. Commanders nearly always approve a board's recommendation, although they will occasionally give a better result if errors are pointed out to them by the service member's attorney.[47]

Does the service member have any rights during the investigation?

Service members have the right to say nothing,[48] to sign nothing, and to get legal assistance[49] if they are questioned about their sexual orientation. In general, this is the best defense if you are questioned.

A service member may consult with a military defense attorney at any time. In many cases, however, service members may not be represented until after an investigation has been conducted. At that point, discharge proceedings may have already started.

Before speaking with a military attorney, the member should ask whether the attorney is a defense counsel and whether their conversations will be confidential.

Service members also have the right to be represented by civilian lawyers or legal workers, but this representation must be arranged by the service member. If you are under investigation, you should contact civilian counsel immediately.

If an enlisted member is called before the administrative discharge board, what rights does he or she have?

Enlisted members have the right to be informed of certain facts prior to appearing before an administrative discharge board. This includes the right to

   • know the reason for the proposed separation, including the circumstances on which it is based and a reference to the applicable regulations;
   • know whether the proposed separation could result in discharge or release from active duty or the reserves and the form and least favorable characterization of the proposed separation; and

• have a "reasonable period of time," not less than two days, in which to respond and to request a hearing before the administrative discharge board.

During the proceeding, the enlisted member has a right to

• submit a written statement and, if being discharged for homosexuality, to appear in person before the board to testify;
• consult with and be represented by qualified military counsel or by civilian counsel of the member's choosing (retained at his or her own expense); and
• question any witness who appears before the board.

Is it different for officers?

Officers who have completed their probationary period are subject to a somewhat better process.[50] In general, if a military commander finds that an investigation has come up with enough evidence to charge an officer with homosexuality, the officer will be ordered to appear before a board of inquiry and explain why he or she should be retained.[51] The officer's rights before a board of inquiry are similar to those of an enlisted member before an administrative discharge board.[52] If the board finds against the officer, he or she has a right to receive a copy of the board's findings and recommendations and to present a written rebuttal to a board of review.

At any time during the proceedings, the officer may resign from the service or request voluntary retirement (if otherwise eligible to retire).[53] The officer may be involuntarily discharged only by the secretary of the military department and only if removal is recommended by the board of inquiry.[54]

Is there any opportunity for appeal or review of the decision?

If a service member receives a less than fully Honorable discharge, he or she may be able to upgrade the discharge characterization by applying to the Discharge Review Board or to the Board for Correction of Military Records for the appropriate branch of service.[55]

Are members of a state national guard governed by the DADT policy?

State national guard units are considered to be both federal and state entities. During any period in which they are on federal active duty, federal law—including the DADT policy—governs their operations. When they are serving solely on state active duty, the federal law does not apply.[56] However, some state national guards may require that each member satisfy the criteria for "federal recognition," which is a determination that she or he is eligible for federal active duty status. Absent that requirement, you may have a claim under your state's constitution for protection from discrimination, but that claim can cover only state active duty employment that does not require federal recognition.[57]

NOTES

1. In 1993, President Clinton pledged to lift the ban on gays and lesbians serving in the military. What followed instead was a political contest between the president and Congress, with Clinton settling on a compromise: the "Don't Ask, Don't Tell" policy. The policy was originally articulated in a U.S. Secretary of Defense memorandum dated July 19, 1993, "Policy on Homosexual Conduct in the Armed Forces," and subsequently became the National Defense Authorization Act for fiscal year 1994, Pub. L. No. 103-160, § 571, 107 Stat. 1547. 1670 (1994) (codified at 10 U.S.C. § 654 (1994)). *See* William N. Eskridge Jr., *Gaylaw: Challenging the Apartheid of the Closet* 173 & 429 n.1 (1999). For a detailed history of the passage of the "Don't Ask, Don't Tell" policy, see Janet E. Halley, *Don't: A Reader's Guide to the Military's Anti-Gay Policy* 1926 (1999).

2. Pub. L. No. 103-160, § 571, 107 Stat. 1547. 1670 (1994) (codified at 10 U.S.C. § 654 (1994)). The implementing regulations are found in the Department of Defense Directive Nos., 1332.14.H (separation of enlisted personnel), 1332.30.H (separation of officers), and 1304.26 (enlistment). *See* Eskridge, *supra* note 1, at 173 & 429 n.1.

3. Department of Defense, *Evaluation Report: Military Environment with Respect to the Homosexual Conduct Policy* (Mar. 24, 2000).

4. The text of the statute follows:

(6) Success in combat requires military units that are characterized by high morale, good order and discipline, and unit cohesion. (7) One of the most critical elements in combat capability is unit cohesion, that is, the bonds of trust among individual service members that make the combat effectiveness of a military unit greater than the sum of the combat effectiveness of the individual unit members. . . . (13) The prohibition against homosexual conduct is a longstanding element of military law that continues to be necessary in the unique circumstances of military service. (14) The armed forces must maintain personnel policies that exclude persons whose presence in the armed forces would create an unacceptable risk to the armed forces' high standards of morale, good order and discipline, and unit cohesion that are the essence of military capability. (15) The presence in the armed forces

of persons who demonstrate a propensity or intent to engage in homosexual acts would create an unacceptable risk to the high standards of morale, good order and discipline, and unit cohesion that are the essence of military capability. 10 U.S.C. § 654(a).

5. 10 U.S.C. § 654(b). The statute provides the following definitions:

(1) The term "homosexual" means a person, regardless of sex, who engages in, attempts to engage in, has a propensity to engage in, or intends to engage in homosexual acts, and includes the terms "gay" and "lesbian". (2) The term "bisexual" means a person who engages in, attempts to engage in, has a propensity to engage in, or intends to engage in homosexual and heterosexual acts. (3) The term "homosexual act" means—(A) any bodily contact, actively undertaken or passively permitted, between members of the same sex for the purpose of satisfying sexual desires; and (B) any bodily contact which a reasonable person would understand to demonstrate a propensity or intent to engage in an act described in subparagraph (A). 10 U.S.C. § 654(f).

6. In addition to the federal regulation, Department of Defense Directive No. 1332.14 (Dec. 21, 1993) implements the policy. It provides:

Homosexual conduct is grounds for separation from the Military Services. . . . Homosexual conduct includes homosexual acts, a statement by a member that demonstrates a propensity or intent to engage in homosexual acts, or a homosexual marriage or attempted marriage. A statement by a member that demonstrates a propensity or intent to engage in homosexual acts is grounds for separation not because it reflects the member's sexual orientation, but because the statement indicates a likelihood that the member engages in or will engage in homosexual acts. A member's sexual orientation is considered a personal and private matter, and is not a bar to continued service under this section unless manifested by homosexual conduct. . . . A service member who has stated that he or she is gay is given the opportunity to rebut the presumption that he or she has a propensity to commit homosexual acts by presenting evidence to an administrative board that he or she "is not a person who engages in, attempts to engage in, has a propensity to engage in, or intends to engage in homosexual acts. DOD Directive No. 1332.14(H)(1)(b)(2).

7. AR 600-443, I, 2 (April 10, 1953).
8. *See* Allan Berube, *Coming Out under Fire: The History of Gay Men and Women in World War II* (1990).
9. *See Pentagon Discharges Record Number of Service Personnel under "Don't Ask, Don't Tell, Don't Pursue, Don't Harass,"* available at <www.sldn.org/templates/law/record.html?record=256>.
10. *See id.*
11. *See Annual Gay Discharges under "Don't Ask, Don't Tell, Don't Pursue, Don't Harass,"* available at <www.sldn.org/binary-data/SLDN_ARTICLES/pdf_file/352.pdf>.
12. Servicemembers Legal Defense Network, *Survival Guide: A Comprehensive Guide to "Don't Ask, Don't Tell, Don't Pursue, Don't Harass" and Related Military Policies* (4th ed. 2003) [hereinafter *Survival Guide*], available at <http://www.sldn.org>.
13. *Id.* at 5.

14. *Id.*

15. *See SLDN Conduct Unbecoming Reports,* available at <http://www.sldn.org/templates/law/record.html?section=22&record=25b>.

16. *Id.*

17. *Survival Guide, supra* note 12, at 5.

18. *Id.* at 32–33.

19. 10 U.S.C. § 654(b)(1).

20. 10 U.S.C. § 654(b)(2).

21. DOD Directive No. 6485.1, encl. 3.2 (Mar. 19, 1991) ("Information obtained from a Service member during, or as a result of, an epidemiological assessment interview may not be used against the Service member (in adverse criminal or administrative actions.")). *See also Survival Guide, supra* note 12, at 28.

22. *See* Exec. Order No. 13,140, 64 Fed. Reg. 55,115 (Oct. 6, 1999).

23. *Survival Guide, supra* note 12, at 28.

24. *Id.* at 14.

25. *Id.*

26. *See Pentagon Discharges, supra* note 9.

27. *Lesbian Baiting: The Disproportionate Impact of the Gay Policies on Women 1994–2000,* available at <www.sldn.org/binary-data/SLDN_ARTICLES/pdf_file/351.pdf>.

28. Department of Defense, *Overview, Directives Implementing the New DoD Policy on Homosexual Conduct in the Armed Forces,* Dec. 21, 1994. *See also Survival Guide, supra* note 12, at 24.

29. 38 U.S.C. § 3001.

30. *Survival Guide, supra* note 12, at 25.

31. *See* Uniform Code of Military Justice (U.C.M.J) art. 92, 125, 133, 134, 10 U.S.C. §§ 892, 925, 933, 934 (1983). *See also Manual for Courts-Martial,* United States 1984, IV-126, IV-131, para. 90.

32. *See* 32 C.F.R. § 41, app. A, pt. 1, § H.3.g.(5) (1990).

33. *Survival Guide, supra* note 12, at 23.

34. *Id.* at 44. *See also* "Gay Doctor Told to Pay Air Force for Education," *San Diego Union & Trib.,* May 30, 2001, at A3 (discussing decision from federal district court requiring former U.S. Air Force captain to pay back the government because he voluntarily came out as gay).

35. *Id.* at 24–25.

36. *Id.* at 25.

37. *See, e.g., Thorne v. United States Dep't of Defense,* 139 F.3d 893 (4th Cir. 1998); *Holmes v. California Army Nat'l Guard,* 124 F.3d 1126 (9th Cir. 1997), *reh'g and suggestion for reh'g en banc denied,* 155 F.3d 1049 (1998), *cert. denied,* 526 US 1067 (1999); *Philips v. Perry,* 106 F.3d 1420 (9th Cir. 1997); *Able v. United States,* 88 F.3d 1280 (2d Cir. 1996); *Richenberg v. Perry,* 97 F.3d 256 (8th Cir. 1996), *reh'g and suggestion for reh'g en banc denied* (1997), *cert. denied,* 522 U.S. 807 (1997); *Selland v. Perry,* 100 F.3d 950 (4th Cir. 1996), *cert. denied,* 520 U.S. 1210 (1997); *Thomasson v. Perry,* 80 F.3d 915 (4th Cir., 1995) (en banc), *cert. denied,* 519 U.S. 948.

38. *See Clackum v. United States,* 296 F.2d 226 (Ct. Claims 1960).

39. *Lawrence v. Texas,* 123 S. Ct. 2472 (2003).

40. DOD Directive 1332.14. Enlisted Administrative Separations. Guidelines for Fact-Finding Inquiries into Homosexual Conduct. Enclosure 4-1. Dec. 21, 1993; DOD Directive 1332.30. Separation of Regulator Commissioned Officers. Enclosure 8-1. Definitions. Guidelines for Fact-Finding Inquiries into Homosexual Conduct.

41. *See Survival Guide, supra* note 12, at 26.

42. *Id.*

43. *Id.*

44. *Id.* at 27.

45. *Id.*

46. *Id.* at 9.

47. *Id.* at 27.

48. Uniform Code of Military Justice (providing that service members have the right to remain silent), Art. 31 10 U.S.C. § 831.

49. Military members may call Servicemembers Legal Defense Network (SLDN) in Washington, D.C. at 202-328-FAIR or the Military Law Task Force (MLTF) in San Diego, California at 619-233-1701 for confidential legal assistance.

50. Probationary officers include regular officers with less than five years' active commissioned service and reserve component officers with less than three years' commissioned service. *See, e.g.,* Army Regulation 635-100, §§ 5–30. Generally, probationary officers are given very few due process rights and can be eliminated quickly by the secretary of the respective service branch on the recommendation of the General Officer Show Cause Authority, after being given an opportunity to consult with counsel and submit a written response to the charges against them. *See* Tesdahl, "Officer Administrative Eliminations— A System in Disrepair," *Army Lawyer,* June 1990, at 4 (Army Pamphlet 27-50-210). However, probationary officers recommended for an OTH discharge are entitled to full due process rights, including a hearing before a board of inquiry, accorded to nonprobationary officers. *Id.*

51. *See* 10 U.S.C. § 1182.

52. *See id.* at § 1185.

53. *See id.* at § 1186.

54. *See id.* at § 1184.

55. *See Survival Guide, supra* note 12, at 27–28.

56. *Perpich v. Department of Defense,* 496 U.S. 334 (1990).

57. *Holmes v. California National Guard,* 109 Cal. Rptr. 2d 154, 90 Cal. App. 4th 297 (2001).

V

Immigration

M any LGBT people living in the United States are not citizens and therefore face a unique set of challenges. Under the Constitution, the federal government has tremendous discretion to determine immigration policy, including almost absolute power to decide who may stay in the country and who may not. Although the rights of immigrants have been under extreme attack since the events of September 11, 2001, other changes in immigration laws and asylum policies have resulted in greater protection for LGBT people who come to the United States seeking refuge because their home country is not safe. Unfortunately, however, the United States still will not recognize binational same-sex couples or extend to them the benefits that are enjoyed by binational heterosexual married couples.

May I be refused entry into the United States or deported because I am gay?

No. Thanks to the work of Representative Barney Frank (D-Mass.) and others, Congress passed the 1990 Immigration Act, which eliminated earlier laws that allowed the Immigration and Naturalization Service (INS) to exclude people based solely on their sexual orientation. At one time, the federal immigration statute forbade anyone "afflicted with a psychopathic personality" from entering the United States.[1] In 1967, the U.S. Supreme Court interpreted that language to include homosexuals.[2] After the American Psychiatric Association's Board of Trustees deleted homosexuality from the list of mental disorders included in its Diagnostic and Statistical Manual of Mental Disorders (commonly called "the DSM") in December 1973, the INS claimed to exclude only those who were openly gay. Even so, many people who simply appeared to be gay were not allowed to immigrate. With the passage of the 1990 Immigration Act, immigration officials are no longer allowed even to ask a person's sexual orientation.

Not all recent changes to the immigration laws have worked in favor of gay and lesbian immigrants. Gay men and lesbians who had entered the country prior to 1990 (and thus illegally) used to be able to apply for a so-called 212(c) waiver of deportation if they could demonstrate seven years of permanent residency in the United States and other factors that would weigh in favor of their being allowed to stay, such as hardship to their family if deported, history of employment, property or business ties, and community service.[3] In 1996, however, Congress repealed the section 212(c) waiver provision, replacing it with a "cancellation of removal" procedure.[4] Although somewhat similar to the prior suspension of deportation remedy, the cancellation provision severely limits the class of people who may seek this type of relief. Applicants must demonstrate that their deportation will cause extreme hardship to a spouse, parent, or child who is a U.S. citizen or permanent resident.[5] Furthermore, only the hardship to the citizen is relevant for consideration, not any hardship suffered by the noncitizen deportee.

Although these statutes do not make any explicit distinction on the basis of sexual orientation, chances of success for gay couples under this provision are dubious, especially in light of the fact that under the earlier, more lenient provision, courts were unreceptive to the argument that deportation of a gay partner should be suspended because of the hardship it would cause the citizen.[6] Gay people who share a child in common may be able to argue that deportation of a parent would cause hardship to the child. However, considering the fact that courts have not always been willing to accept this argument even for biological parents,[7] adoptive gay parents may have a difficult time convincing immigration officials that undue hardship will result from deportation, with nonbiological/psychological gay parents facing even greater likelihood that these arguments will fail. Although the ACLU and other organizations have been successful in challenging some portions of the 1996 immigration amendments,[8] under the current law it is clearly more difficult for long-time residents of the United States whose initial entry was illegal to avoid deportation than it was prior to the elimination of the 212(c) waiver.

There are also two other ostensibly neutral provisions in current immigration law that have a disproportionate effect on LGBT people. The first is the "good moral character" provision. An immigrant must prove that he or she has had "good moral character" for a certain amount of time to qualify for naturalization;[9] to suspend a deportation action and convert it to a voluntary departure so as to take advantage of the "registry," a process available to undocumented immigrants;[10] and for other assorted purposes. At one point, the mere existence of sodomy laws within a state was sufficient evidence of a person's poor moral character, even if that person had not been convicted. Consequently, until the 1970s, this provision had been used against all gay men and lesbians, without any consideration of their individual conduct.[11] The sole fact that an individual engages in private consensual sodomy may no longer be used to prove poor moral character;[12] however, the INS regulations still provide that homosexual conduct involving minors, public solicitation, the violation of marital vows, or other "adverse public effects" may preclude a finding of good moral character.[13] Furthermore, lying under oath on immigration documents about any previous convictions for sex crimes may also result in a negative determination regarding "good moral character."[14]

The other potentially problematic provision requires that immigrants convicted of "crimes involving moral turpitude" be deported.[15] With the Supreme Court's announcement in Lawrence v. Texas, states may no longer criminalize private consensual acts of sodomy (see chapter 2). But violations of public sex, lewdness, or solicitation laws will still qualify as crimes involving moral turpitude.[16] If you have been convicted of one of these crimes, you are at risk of deportation. Therefore, you should consult with an immigration attorney before doing anything that would draw the INS's attention to you, such as applying for naturalization or leaving the country.

The INS has threatened to deport my partner. May we get married so that my partner can stay in the country? If we register for a civil union, will that be enough to stop the deportation proceedings?

Presently, no state allows citizens to enter into a civil marriage with their same-sex partner, which means that lesbian and gay couples do not have the option of marrying to avoid separation. Entering into a civil union in Vermont will not enable a person to sponsor his or her spouse for immigration purposes. The Defense of Marriage Act (DOMA) defines the term spouse for all federal law purposes (including immigration law) as limited to a married partner of the opposite sex.[17] Moreover, courts in immigration cases have ruled that a spouse must be someone of the opposite sex to qualify for special consideration.[18] Therefore, even if a state were to permit same-sex marriage under its laws, the marriage would not be recognized for immigration purposes.

May my partner (who is not a U.S. citizen) marry someone of a different sex to remain in the country?

Although some gay people do acquire lawful status as a result of marriage to someone of a different sex, and even though there are different reasons for marrying and different kinds of marriage, the INS considers "marriages of convenience" or "sham marriages" to be fraudulent if entered into solely for the purpose of obtaining immigration privileges. A marriage is a sham, according to the INS, "if the bride and groom did not intend to establish a life together at the time they were married."[19] The agency will examine the parties' "conduct and lifestyle before and after the marriage" to determine the parties' intent.[20] If the INS decides that a marriage is a sham, the noncitizen involved may be deported and barred forever from returning to the United States, and the individual he or she married faces a possible $250,000 fine and up to five years' imprisonment.[21]

My partner (who is not a U.S. citizen) and I were married or registered as partners in a foreign country (e.g., Canada, Denmark, France, Germany, the Netherlands, Norway, Sweden). Will that make it easier for my partner to come to the United States permanently?

No. Despite changes in the laws of many countries throughout the world, U.S. immigration law does not yet recognize same-sex marriage (or registered partnership) as the equivalent of heterosexual marriages. The federal DOMA restricts the definition of marriage for all federal law purposes, including immigration law.

Which countries recognize same-sex partners for the purposes of determining immigration benefits?

A number of countries, in addition to those that allow gay and lesbian couples to marry or to register as partners, treat same-sex couples as the equivalent of spouses when determining immigration issues. As of 2003, a total of fifteen counties recognized lesbian and gay relationships for purposes of immigration: Australia, Belgium, Canada, Denmark, Finland, France, Germany, Iceland, Israel, the Netherlands, New Zealand, Norway, South Africa, Sweden, and the United Kingdom.[22]

Are there any attempts being made to improve the situation in the United States?

Yes. Beginning in 2000, Representative Jerrold Nadler (D-N.Y.) has introduced legislation that would recognize same-sex "permanent partners" as the equivalent of spouses for immigration purposes and would extend all of the benefits currently offered to spouses to the permanent partners of gay and lesbian citizens.[23] A *permanent partner* is defined in the bill as any person who is (1) in an committed, intimate relationship with another adult in which both parties intend a lifelong commitment; (2) financially interdependent with that person; (3) not married to or in a permanent partnership with anyone other than that person; (4) unable to contract with that person to marry; and (5) not a first, second, or third degree blood relation of that person.[24]

Lesbian, gay, and bisexual people suffer tremendous persecution in my home country, and if I am deported, I fear for my safety. May I qualify for political asylum?

Possibly. As Amnesty International has reported,[25] it is a struggle in many countries simply to stay alive as an openly (or even as a closeted) lesbian, gay, or bisexual person. More and more lesbian, gay, and bisexual people from around the world are coming forward with stories of persecution, mutilation, shock therapy, and sometimes even execution of people for their sexual orientation. Under U.S. immigration law, the attorney general may grant political asylum to any person who has fled his or her home country because of persecution or a well-founded fear of persecution on account of race, religion, nationality, membership in a particular social group, or political opinion.[26]

Under the asylum statute, men and women who are targeted by their home government for persecution because of advocacy on behalf of LGBT rights may be protected on the basis of their political opinion. Increasingly, the INS has acknowledged that lesbian, gay, and bisexual people can also qualify as members of a particular social group that should be entitled to asylum.[27] In *Matter of Toboso-Alfonso,* the Bureau of Immigration Appeals allowed a Cuban gay man to stay in the United States rather than go home to face the Cuban government's persecution of homosexual men.[28] In 1993, an immigration judge granted asylum to a Brazilian man who feared persecution because of his membership in a particular social group, that is, of LGBT people.[29]

The immigration statute requires that individuals seeking asylum file their application within one year of arriving in the United States, unless the delay was caused by "extraordinary" or "changed" circumstances (e.g., only recently coming out).[30] The applicant must show not only that he or she personally fears persecution but also that an outsider would agree that the fear of persecution is reasonable. In the 1990s, federal courts started to accept the idea that lesbian, gay, and bisexual people may qualify as a particular social group entitled to asylum. However, the individual must make a specific showing that there is a likelihood of persecution in the home country. For instance, in 1997 the U.S. Court of Appeals for the Ninth Circuit rejected the claims of a Bulgarian gay man, finding that he had not given enough specific evidence to justify his fears of persecution.[31] In another 1997 case, a panel of immigration judges refused to grant a Russian lesbian asylum because it believed that the recent changes in the Russian government should decrease her fear of persecution.[32] The Ninth Circuit did not disturb the panel's findings on this point but sent the case back to the panel for further consideration after ruling that "medical" treatment designed to "cure" homosexuality, such as shock therapy, could establish grounds for an asylum claim even though the treatment was purportedly designed to cure rather than to punish.[33]

For more detailed advice, contact the Lesbian and Gay Immigration Rights Task Force. (See the list of LGBT legal groups in appendix A.)

I am a transgender person. May I obtain asylum?

Yes. In *Hernandez-Montiel v. INS,* the Ninth Circuit Court of Appeals ruled that "gay men with female sexual identities" constituted a "particular social group" that could qualify for asylum.[34] The court rejected the lower court's determination that the petitioner had been mistreated simply because he cross-dressed and found instead that the petitioner "manifest[ed] his sexual orientation by adopting gendered traits characteristically associated with women."[35] Because female-identified men had suffered past persecution in Mexico, and because there was a "clear probability" that the persecution would continue in the future, the court granted the petitioner's application for asylum and terminated the deportation proceedings against her.

I am an undocumented immigrant, and I am working off the books. I am being sexually harassed because my employer thinks I am gay, and he threatens to call the INS on me if I complain. What can I do?

All undocumented immigrants are living dangerously, especially those who are working off the books. Federal workplace laws setting wages and hours and regulating working conditions protect all employees, even undocumented immigrants. Enforcement of these laws can be difficult, however, when the workers victimized by these practices are themselves vulnerable to deportation. If you are being harassed because you are gay, it is quite possible that other workers are also being sexually harassed, mistreated, underpaid, or abused in some way. Consider working together with fellow coworkers for protection and contacting local agencies designed to enforce the law. If you are being sexually harassed, you may want to consider contacting the Equal Employment Opportunity Commission. That agency has no formal agreement to share information with the INS. You can also contact local organizations designed to serve the needs of the immigrant population in your area.

Notes

1. This provision was found in § 212(a)(4) of the Immigration and Nationality Act of 1952 [hereinafter INA], 8 U.S.C. § 1182(a)(4). The new list of grounds for exclusion can now be found at 8 U.S.C. § 1182 (2000).

2. *See Boutilier v. INS*, 387 U.S. 118, 119–20 (1967).

3. *See* INA § 212(c) (codified as amended at 8 U.S.C. § 1182(c) (1994)).

4. The 212(c) waiver provision was repealed by the illegal Immigration Reform and Immigrant Responsibility Act of 1996 [hereinafter IIRIRA] § 304(b), 110 Stat. at 3009-597 (Supp. III 1997).

5. *See* 8 U.S.C. § 1129b(1) (2001).

6. *See Sullivan v. INS*, 772 F.2d 609 (9th Cir. 1985).

7. *See, e.g., Perez v. INS*, 96 F.3d 390 (9th Cir. 1996).

8. *See INS v. St. Cyr*, 533 U.S. 289 (2001) (challenging retroactive application of the elimination of 212(c) waiver provision).

9. 8 U.S.C. § 1427(a) (1988 & Supp. II 1990).

10. 8 U.S.C. § 1259 (2000).

11. *See In re Longstaff,* 538 F. Supp. 589 (N.D. Tex. 1982) ("The citizens of Texas have long regarded the crime of homosexual conduct or sodomy, as it is commonly and historically referred to, to be immoral."), *aff'd,* 716 F.2d 1439 (5th Cir. 1983). *But see Nemetz v. INS,* 647 F.2d 432 (4th Cir. 1981) (overruling finding that homosexual applicant for naturalization lacked "good moral character" in light of the fact that applicant's conduct had been purely private, consensual, and without harm to the public); *In re Brodie,* 394 F. Supp. 1208 (D. Ore. 1975) (examining specific conduct of homosexual applicant and finding him to be of good moral character); *In re Labady,* 326 F. Supp. 924, 926 (S.D.N.Y. 1971) (accord).

12. *See Nemetz, supra* note 11; *see also Yepes-Prado v. INS,* 10 F.3d 1363, 1369 (9th Cir. 1993) (noting that 1990 amendment to federal immigration law eliminating "sexual deviancy" as a ground for exclusion "evidence[s] Congress's intent that private sexual conduct among consenting adults should no longer be considered a legitimate basis for making immigration decisions").

13. *See* INS Interpretations 316.1(f)(7), cited in Denise C. Hammond, "Immigration and Sexual Orientation: Developing Standards, Options, and Obstacles," 77 *No. 4 Interpreter Releases* 113, 116 (2000).

14. *See Kovacs v. United States,* 476 F.2d 843 (2d Cir. 1973) (purportedly penalizing applicant for lying about his criminal past, which included convictions for public sex, and not for his sexual orientation).

15. 8 U.S.C. § 1182(a)(2)(A) (2000).

16. *See Matter of Leyva,* 16 I. & N. Dec. 118 (BIA 1977); *Velez-Lozano v. INS,* 463 F.2d 1305 (D.D.C. 1972). *But cf. Yepes-Prado v. INS,* 10 F.3d 1363 (9th Cir. 1993) (private sexual conduct is not a grounds for deportation of an immigrant).

17. *See* 1 U.S.C. § 7 (Supp. V 1999).

18. *See Adams v. Howerton,* 673 F.2d 1036 (9th Cir. 1982).

19. *Garcia-Jaramillo v. INS,* 604 F.2d 1236, 1238 (9th Cir. 1979) (citing and quoting *Bark v. INS,* 511 F.2d 1200, 1201 (9th Cir. 1975)).

20. *Id.*

21. *See* 8 U.S.C. § 1325(c) (2001).

22. For more information about the rights of binational couples, go to the Lesbian and Gay Immigration Rights Task Force Web site, available at <www.lgirtf.org>.

23. *See* H.R. 832, 108th Cong. (2003).

24. Text of pending federal legislation is available at <http://thomas.loc.gov>.

25. *See* Amnesty Int'l, *Crimes of Hate, Conspiracy of Silence: Torture and Ill Treatment Based on Sexual Identity* (2001), available on-line at <www.amnesty.org>.

26. 8 U.S.C. § 1158(b) (1988).

27. *See generally* Suzanne B. Goldberg, "Give Me Liberty or Give Me Death: Political Asylum and the Global Persecution of Lesbians and Gay Men," 26 *Cornell Int'l L.J.* 605 (1993).

28. *Matter of Toboso-Alfonso,* 20 I. & N. Dec. 819 (BIA 1990).

29. *In re Tenorio,* No. A72-093-558 (Immigr. Ct., San Francisco July 26, 1993), reprinted in *Refugee Law and Policy* 713–20 (Karen Musalo et al., eds. 1997).

30. *See* 8 U.S.C. § 1158(a)(2)(B) (2001).

31. *See Vassilev v. INS,* 110 F.3d 72 (9th Cir. 1997).

32. *See Pitcherskaia v. INS.* 118 F. 3d 641, 645 (9th Cir. 1997) ("The BIA majority also concluded that recent political and social changes in the former Soviet Union make it unlikely that she would be 'subject to psychiatric treatment with persecutory intent upon [her] return to the present-day Russia.'").

33. *See id.* at 647–48.

34. *Hernandez-Montiel v. INS,* 225 F.3d 1084 (9th Cir. 2000).

35. *Id.* at 1096 (noting, "This case is about sexual identity, not fashion").

PART 2
Civil Rights in the Private Sector

VI

Employment in the Private Sector

LGBT people, just like everyone else, spend the vast majority of their waking hours at work. Jobs have also become an important mechanism for the distribution of social benefits, such as health insurance. Therefore, one can look to how people are treated at work as an important indicator of whether they are treated as equals. Although federal law does not yet protect workers from discrimination on the basis of sexual orientation, many states and municipalities have taken the lead by requiring equal treatment for gay and straight employees. Sexual-harassment law, which was once understood as only protecting women from men, also offers some protection for LGBT employees who are targeted for mistreatment by their supervisors or coworkers. In addition, an increasing number of private employers offer domestic-partner benefits, having realized that these policies make "good business sense" because many highly desirable gay employees would prefer to work in friendly environments. Some progress is also being made in protecting transgender people. (For a fuller discussion of those issues, see chapter 12.) Nevertheless, many jurisdictions still allow employers to treat their workers unequally solely because of their sexual orientation, placing LGBT employees at risk on a daily basis of being harassed or fired for no other reason than the fact that they are not heterosexual.

May my employer discriminate against me because I am lesbian or gay?

Unfortunately, in many cases, the answer is yes. Most employees, unless they have a union contract, are employed "at will." This means that their employer can fire them or treat them differently for almost any reason, including the fact that they are gay. As this book goes to press in 2003, there is no national law against employment discrimination on the basis of sexual orientation. The federal civil rights law that bans employment discrimination, Title VII,[1] prohibits employers from discriminating on the basis of race, sex, religion, or national origin, but not sexual orientation.[2] (See below for discussion of when LGBT employees can assert sex-discrimination claims.) Another federal law, the Americans with Disabilities Act, prohibits discrimination based on disability.[3] The Employment Non-Discrimination Act (ENDA), which has been pending in Congress for years, would extend civil rights law to ban discrimination based on sexual orientation.

Some states and cities, however, have passed laws prohibiting companies that operate within their borders from discriminating against LGBT people. Fourteen states—California, Connecticut, Hawaii, Maryland, Massachusetts, Minnesota, Nevada, New Hampshire, New Jersey, New Mexico, New York, Rhode Island, Vermont, and Wisconsin—plus the District of Columbia forbid private employers from discriminating against employees because of their sexual orientation as a matter of state law. In a fifteenth state—Oregon—an appellate court has ruled that the state law prohibiting sex discrimination in the workplace covers sexual orientation as well.[4] Minnesota, New Mexico, and Rhode Island have also outlawed employment discrimination based on gender identity.

Many large metropolitan areas—including Atlanta, Baltimore, Boston, Chicago, Detroit, New York, Los Angeles, Miami/Dade County, New Orleans, Philadelphia, San Diego, San Francisco, and Seattle—have antidiscrimination ordinances as well. Statutes continue to be adopted throughout the country, so you should check on whether there has been recent legislative activity in your area.

What kinds of work policies are covered by these laws?

The forms of employment discrimination banned by these laws include a variety of actions by an employer. The definition of discrimination includes firing, failing to hire or promote, offering a lower salary or benefits, or offering inferior work terms (such as less-convenient scheduling) and conditions. Inferior work terms can also include harassment on the job, if employers ignore such behavior and allow a hostile environment to develop in the workplace (see below). An employer also may not "limit, segregate, or classify" its employees or applicants for employment in any way that would limit their opportunities within the company because of a protected characteristic. An example of such impermissible treatment would be if Latino workers were given the heaviest or dirtiest jobs. Employment agencies are also covered; they may not discriminate in the placement of workers based on their membership in a protected group. Likewise, labor unions may not exclude or treat individuals differently based on these protected characteristics.

May I bring a claim against my union if it fails to process my grievance because I am gay?

Yes. The Supreme Court has made clear that the Labor Management Relations Act,[5] which gives a union the authority to negotiate on behalf of its members, also implicitly imposes on union leadership a "duty of fair representation [that] requires a union to serve the interests of all members without hostility or discrimination toward any, to exercise its discretion with complete good faith and honesty, and to avoid arbitrary conduct . . . [meaning that] a union breaches the duty of fair representation when its conduct toward a member of the bargaining unit is arbitrary, discriminatory, or in bad faith."[6] Therefore, a union may not ignore your grievance (or simply "go through the motions") just because you are gay. Moreover, unions have similar duties to their members under state law. For example, a union that forced a gay member to pursue his own grievance, when other members had been able to rely on the union to draft and research their complaints, may be held liable under state law for breach of the duty of fair representation.[7]

May I talk about my partner or personal life at work? May I bring my partner to company events?

It depends on whether sexual-orientation discrimination is prohibited where you work. In addition to state and city laws, a company's own internal policy or a union contract may prohibit discriminatory treatment. Of course, if no employees are permitted to put up pictures of family and friends in their office, then the policy is not discriminatory even if it is unreasonable. If there is no law or policy that covers you, you should realize that talking about your partner or personal life at work may result in your employer discriminating against you for being lesbian or gay.

Some businesses specifically permit spouses but not "significant others" to come to company events. Although such a policy affects unmarried heterosexual couples as well as same-sex couples, the impact is obviously greater on the latter because there is no option to marry. Again, you should consult state or local law or company policy. Absent that, LGBT employees should consider lobbying the management of their company to make accommodations for couples who do not fall within a "spouses only" policy, perhaps in alliance with unmarried heterosexual couples who are also affected.

May my company keep me off certain assignments or accounts because our customers do not like LGBT people?

Again, as sexual-orientation discrimination is not illegal in most places, private employers generally may use sexual orientation as an excuse to treat lesbian, gay, or bisexual employees differently, without breaking the law. Where it is illegal to discriminate against LGBT employees, however, a general concern about customer discomfort cannot justify inferior work assignments. Although all businesses are unique, in most situations, the sexual orientation of the employee should be irrelevant to his or her ability to perform the job. Some states, such as Massachusetts, explicitly prohibit employment discrimination against gay men and lesbians on the ground that customers "are uncomfortable working with people of different sexual orientation."[8] It is a well-established principle under most civil rights laws that customer preference is not an acceptable reason for discrimination.[9]

My state or city does have a nondiscrimination law that covers sexual orientation. Must I tell my employer that I am gay?

No. Laws that prohibit sexual-orientation discrimination protect everyone, no matter what their sexual orientation, from being treated differently because they are straight or because they are lesbian, gay, or bisexual. They also protect you if you are perceived as lesbian, gay, or bisexual, even if you are not. Thus, you do not have to come out to be protected. The decision to come out is a private one, and each individual should make that choice for himself or herself.

One of the disadvantages of *not* coming out, however, is that an employer who treats you negatively because he or she suspects that you are gay may be able to claim ignorance of your sexual orientation as a defense to a discrimination complaint. Coming out to an employer may also avoid awkward situations by deterring people from making homophobic remarks in your presence.

Does the law forbid harassment against LGBT employees in the workplace?

If the law in your area covers discrimination on the basis of sexual orientation, then harassment will be prohibited because it is considered to be a form of discrimination. In any location, you will be protected by federal law from harassment based on race, sex, religion, or national origin.

What kinds of harassing activities are prohibited?

Forbidden harassment can take many forms. Verbal abuse or physical violence, regardless of whether it is sexual in nature, is prohibited if it creates a *hostile work environment.*[10] A hostile work environment is one in which an employer allows workers to be verbally taunted and/or physically assaulted because of a protected characteristic, and the harassment is so severe and pervasive that it materially alters the employee's work environment.[11] Another forbidden form of harassment is what is called *quid pro quo* (a Latin phrase meaning "something for something") harassment, which occurs when an employer or supervisor demands sex in return for promoting or not firing an employee or for other job benefits.

What should I do if I have been the victim of discrimination or harassment?

If you feel that you have suffered from discriminatory treatment or harassment, you should do two things to start to protect yourself. The first is to document what happens: keep records of any incidents that you think show discrimination and gather important documents. You should compile a copy of all of your personnel records, especially positive work evaluations, to prevent any tampering and to avoid any surprise additions (such as backdated reprimands) to your file. You should also obtain copies of any employee handbooks or nondiscrimination policies maintained by your employer.

The second is to seek help, first from your employer. Some companies have an officer who is specifically responsible for dealing with discrimination or harassment claims. You may be able to solve the problem internally. Also, the fact that you complained can be important later on, depending on how your employer responds, particularly in harassment cases; therefore, be sure to lodge your complaint with the appropriate supervisor. It is critical to develop a written record, because the success or failure of many employment-discrimination claims hinges on sufficient proof. Employers can often come up with multiple reasons why an employee was treated badly, ranging from poor performance to "bad attitude." The complaints that you filed can help prove that the reason for any adverse employment action was sexual-orientation discrimination, and not other factors that would provide a legally permissible basis for negative treatment on the job.

You should also consider contacting a lawyer. Both local and national LGBT law associations have referral directories. There are different options, depending on where you work and live, and an attorney will be able to help you decide what is the best way to proceed. Some employers have internal processes that may need to be used before outside legal action can be taken. Most states and cities have a civil rights or human rights commission where individuals can file complaints if there is a local law that covers you. Some of the processes require the services of a lawyer; others do not. Nevertheless, it is a good idea to develop a strategy after consulting with an attorney who can advise you on the pros and cons of the different options.

If there is no local law prohibiting discrimination on the basis of sexual orientation, could I be protected from harassment based on my sex?

The simple answer is yes, because "although Title VII does not include a prohibition of discrimination based on sexual orientation, homosexuals are just as protected by Title VII's [other] existing protections as anyone else."[12] For example, if you are being discriminated at work because of your race, it is irrelevant to your right to sue that you are gay. Therefore, if the discrimination you suffered included discrimination for any of the reasons covered by Title VII, you will be protected.

In 1989, the Supreme Court ruled that discrimination based on sexual stereotyping violated Title VII. In that case, a woman was denied a promotion because her supervisors believed that she was not feminine enough.[13] Since then, courts have begun to recognize on a more consistent basis that harassment against individuals who do not conform to gender expectations, either through their dress (e.g., a man wearing an earring) or mannerisms (e.g., a woman acting "too aggressive"), is a form of sex discrimination and, therefore, a violation of existing federal law.

Complicating matters is the fact that under federal law an employee may bring a claim for sexual harassment "on the basis of sex,"[14] but discrimination based on sexual orientation is not prohibited.[15] The court decisions are mixed on whether harassment of lesbians and gay men (or people perceived as lesbian or gay) who deviate from gender norms counts as sexual harassment based on sex.[16] It seems likely that the Supreme Court will need to resolve this issue and provide further guidance. And just to make it even more perplexing, it is possible that a state or local law prohibiting sex discrimination could be interpreted to include harassment-based on sexual stereotyping, even if the federal law is not interpreted that way.[17]

Another possible basis for a sex-discrimination claim focuses on the differential nature of the employer's response to a complaint of harassment rather than on the motivation of the individual harasser(s). If an employer refused to take action to stop certain kinds of harassment being directed against a man (e.g., grabbing at the genital area) that the employer would take and/or had taken when they had been directed against women employees, this would constitute discrimination against the male employee on the basis of sex.[18]

Can it be considered discrimination if I am being harassed at work by someone of the same sex?

Yes. Sexual harassment violates Title VII regardless of whether the harasser and victim are of different sexes or the same sex.[19] Increasing numbers of sexual-harassment cases involving male-on-male harassment are being filed. According to the Equal Employment Opportunity Commission (EEOC), the number of sexual harassment claims brought by men doubled during the 1990s to 13.5 percent, with the vast majority of those claims apparently involving same-sex harassment.[20] For the most part, these are hostile environment cases in which a group of men single out a particular man for harassment, often including sexualized assaultive conduct and sexual or antigay epithets. This can occur regardless of whether the victim is gay or is perceived as being gay. For example, the Eighth Circuit Court of Appeals recognized a claim of sexual harassment brought by a heterosexual male employee; he was continuously called "homo," asked to perform sexual acts, and subjected to other inappropriate sexualized behavior by male coworkers.[21] As the answer to the previous question indicates, however, the courts are split on whether such behavior satisfies the "because of sex" requirement of Title VII. This is likely to be an area of law with many continuing developments after this book is published, so consult an attorney if you are being harassed at work to find out the current state of the law.

My jurisdiction does not have a nondiscrimination law that covers sexual orientation. What can I do if I have been fired or denied a promotion?

While you may not be able to bring a lawsuit for sexual-orientation discrimination, your employer may have violated some other law, a contract, or a collective-bargaining agreement. If you have experienced discriminatory treatment at work, you should consult with an attorney. If you have an employment contract, or sometimes even just an employee manual, you may have a guarantee you will be fired only for good cause or that you will have a hearing before termination. Some states have general contract law that is sympathetic to employees fired for reasons "violating public policy"[22] or that favors employees who relied on assurances by employers that they would not be fired for arbitrary reasons.[23] Labor laws sometimes prohibit or prevent employers from interfering with the political activities of their employees, and these laws can offer you some protection if you suffered discrimination because you came out or did progay political work.

In at least one state, discrimination based on sexual orientation is included within the state law's prohibition of sex discrimination (for all discriminatory actions, not just sexual harassment). An Oregon state appeals court ruled that the state law that prohibits discrimination based on sex, including the sex of one's associates, includes a prohibition of antigay discrimination.[24] Accordingly, LGBT rights advocates have increasingly argued that courts should interpret existing state law prohibitions of sex discrimination in this way.[25]

Laws other than civil rights laws may also be useful in challenging discrimination. For example, California attorneys relied on state regulatory law to classify Pacific Telephone as a quasi monopoly and therefore as a governmental actor for purposes of whether the state constitution applied. As a result, the company was prohibited from engaging in "arbitrary employment discrimination," including sexual-orientation discrimination.[26]

May a private employer offer benefits to married employees, such as insurance coverage for their spouses, and refuse to extend that coverage to partners of lesbian and gay employees?

The answer is usually yes, even in places with laws that prohibit sexual-orientation discrimination, but the reason is fairly complicated.

First, as to health insurance that you get through your job, there is a federal law that controls the regulation of health insurance policies offered through private sector jobs. The Supreme Court has held that this federal law, the Employee Retirement Income Security Act, known as ERISA,[27] preempts (or trumps) any state or local antidiscrimination law that would mandate particular benefits or forms of coverage, such as domestic-partner coverage.[28] As a result, states and localities with antidiscrimination laws currently cannot require private-sector employees to cover domestic partners. Nor can a company's internal nondiscrimination policy currently be used as a basis for requiring domestic-partner policies, because invoking such a policy as a mandate for health benefits has been found to be in conflict with ERISA.[29] A federal antidiscrimination law (or changes in insurance laws) would be necessary to alter that preemption rule. Hundreds of employers, however, have chosen to offer domestic-partner coverage voluntarily.[30]

One mechanism by which state or local civil rights laws can reach private employers' health insurance policies is by using the power of government as a purchaser rather than as a regulator. Several cities have enacted provisions that require all businesses that contract with the city to offer domestic-partner coverage. San Francisco was the first jurisdiction to enact such an ordinance, and Los Angeles, Oakland, and Seattle passed similar laws.[31] This kind of provision is not a mandate: it merely conditions the awarding of city contracts on whether the prospective contractor offers domestic-partner coverage. A business can choose not to bid on the contracts and thereby remain unaffected by the law. Although a number of businesses seeking city contracts banded together to challenge the San Francisco ordinance, it was sustained by the federal courts.[32] However, such an ordinance can reach only the employees who work either in the city itself or, if at another location, on the particular project or service provided to the city.[33] California will require all businesses with state contracts to offer domestic partner benefits to their employees starting in 2007.[34]

For most benefits other than health insurance or pensions, however, ERISA is irrelevant. The question then becomes whether a private employer can be required to recognize domestic partners in the context of other benefits (bereavement leave, for example).[35] Thus, for purposes of analyzing whether non-health-care benefits can be required, one turns to antidiscrimination law.

Limiting benefits to spouses is usually considered to be discrimination on the basis of marital status, rather than discrimination based on sexual orientation, because, it is argued, unmarried heterosexual couples are also adversely affected.[36] Twenty states and the District of Columbia have laws prohibiting marital-status discrimination in employment.[37] Even in those states, however, the courts have tended to interpret the laws narrowly, ruling that domestic partners are not "similarly situated" to married persons and thus not covered by the marital-status laws.[38] As for sexual-orientation claims, there has been only one success so far in persuading courts that the denial of domestic-partner benefits constitutes sexual-orientation discrimination because of the heavier impact on lesbian and gay couples.[39] This argument may meet with greater success in the future, however, as creating the first precedent is the most difficult.

In sum, your best chances of securing domestic-partner benefits from a private-sector employer probably will come from applying pressure, together with other employees, to persuade the company to institute such a policy if it does not have one already. When considering whether to recognize domestic partners, companies tend to be motivated by the desire to foster their image as a forward-thinking company and by the need to compete for skilled workers. Alternatively, investigate whether the company contracts with cities that require such policies, as well as whether your state or city has an antidiscrimination law that covers marital status or sexual orientation.

May the government deny a professional license because of the applicant's sexual orientation?

No. Many professions, from massage therapy to real estate brokerage to the practice of law, require a license. Frequently, the person seeking the license must certify that he or she possesses a "good moral character." In the past, homosexuality was considered synonymous with immorality, posing a significant problem for LGBT people who sought professional licenses. As those stereotypes have changed, however, so too have licensing requirements surrounding sexual orientation.

For example, LGBT people cannot be disqualified from the practice of law solely on the basis of their sexuality. The U.S. Supreme Court declared more than forty years ago that although a state may require a good moral character and proficiency in its laws, it may not prevent someone from practicing law unless the particular qualification requirement has a "rational connection with the applicant's fitness or capacity to practice law."[40] State supreme courts have extended this rationale to apply to LGBT people,[41] with the Florida court holding that "[p]rivate noncommercial sex acts between consenting adults are not relevant to prove fitness to practice law."[42]

I need a security clearance to keep my job or be promoted. Will I be able to get a security clearance as an LGBT person?

Yes. It used to be a common practice that security clearances were denied to LGBT people, on the theory that they were especially vulnerable to blackmail.[43] As more gay people came out of the closet, the blackmail theory lost credibility. In 1995, President Clinton ended this practice when he amended the security clearance regulations through executive order to prevent discrimination on the basis of sexual orientation[44] and commanded, "No inference concerning the standards in this section may be raised solely on the basis of the sexual orientation of the employee."[45] President Bush retained these Clinton administration orders, so these protections against discrimination are still in place.[46]

Do antidiscrimination laws cover religious organizations?

They only sometimes cover religious organizations. Persons who work for religiously affiliated organizations will have a more difficult time in court than those working for secular employers. Even in states and cities where sexual-orientation discrimination is outlawed, the law might contain a religious exemption that allows faith-based organizations to discriminate against gay people.[47] This is because some religious organizations consider opposition to homosexuality to be part of their religious beliefs, and they argue that forcing them to hire gay people would infringe on their right to practice their religion without government interference.[48] Religious organizations are exempt from other antidiscrimination provisions as well.[49] The result is that employees of religious groups have little protection from discrimination.

NOTES

1. 42 U.S.C. § 2000e.

2. *Bibby v. Philadelphia Coca-Cola Bottling Co.*, 260 F.3d 257 (3d Cir. 2001); *Higgins v. New Balance Athletic Shoe, Inc.*, 194 F.3d 252, 259 (1st Cir. 1999); *Hopkins v. Baltimore Gas & Elec. Co.*, 77 F.3d 745, 751–52 & n.3 (4th Cir. 1996); *Williamson v. A. G. Edwards & Sons*, 876 F.2d 69, 70 (8th Cir. 1989).

3. 42 U.S.C. § 12112.

4. *Tanner v. Oregon Health Sci. Univ.*, 157 Or. App. 502, 971 P.2d 435 (1998).

5. *See* 28 U.S.C. § 185(b).

6. *Marquez v. Screen Actors Guild, Inc.,* 525 U.S. 33, 44 (1998) (quoting *Vaca v. Sipes,* 386 U.S. 171, 177, 190 (1967), (discussing 29 U.S.C. § 158(b)).

7. *See Martin v. New York State Dep't of Corr. Servs.,* 115 F. Supp. 2d 307, 316–18 (N.D.N.Y. 2000) (discussing New York State Labor Relations Act, N.Y. Labor Law § 700, *et seq.* (2000)). *But see Wilhelm v. Sunrise Northeast, Inc.,* 923 F. Supp. 330 (D. Conn. 1995) (holding that a state's general antidiscrimination law protecting LGBT people from unfair employment practices is preempted by the federal labor law statute, which does not prohibit sexual-orientation discrimination, when the issue is a union's duty of fair representation).

8. 804 Code of Mass. Reg. § 3.01(3)(b)(2) (2001).

9. *See Fernandez v. Winn Oil,* 653 F.2d 1273, 1276 (9th Cir. 1981); *Diaz v. Pan Am. World Airways,* 442 F.2d 385, 389 (5th Cir. 1971).

10. *See Meritor Savings Bank v. Vinson,* 447 U.S. 57 (1986).

11. *See Harris v. Forklift Sys., Inc.,* 510 U.S. 17 (1993).

12. *Tanner v. Prima Donna Resorts, Inc.,* 919 F. Supp. 351, 355 (D. Nev. 1996). *But cf. Vandeventer v. Wabash Nat. Corp.,* 887 F. Supp. 1178, 1180 (N.D. Ind. 1995) ("[B]eing homosexual does not deprive someone of protection from sexual harassment under Title VII, it is merely irrelevant to it. The issue is and remains whether one is discriminated against because of one's gender.").

13. *Price Waterhouse v. Hopkins,* 490 U.S. 228 (1989).

14. *Oncale v. Sundowner Offshore Servs., Inc.,* 523 U.S. 75, 81 (1998) ("[The plaintiff] must always prove that the conduct at issue was not merely tinged with offensive sexual connotations, but actually constituted discrimination because of sex.").

15. *See, e.g., Bibby, supra* note 2; *Higgins, supra* note 2, at 259; *Hopkins, supra* note 2, at 751–52 & n.3; and *Williamson, supra* note 2, at 70.

16. Courts have struggled with how to classify particular cases. In a very fractured opinion, in which no one theory commanded a majority, an eleven-judge en banc panel of the Ninth Circuit held that a gay man who was subject to sexualized physical assault and antigay slurs could sue for sex discrimination. The court could not agree whether it was the sexualized nature of the assaults or the gender stereotyping behind them that provided a basis for the claim. *Rene v. MGM Grand Hotel, Inc.,* 305 F.3d 1061 (9th Cir. 2002) (en banc), *cert. denied,* 123 S.Ct. 1573 (2003). The Third Circuit ruled that in a case in which the harassment consisted of nonsexual physical assault and being called "faggot," "sissy," and other antigay epithets, plaintiff failed to prove that he was harassed because he did not conform to gender-role stereotypes. *Bibby, supra* note 2.

17. A similar divergence between state and federal interpretations of discrimination has happened before. Prior to an amendment by Congress that explicitly made pregnancy a prohibited basis for discrimination, the U.S. Supreme Court interpreted Title VII to mean that discrimination on the basis of pregnancy would not qualify as sex discrimination under that statute. *See General Elec. Co. v. Gilbert,* 429 U.S. 125 (1976). Numerous state courts interpreted their civil rights laws more broadly, however, finding that the prohibition on sex-based discrimination also covers discrimination based on pregnancy. *See, e.g., Quaker Oats Co. v. Cedar Rapids Human Rights Comm'n,* 268 N.W.2d 862, 866–67 (Iowa 1978); *Massachusetts Elec. Co. v. Massachusetts Comm'n Against Discrimination,* 375 Mass. 160, 165–66; 375 N.E.2d 1192, 1198–99 (1978). A broader interpretation under state law could happen with sexual-harassment law as well.

18. *See, e.g., Quick v. Donaldson Co., Inc.,* 90 F.3d 1372 (8th Cir. 1996) (reviving sexual-harassment claim in which employer allowed abusive conduct toward male employees); *Wilcox v. Dome Ry. Servs.,* 987 F. Supp. 682, 689 (S.D. Ill. 1997) (finding that plaintiff stated a claim of disparate treatment regarding the employer's treatment of male-on-male sexual harassment claims but dismissing claim because plaintiff had not raised it in preliminary administrative proceedings); *Cummings v. Koehnen,* 568 N.W.2d 418, 410 n.1 (Minn. 1997) (reversing trial court's summary dismissal of plaintiff's claim of sexual harassment and failure of employer to investigate harassing conduct).

19. *See Oncale,* supra note 14.

20. *See* Reed Abelson, "Men, Increasingly, Are the Ones Claiming Sex Harassment by Men," *N.Y. Times,* June 10, 2001, at A1.

21. *See Schmedding v. TNEMEC Co., Inc.,* 187 F.3d 862, 864–65 (8th Cir. 1999); *see also Doe v. City of Belleville,* 119 F.3d 563, 592 (7th Cir. 1997) (acknowledging that the victim of harassment was perceived to be, but was not in fact, gay), *vacated,* 523 U.S. 1001 (1998) *and abrogated by Oncale, supra* note 14.

22. *See, e.g., Peterman v. International Bhd. of Teamsters,* 174 Cal. App. 2d 184, 344 P.2d 25 (1959) (dismissal based on employee's refusal to perjure himself violates public policy); *Payne v. Rozendaal,* 147 Vt. 488, 520 A.2d 586 (1986) (termination of an employee based solely on age violates public policy). *But see Hicks v. Arthur,* 843 F. Supp. 949 (E.D. Pa. 1994) (finding no public policy exceptions to general at-will employment because there is no clearly established public policy against sexual-orientation or pregnancy discrimination).

23. *See, e.g., Touissant v. Blue Cross & Blue Shield of Mich.,* 408 Mich. 579, 292 N.W.2d 880 (1980); *Rabago-Alvarez v. Dart Indus., Inc.,* 55 Cal. 3d 91, 127 Cal. Rptr. 222 (1976).

24. *See Tanner, supra* note 4.

25. *See, e.g., Baehr v. Lewin,* 74 Haw. 530 (1993). See chapter 9 for a fuller discussion of the use of sex- and gender-discrimination arguments to attack discrimination against lesbians and gay men.

26. *Gay Law Students Ass'n v. Pacific Tel. & Tel. Co.,* 24 Cal. 3d 458, 472 (1979).

27. 29 U.S.C. § 1001 *et seq.* ERISA is primarily concerned with pension rights; however, it also has a major impact on health-care benefits.

28. *See Shaw v. Delta Airlines, Inc.,* 463 U.S. 85 (1983).

29. *See Rovira v. AT&T,* 817 F. Supp. 1062 (S.D.N.Y. 1993) (finding that despite company's nondiscrimination policy, gay life partner of deceased employee not entitled to benefits under employee's death benefits plan governed by ERISA).

30. *See* Human Rights Campaign, *The State of the Workplace for Lesbian, Gay, Bisexual and Transgendered Americans, 2002* (addressed in appendix A) (listing Fortune 500 Companies that provide domestic-partner health benefits), available at <www.hrc.org>.

31. *See* Joseph Hanania, "Bias Against Gays Today Often Subtle, Sometime Not So: Some Defuse Tensions by Confronting, Ignoring or Sidestepping Their Harassers," *L.A. Times,* Feb. 18, 2001, at W1. Other cities are considering such legislation. *See, e.g.,* Winnie McCroy, "Vendor Partner-Benefits Bill Now 'Veto Proof,'" *N.Y. Blade,* May 9, 2003 (noting that New York City Council on the verge of passing legislation requiring city contractors to provide health benefits to employees' domestic partners).

32. *S. D. Myers, Inc. v. City and County of San Francisco,* 253 F.3d 461 (9th Cir.

2001); *Air Trans. Ass'n of Am. v. City and County of San Francisco,* 266 F.3d 1064 (9th Cir. 2001), *aff'g* 992 F. Supp. 1149 (N.D. Cal. 1998) [hereinafter *Air Transport*].

33. *See Myers, supra* note 32.

34. *See* Ethan Rarick, "Davis Signs Bill to Expand Benefits for Domestic Partners," *San Jose Mercury News,* Oct. 13, 2003, at 18.

35. *See Air Transport, supra* note 32, at 1163–64.

36. *See Ross v. Denver Dep't of Health & Hosp.,* 883 P.2d 516 (Colo. Ct. App. 1994); *Rutgers Council of AAUP Chapters v. Rutgers Univ.,* 298 N.J. Super. 442, 452+ (1997).

37. The twenty states are Alaska, California, Connecticut, Delaware, Florida, Hawaii, Illinois, Maryland, Michigan, Minnesota, Montana, Nebraska, New Hampshire, New Jersey, New York, North Dakota, Oregon, Virginia, Washington, and Wisconsin. Indiana prohibits marital-status discrimination only with regard to the employment of teachers. The American Association for Single People has an extensive Web site documenting how the law currently favors married over nonmarried people. *See* <www.singlesrights.com>.

38. *See Funderburke v. Uniondale Union Free Sch. Dist.,* 676 N.Y.S.2d 199, 251 A.D.2d 622 (App. Div. 1998); *Phillips v. Wisconsin Pers. Comm'n,* 167 Wis. 2d 205, 482 N.W.2d 121 (Ct. App. 1992).

39. *See Levin v. Yeshiva Univ.,* 96 N.Y.2d 484 (2001) (finding that denial of married-student housing to domestic partners of homosexual students violated New York City statute prohibiting practices that had a disparate (differentially heavy) discriminatory impact due to sexual orientation); *Tanner, supra* note 4, at 516, 971 P.2d at 443 (finding that the denial of benefits constituted sexual-orientation discrimination because it had a disparate effect on same-sex couples but that the civil rights statute did not apply because it exempted bona fide benefits plans from its scope).

40. *Schware v. Board of Bar Examiners,* 353 U.S. 232, 239 (1957).

41. *See, e.g., Application of Kimball,* 347 N.Y.S.2d 453, 301 N.E.2d 436 (1973).

42. *Florida Bd. of Bar Examiners Re N.R.S.,* 403 So. 2d 1315 (Fla. 1981).

43. *See, e.g., McKeand v. Laird,* 490 F.2d 1262 (9th Cir. 1973); *Adams v. Laird,* 420 F.2d 230 (D.C. Cir. 1969).

44. *See* Exec. Order 12,968 (Aug. 2, 1995).

45. Marlene Cimons, "Clinton Ends Prohibition of Security Clearances for Gays," *L.A. Times,* Aug. 5, 1995, at 4. *See also* Jill Zuckman, "US Security Ban on Gays to End: Clinton to Change Clearances Policy," *Boston Globe,* Aug. 4, 1995, at 1.

46. Shawn Zeller, "A New GOP 'Tone' on Gay Rights?" *National Journal,* May 26, 2001, available at 2001 WL 7182194.

47. *See, e.g.,* Cal. Gov't Code § 12926(d); Nev. Rev. Stat. Ann. § 613.320(1)(b). Wisconsin is currently the only state whose antidiscrimination law covers both religious and secular employers. *See* Wis. Stat. Ann. § 111.31 *et seq.*

48. *See Hall v. Baptist Mem. Health Care Corp.,* 215 F.3d 618, 626 (6th Cir. 2000). Business owners who claim a right to discriminate based on their personal religious beliefs will not be granted an exemption from an antidiscrimination law. *See Hyman v. City of Louisville,* 132 F. Supp. 2d 528 (W.D. Ky. 2001), *judgment vacated on other grounds by* 53 Fed. Appx. 740 (6th Cir. 2002) (unpublished decision).

49. *See Corporation of the Presiding Bishop of the Church of Jesus Christ of Latter Day Saints v. Amos,* 483 U.S. 327 (1987).

VII

Housing and Credit

Many people find it difficult to locate safe and affordable housing and secure credit, but these projects can be particularly stressful when one fears that he or she will be discriminated against because of his or her sexual orientation or gender identity. In 1968, Congress passed the Fair Housing Act, which prohibited discrimination on the basis of race, color, religion, sex, or national origin.[1] This law was amended in 1989 to add disability, including HIV and AIDS, to the list of protected categories. Congress has never amended these provisions to prohibit discrimination on the basis of sexual orientation or gender identity. As a result, LGBT people have had to rely on state and local laws for protection from discrimination in housing. Twelve states and numerous cities and counties prohibit sexual-orientation discrimination; three states also explicitly outlaw housing discrimination against transgender people. Unfortunately, however, many LGBT people are still vulnerable to the arbitrary and irrational prejudices of some landlords.

Congress passed similar legislation concerning credit in 1974 called the Equal Credit Opportunity Act;[2] its purpose was to "promote the availability of credit to all creditworthy applicants without regard to race, color, religion, national origin, sex, marital status, or age."[3] Although this provision also does not list sexual orientation or gender identity as a protected category, at least one federal court thus far has interpreted these provisions as protecting individuals who are discriminated against because they do not conform to gender stereotypes. In addition, seven states have passed laws prohibiting sexual-orientation discrimination regarding credit, and three states specifically protect transgendered individuals. As a general matter, however, LGBT people are still at risk of unequal treatment at the hands of creditors.

HOUSING

Are there any places that forbid sexual-orientation discrimination in housing?

Twelve state statutes prohibit housing discrimination on the basis of sexual orientation: Connecticut, Hawaii, Maryland, Massachusetts, Minnesota, New Hampshire, New Jersey, New Mexico, New York, Rhode Island, Vermont, and Wisconsin. There is also statutory protection in the District of Columbia. In addition, California courts have interpreted the state's housing law to outlaw all forms of arbitrary discrimination by landlords, including discrimination against gay men and lesbians.[4] The statutes in Minnesota, New Mexico, and Rhode Island specifically prohibit discrimination in housing based on gender identity and expression as well. Likewise, a growing number of cities and counties have extended protection to LGBT people. Among the cities where sexual-orientation discrimination in housing is prohibited are Alexandria, Virginia; Atlanta; Baltimore; Boston; Boulder; Chicago; Columbus; Denver; Hartford; Los Angeles; Miami; Milwaukee; Minneapolis; New Orleans; New York; Oakland; Philadelphia; Pittsburgh; Portland; San Diego; San Francisco; San Jose; Seattle; St. Paul; and Tucson.

May a private landlord in other places refuse to rent to a same-sex couple or an LGBT individual?

Often the answer is yes. American law offers property owners tremendous discretion to decide who their tenants will be. So long as the landlord does not explicitly discriminate on the basis of a characteristic that the federal, state, or local government has specifically protected, such as race, a landlord may deny a rental to anyone for any reason.

LGBT people can sometimes protect themselves by using other laws. For example, approximately half of the states prohibit housing discrimination on the basis of marital status.[5] Consequently, a same-sex couple denied a lease because they are not married may have a claim against the landlord. Some landlords have maintained that their right to freedom of religion means that they cannot be required to rent to people who may have nonmarital sex, but the courts have been mixed on whether this argument has merit.[6] Other landlords have attempted to refuse to rent to gay men because of fears about contamination by HIV. When faced with such a case, however, a New Jersey court decided in favor of the two gay prospective tenants, finding that the state's disability discrimination statute protected them from being turned down because of a "perceived disability."[7]

May I be excluded from public or federally subsidized housing because of my sexual orientation?

No. Public-housing authorities (PHAs) have the authority, subject to the review of the Department of Housing and Urban Development (HUD), to consider various factors in determining whether an applicant is eligible for housing.[8] For example, PHAs may (and in some cases must) exclude individuals who have prior drug convictions or who are subject to a lifetime registration requirement for a sex crime (see chapter 2). The regulations make clear, however, that "[t]he tenant selection criteria to be established and information to be considered shall be reasonably related to individual attributes and behavior of an applicant and shall not be related to those which may be imputed to a particular group or category of persons of which an applicant may be a member."[9] These protections regarding public housing also apply to Section 8 housing, which is privately owned but heavily subsidized by the federal government.[10]

Therefore, an exclusion based on the sole ground that the applicant is an LGBT person is impermissible; officials would have to show that a particular applicant threatens "the health, safety or welfare of other tenants."[11] PHAs are empowered to investigate applicants only to the extent that verification of eligibility is necessary. You should not be questioned about your private sexual acts because they should not constitute a reason for exclusion. If you are asked questions that you believe may have been inappropriate attempts to glean your sexual orientation, contact one of the groups listed in appendix A.

For couples, however, there are additional considerations. Throughout much of federal housing law, the term *family* is defined as "two or more persons related by blood, marriage, or operation of law, who occupy the same dwelling or unit."[12] For purposes of determining eligibility for federal public housing, however, the term *family* is defined so as also to include "families consisting of a single person."[13] Therefore, ironically, gay and lesbian couples probably do not qualify as "families" for public housing under these statutory eligibility requirements unless both are parents (biological and/or adoptive) of the same child, but individual LGBT people can qualify as a one-person "family."

What rights do I have regarding my application for public housing?

Applicants for public housing are entitled to certain due process rights; that is, the PHA is constitutionally required to do or not to do certain things in dealing with applications. For example, the selection criteria used by a PHA must be specified in writing and be publicized, meaning that the PHA must make copies of the admissions policy available upon request.[14] The PHA must inform the applicant of the disposition of his or her application within a reasonable amount of time and provide the reasons for that disposition.[15] Moreover, as mentioned earlier, the PHA may not automatically exclude all persons who are members of a particular group, such as unwed mothers, welfare recipients, or LGBT people. Instead, each applicant must be evaluated as an individual.

Many state and local governments have their own housing programs. The eligibility requirements for those programs vary, and a complete survey of each jurisdiction is beyond the scope of this chapter. If you believe that impermissible standards were applied to your application for housing or that you were denied due process rights by a government agency, you should determine whether there are administrative appeals rights. If there are not, the only recourse may be to challenge the governmental action in court. Again, you can contact one of the organizations listed in appendix A.

May a private landlord evict an LGBT tenant because of his or her sexual orientation or gender identity?

That depends on the terms of the lease. If a tenant is protected by a written lease, the landlord usually cannot evict him or her without proof that the lease has been violated. Unfortunately, many leases are written in ways that favor the landlord, such as including specific instructions on how the apartment may be used and how many people may share it. Some leases restrict occupancy to the person who signed the lease or to those related "by blood or by marriage." If the lease has such a provision and the tenant's lover or roommate moves in, the landlord may try to evict both the tenant and the roommate.

Some lease provisions, however, may be unenforceable in the courts. All states have laws governing the rental of property, and some seriously limit the ability of a landlord to take arbitrary or discriminatory action against a tenant. For example, in 1983, New York passed a statute that permits every tenant to have at least one other person living in the apartment, regardless of the nature of the relationship between them and regardless of any terms to the contrary in the lease.[16]

People living in rent-controlled or rent-stabilized apartments may have more legal protections. Because people who live in these units are benefiting from subsidized rents that may be increased if the tenant leaves, courts pay particular attention to their claims when a landlord attempts to eject them. In *Braschi v. Stahl Associates,* New York's highest court found that a landlord could not evict Miguel Braschi, the long-term lover of the tenant of a rent-controlled apartment who had died of AIDS.[17] Although Braschi's name had never been added to the lease, he argued that the landlord was prohibited from evicting "either the surviving spouse of the deceased tenant or some other member of the deceased tenant's family who had been living with the tenant."[18] The court accepted Braschi's argument that, for the purposes of rent-control laws, he should be considered family of his deceased partner:

The term family . . . should not be rigidly restricted to those people who have formalized their relationship by obtaining, for instance, a marriage certificate or an adoption order. The intended protection against sudden eviction should not rest on fictitious legal distinctions or genetic history, but instead should find its foundation in the reality of family life. In the context of eviction, a more realistic, and certainly equally valid, view of a family includes two adult lifetime partners whose relationship is long term and characterized by an emotional and financial commitment and interdependence.[19]

After the *Braschi* decision, New York courts considered on a case-by-case basis which factors were appropriate to take into account when determining who should qualify as a "family member."[20] Later, the Division of Housing and Community Renewal codified the *Braschi* principles in its regulations and extended them to rent-stabilized as well as rent-controlled housing. The New York law now defines *family member* to include a "person residing with the tenant in the housing accommodation as a primary residence who can prove emotional and financial commitment, and interdependence between such person and the tenant."[21] It lists eight factors as suggested bases for a determination of commitment and interdependence, such as longevity of the relationship; whether the couple shared household expenses and intermingled finances; whether they formalized legal obligations toward each other; and whether they held themselves out as family members and regularly performed family-type activities and family functions. The law specifically excludes evidence of a sexual relationship. The test is not toothless; courts have found insufficient evidence of a family connection in some cases.[22] Nevertheless, this extended definition of family offers important protections to gay men and lesbians.

More recent cases have continued this trend. Two New York housing court judges have ruled that a law prohibiting the eviction of a married couple when one spouse is disabled applies equally to lesbian and gay couples.[23] In the more recent of these two cases, *Mandell v. Cummins,* the judge cited *Levin v. Yeshiva University,* an important 2001 case holding that a policy requiring a couple to be married to qualify for subsidized married-student housing violated the prohibition on sexual-orientation discrimination (see question below on student housing), as the basis for his ruling that the city's antidiscrimination statute mandated that result.[24] Regardless of the reasons the landlord gives for eviction, every tenant is entitled to a court hearing prior to eviction. Furthermore, no tenant may be evicted unless a formal court order has been issued. The tenant is *always* entitled to adequate notice of the hearing and must be allowed to participate in the proceedings. If a landlord threatens eviction or serves a notice of eviction, legal advice should be sought immediately.

If I am already in public and federally subsidized housing, may I be evicted simply because I am an LGBT person?

No. If a person meets the eligibility requirements and is a public-housing tenant, he or she may not be evicted solely on the basis of his or her sexual orientation or gender identity.

A series of cases from the 1970s clarified the protections required by the Constitution for beneficiaries of public-housing programs. In 1970, a federal appellate court ruled in *Escalera v. New York City Housing Authority* that along with notice for the reasons for eviction, due process demands that public-housing tenants be given access to PHA files that relate to them and be given an opportunity to confront and cross-examine those who provide information adverse to them.[25] Three years later, in *Joy v. Daniels,* another federal court of appeals made clear that a tenant could not be evicted from public housing unless good cause had been shown.[26]

Later cases have extended the rationale of the *Joy* court to Section 8 hous-ing[27] and other federally subsidized private housing units.[28]

Since these cases were handed down, HUD has incorporated this standard into its governing regulations. A landlord may only evict a tenant from public housing for material noncompliance with the rental agree-ment, any drug-related criminal activity on or near the premises, any other type of criminal activity that would threatens the safety or well-being of other residents, or "other good cause."[29] A conviction for sexual conduct in public, for example, may constitute grounds for eviction under the criminal activity provision. The regulations define "material noncompli-ance with the rental agreement" to include "adversely affect[ing] the health or safety of any person or the right of any tenant to the quiet en-joyment of the leased premises and related project facilities."[30]

As is true for applications to get into public housing (see previous question), such determinations must be made on the basis of individual, and not group, considerations. Therefore, merely being LGBT would not justify eviction without an evaluation of how an individual's conduct is allegedly interfering with the other tenants' enjoyment of their apart-ments. The Supreme Court has made clear that irrational animus against homosexual people is a constitutionally impermissible basis for state dis-crimination.[31]

May I be turned down by a co-op board because of my sexual orientation?

In most places, you may. Co-op boards have as much discretion in selecting a buyer as an individual selling a house. Co-ops are unique forms of property ownership, in which the interest of any one individual prop-erty owner is linked to those of the other owners of the property. As one court said, "In the absence of discriminatory practices prohibited by law, the directors of a residential housing cooperative have the contractual and inherent power to approve or disapprove the transfer of shares and the assignment of proprietary leases."[32] This means that in most cases, there is little an LGBT person can do to challenge an owner or co-op board's refusal to sell, unless there is a state or local statute specifically outlawing housing discrimination on account of sexual orientation or gender iden-tity.[33]

A co-op board may also have the ability to prevent owners from transferring or selling their property to the person of their choice. Boards usually have the right to review any transaction in advance and to veto a transfer. As a result, LGBT people may not even be able to leave an apartment to their partners under a will or to sell a half-interest when their partners move in without first securing the approval of the co-op board. Anyone who wants to prepare a will with such a transfer clause should either seek preapproval from the board or try to make the partner a joint owner of the apartment.

My partner and I own a home in an area that is zoned for "single families" only. Are we violating the zoning laws because we are not married?

As our definitions of family evolve to include same-sex couples and other kinds of nontraditional relationships, the answer to this question should be no. But lingering Supreme Court precedents may still mean that some families could be at risk under restrictive zoning laws. In *City of Belle Terre v. Boraas,* the Supreme Court decided that it is legal for a neighborhood to limit houses in its area only to those related by "blood, adoption or marriage" without interfering with an individual's right of association to determine what kind of family he or she will construct.[34] A community may not, however, limit the ability of extended family members who share a biological link to live together.[35] Therefore, same-sex partners living in an area zoned for "single families," but who do not, for example, have a child in common, could face problems. More recently though, some courts have taken a more liberal view of family. A New York court found that a gay male couple could not be evicted because of an "immediate family" clause, unless there was some other evidence of harm by their presence. The court found that it was not "productive to spend judicial time conjuring up artificial distinctions among various types of sexual, fraternal, and economic relationships."[36]

May my university exclude my partner and me from our school's married-student housing?

Many universities all over the country have voluntarily changed their married-student housing policies so that same-sex couples may take advantage of this highly subsidized housing. Unfortunately, however, ACLU estimates indicate that approximately half of the universities nationwide that offer family housing discriminate against same-sex couples.[37] As this book goes to press, ACLU campus groups and LGBT student groups are actively working to change policies at University of California-Berkeley, University of Texas in Austin, University of Kansas in Lawrence, Iowa State University in Ames, Ohio University, University of Kentucky in Lexington, and elsewhere.[38]

Few courts have explicitly addressed the issue of whether schools are required by law to offer such housing to same-sex couples. Prior to 2001, in cases of housing and other types of discrimination against same-sex couples, courts typically compared gay and lesbian plaintiffs to single heterosexual people and concluded that there was no impermissible discrimination because all unmarried people, gay and straight alike, were denied access to a particular benefit (e.g., subsidized housing). Some courts have also justified their decisions by asserting that the state has the right to express a policy preference for marriage by distributing benefits in a manner that benefits married people.[39] In 2001, however, New York's highest court, the Court of Appeals, issued a breakthrough opinion by ruling that Yeshiva University's policy excluding same-sex couples from the housing available to married students at its medical school violated the New York City law prohibiting discrimination based on sexual orientation.[40] While determining that the housing policy did not discriminate on the basis of marital status, the court ruled that a policy offering subsidized housing exclusively to married students and their spouses had a disparate impact—that is, a disproportionately negative effect—on gay men and lesbians, who could not marry their partners, and thereby the policy violated New York City law.

As public awareness increases about the harms that result from the exclusion of gay and lesbian couples from the institution of civil marriage, other courts will likely start to recognize that the distribution of benefits on basis of the marital status of an individual or couple can no longer be considered a neutral policy decision.

CREDIT

May I be denied a mortgage because of my sexual orientation?

Yes, you may, except in those places that have specifically outlawed sexual-orientation discrimination. Even then, a local antidiscrimination ordinance may not apply to mortgage applications if a different state regulatory scheme controls them.[41] As of 2003, state laws in Connecticut,

Massachusetts, Minnesota, New Mexico, New York, Rhode Island, Vermont, and Wisconsin specifically prohibit sexual-orientation discrimination with regard to credit, as do local ordinances in cities such as Alexandria (Virginia), Chicago, Columbus, Detroit, and Portland (Maine), and in the District of Columbia. The laws in Minnesota, New Mexico, and Rhode Island also explicitly prohibit credit discrimination against transgender applicants.

If you and your partner are applying together and you want to have both incomes considered, you may have some protection under the federal Equal Credit Opportunity Act (ECOA) of 1975. This law prohibits discrimination on the basis of race, color, religion, national origin, sex, or marital status, as well as other conditions, and prohibits lenders from turning down two applicants for a joint mortgage simply because they are not married.[42] (See next question.) Many states have similar laws protecting against discrimination with regard to obtaining credit. Therefore, if you have been denied credit, one or more of these laws may apply even if it does not expressly protect sexual orientation or gender identity. For example, in 2001, a federal court of appeals ruled that the ECOA's protections against sex discrimination also prohibited unequal treatment based on the fact that an applicant does not conform to gender stereotypes.[43]

As a general matter, the personal life of an applicant for a mortgage should be irrelevant to whether he or she is creditworthy. In the past, however, banks and other lenders claimed that unmarried people, and in particular single women, were financially unreliable.[44] As a result, all unmarried women and, to a lesser degree, gay men have historically found it relatively more difficult to secure credit. The economic irrationality of this position has helped to eradicate this type of discriminatory treatment. If such antiquated arguments are used against you, and no state or local law protects you, you may want to consider complaining to the bank's corporate management.

May my partner and I be denied a joint mortgage because we are not married?

Unmarried couples are protected from discrimination when seeking credit under both federal law, that is, the ECOA, and under the laws of many states. Therefore, two people applying for a joint mortgage may not be denied simply because they are not married. In *Markham v. Colonial Mortgage Service Co.,* a federal court of appeals ruled that although "judicially-enforceable rights such as support and maintenance are legal consequences of married status, they are irrelevancies as far as the credit-worthiness of joint applicants is concerned."[45] Thus, the fact that one applicant does not have a duty to support the other should be irrelevant. Furthermore, unmarried couples have a right to demand that their incomes be combined when the lender assesses their creditworthiness in a joint mortgage application.[46] Some courts, however, have held that a bank may refuse to offer an unmarried couple the discounted rate that it would offer to a married couple without violating the ECOA.[47]

NOTES

1. *See* Fair Housing Act of 1968, 42 U.S.C. § 3601 *et seq.* (1994 & Supp. IV 1999).

2. *See* Equal Credit Opportunity Act, 15 U.S.C. § 1691 *et seq.* (1994 & Supp. IV 1999).

3. *See* 12 C.F.R. § 202.1(b) (2003).

4. *See* Cal. Civ. Code § 51, as interpreted by *Hubert v. Williams,* 133 Cal. App. 3d (Supp.) 1, 184 Cal. Rptr. 161 (Super Ct. 1982).

5. These states are Alaska, California, Colorado, Connecticut, Delaware, Hawaii, Illinois, Maryland, Massachusetts, Michigan, Minnesota, Montana, Nebraska, New Hampshire, New Jersey, New York, North Dakota, Oregon, Rhode Island, Vermont, Virginia, Washington, and Wisconsin.

6. *See, e.g., Smith v. Fair Employment & Hous. Comm'n,* 12 Cal. 4th 1143, 913 P.2d 909 (1996) (rejecting free exercise challenge); *Swanner v. Anchorage Equal Rights Comm'n,* 874 P.2d 274 (Alaska 1994) (accord); *Attorney Gen. v. Desilets,* 418 Mass. 316, 636 N.E.2d 233 (1994) (reversing summary judgment in favor of landlords, who had raised Free Exercise defense to charge of housing discrimination); *Thomas v. Anchorage Equal Rights Comm'n,* 165 F.3d 692, 712+ (9th Cir. 1999) (rejecting Free Exercise Clause challenge to law prohibiting housing discrimination based on marital status but invalidating law as impermissible infringement of religious speech), *opinion withdrawn by* 220 F.3d 1134, *and vacated,* 220 F.3d 1134 (9th Cir. 2000) (dismissing landlord's complaint as unripe). *But see McCready v. Hoffius,* 459 Mich. 1235, 593 N.W.2d 545 (1998) (vacating portion of lower court opinion that had sustained discrimination statute against Free Exercise Clause challenge and remanding for "further consideration"); *cf. North Dakota Fair Hous. Council v. Peterson,* 625 N.W.2d 551 (N.D. 2001) (finding that landlords' refusal to rent to unmarried couple did not violate Human Rights Act's prohibition on marital-status discrimination because state law still prohibited cohabitation by unmarried individuals of the opposite sex).

7. *See Poff v. Caro,* 228 N.J. Super. 370, 549 A.2d 900 (1987).

8. *See* 42 U.S.C. § 1437d(c)(2) (2003).

9. *See* 24 C.F.R. § 960.203(a) (2003).

10. *See, e.g., Jeffries v. Georgia Residential Fin. Auth.,* 678 F.2d 919, 924–25 (11th Cir. 1982).

11. *See* 24 C.F.R. § 960.203(c) (2003).

12. *See, e.g.,* 24 C.F.R. § 235.1206(c)(1) (2003), cited in *Diaz v. Virginia Hous. Auth.,* 101 F. Supp. 2d 415, 421 n.13 (E.D. Va. 2000) (pointing out examples in federal law in which benefits were distributed unequally based on marital status). It is unclear whether a civil union or registered domestic partnership would suffice to support a classification as a family "by operation of law," although the Defense of Marriage Act may pose a significant obstacle to those trying to argue in favor of such an interpretation of federal housing law.

13. *See* 42 U.S.C. § 1437a(b)(3) (2003).

14. *See* 24 C.F.R. § 960.202.

15. *See id.* at § 960.208.

16. *See* N.Y. Real Prop. Law § 235-f.

17. *Braschi v. Stahl Assocs.,* 544 N.Y.S.2d 784, 543 N.E.2d 49 (1989).

18. *Id.* at 785.

19. *Id.* at 788–89.

20. *See Rent Stabilization Ass'n v. Higgins,* 608 N.Y.S.2d 930, 933, 630 N.E.2d 626, 629 (1993).

21. New York Rent Stab. Regulations, § 2500.2(n)(2). Other states' laws reflect an evolving definition of family. For example, under Massachusetts housing law, a *family* consists of "two or more persons who live or will live regularly in a unit as their primary residence whose income and resources are available to meet the household's needs; and who are either related by blood, marriage, or operation of law, or who have otherwise evidenced a *stable inter-dependent relationship.*" 760 Code of Mass. Reg. 5.03 (2003) (emphasis added).

22. *See, e.g., 390 West End Assocs. v. Wildfoerster,* 661 N.Y.S.2d 202, 241 A.D.2d 402 (App. Div. 1997) (surviving partner in gay relationship that satisfied most relevant factors was not a *family member* for rent stabilization because deceased partner died without a will and had not named his partner as the beneficiary of his life insurance policy); *521 East 72nd St. Realty Co. v. Weltsek, N.Y.L.J.,* July 3, 1996, at 29 (N.Y. Civ. Ct. June 1996) (surviving gay partner not a *family member* because couple had not opened joint bank accounts, pooled their individual government benefits, or held themselves out as a family to their landlord).

23. *Knafo v. Ching, N.Y.L.J.,* Dec. 6, 2000, at 28 (N.Y. Civ. Ct. Nov. 2000); *Mandell v. Cummins, N.Y.L.J.,* July 25, 2001, at 18 (N.Y. Civ. Ct. July 2001).

24. "[T]he Court of Appeals construed [the city code] to recognize the status of lesbian life partners and to advance public policy considerations substantially identical to those herein where this court must construe the City Human Rights Law and the Rent Stabilization Code to avoid disparate impact upon a protected class." *Mandell, supra* note 23.

25. *Escalera v. New York City Hous. Auth.,* 425 F.2d 853 (2d Cir. 1970).

26. *See Joy v. Daniels,* 479 F.2d 1236 (4th Cir. 1973).

27. *See Jeffries, supra* note 10, at 925; *Christian v. Silver Maples Ltd. Dividend Hous.*

Ass'n, 1986 U.S. Dist Lexis 27154 (E.D. Mich 1986) (finding state action under the Section 8 New Construction program, despite lack of direct government involvement in the eviction decision).

28. *See Joy, supra* note 26, at 1243 (holding that tenants of privately owned units receiving federal subsidies under Section 221(d)(3) of the National Housing Act are entitled to due process protections); *Green v. Copperstone, Ltd.,* 28 Md. App 498, 346 A.2d 686, 697 (1975) (holding that tenant of unit that received construction and financing subsidy under Section 236 of the National Housing Act is entitled to good-cause eviction protection).

29. *See, e.g.,* 24 C.F.R. § 982.310 (2003) (grounds for eviction from Section 8 housing); *see also id.* at § 966.4(l)(2)(i) (2003) (listing tenant's obligations); *id.* at § 247.3 (2003) (delineating conditions under which tenant is entitled to occupancy). For a more extensive discussion of good cause eviction, see Marc Jolin, "Good Cause Eviction and the Low Income Housing Tax Credit," 67 *U. Chi. L. Rev.* 521, 529+ (2000).

30. *See* 24 C.F.R. § 247.3(c) (2003).

31. *See Romer v. Evans,* 517 U.S. 620, 634 (1996)

32. *See Bachman v. State Div. of Human Rights,* 481 N.Y.S.2d 858, 860, 104 A.D.2d 111, 114 (App. Div. 1984).

33. *See id.*

34. *City of Belle Terre v. Boraas,* 416 U.S. 1 (1974).

35. *See Moore v. City of East Cleveland,* 431 U.S. 494 (1977).

36. *See 420 East 80th Co. v. Chin,* 455 N.Y.S.2d 42, 43, 115 Misc. 2d 195, 196 (App. Div. 1982). *See also Borough of Glassboro v. Vallorosi,* 117 N.J. 421, 568 A.2d 888 (1990) (group of students living together show "stability and permanency" as the "functional equivalent of a family" for purposes of restrictive ordinance); *Baer v. Town of Brookhaven,* 540 N.Y.S. 2d 234, 537 N.E.2d 619 (1989) (elderly unrelated persons living together are "functionally equivalent family" who cannot be excluded from "family" zone).

37. *See* ACLU Press Release, "New York High Court Hears Arguments in ACLU Case Charging Yeshiva University with Anti-Gay Housing Bias," April 24, 2001, available at <www.aclu.org/news/2001/n042401a.html>.

38. *See id.*

39. *See, e.g., Beaty v. Truck Ins. Exch.,* 6 Cal. App. 4th 1455, 1465 (3d Dist. 1992) ("Our refusal to grant plaintiffs the relief they seek reaffirms our recognition of a strong public policy favoring marriage. No similar policy favors the maintenance of nonmarital relationships. . . . In the absence of legislation which grants to members of a nonmarital relationship the same benefits as those granted to spouses, no basis exists in this context for extending to nonmarital relations the preferential status afforded to marital relations.") (internal quotations and citations omitted).

40. *See Levin v. Yeshiva Univ.,* 96 N.Y.2d 484 (2001).

41. *See, e.g., Anchor Sav. & Loan Ass'n v. Equal Opportunities Comm'n,* 120 Wis. 2d 391, 355 N.W.2d 234 (1984).

42. 15 U.S.C. § 1691 (1997).

43. *See Rosa v. Park West Bank & Trust Co.,* 214 F.3d 213 (1st Cir. 2000).

44. *See generally* Laura Eckert, "Inclusion of Sexual Orientation in the Equal Credit

Opportunity Act," 103 *Comm. L.J.* 311 (1998); Elwin Griffith, "The Quest for Fair Credit Reporting and Equal Credit Opportunity in Consumer Transactions," 25 *U. Mem. L. Rev.* 37, 41 (1994).

45. *Markham v. Colonial Mortg. Serv. Co.,* 605 F.2d 566, 569 (D.C. Cir. 1979).

46. *See id.*

47. *See, e.g., Bagley v. California Fed. Bank,* CV 93-7027 (C.D. Calif. Mar. 3, 1995) (employer's denial of discounted loan to gay couple is not marital-status discrimination, prohibited by federal ECOA, because employee would have been eligible for the loan if he had applied alone as a single person).

VIII

Public Accommodations

Title II of the Civil Rights Act of 1964 states that all people are entitled to the "full and equal enjoyment of the goods, services, privileges, advantages and accommodations of any place of public accommodation," and shall not be discriminated against because of their race, color, religion, or national origin.[1] Although the failure of this statute to cover sexual orientation may come as no surprise, Title II is also one of the few federal civil rights statutes that specifically does *not* include sex or gender as a protected category. Therefore, individuals who do not conform to gender stereotypes, whether lesbian, gay, bisexual, or transgender, find little protection under Title II. The vast majority of states, however, prohibit discrimination in public accommodations on the basis of sex or gender,[2] and an increasing number of states and municipalities include sexual orientation as a protected category.

In addition, the federal Americans with Disabilities Act (ADA) has ensured that public accommodations remain open to LGBT people and those living with HIV and AIDS (see below). As a result of changing attitudes in society, LGBT people rightly expect to be served on an equal basis with any other person when shopping, having a drink at a bar, going to the movies, or attending a doctor's appointment.[3] Unfortunately, however, in many places, LGBT people must still endure homophobic and/or transphobic treatment at the hands of business owners.

What is a public accommodation?

A *public accommodation* is an item, service, or benefit offered generally to the public. "Places of public accommodation" include hotels and motels, restaurants, stores, and other businesses and facilities open to the public. Private social clubs are exempt from public-accommodations laws but only if they are genuinely private. The exemption does not apply to quasi-public organizations that only claim to be private for the purpose of avoiding antidiscrimination laws.[4] The term *public accommodation* is defined somewhat differently from state to state or city to city but generally covers most businesses and social or recreational facilities open to the public. It is true, however, that an entity subject to the antidiscrimination law of one state or city might be exempt from a similar law elsewhere.

What legal protection is there against discrimination by public accommodations?

No federal law prohibits discrimination by public accommodations based on sex or sexual orientation. One federal law prohibits such discrimination based on race, color, religion, or national origin;[5] another federal law prohibits discrimination against persons with disabilities, which includes individuals living with HIV and AIDS (see chapter 13).[6]

Twelve states—California, Connecticut, Maryland, Massachusetts, Minnesota, New Hampshire, New Jersey, New Mexico, New York, Rhode Island, Vermont, and Wisconsin—prohibit sexual-orientation discrimination in all public accommodations, as does the District of Columbia. Two other states' laws provide more limited protection to gay men and lesbians: Hawaii's statute prohibits sexual-orientation discrimination by any public accommodation that receives state financial assistance,[7] and Maine's public accommodations law includes sexual orientation but carves out an exemption for religious entities.[8] In addition to these state statutes, a number of municipal public-accommodations laws cover gay, lesbian, and bisexual people. Examples include Ann Arbor, Austin, Baltimore, Boston, Chicago, Cedar Rapids, Cleveland, Detroit, Denver, Los Angeles, New Orleans, New York City, Philadelphia, Portland, St. Louis, San Diego, and San Francisco. The laws in Minnesota, New Mexico, and Rhode Island also specifically protect individuals from unequal treatment based on their gender identity.

Are doctor's offices and other medical facilities covered by these laws?

Under the laws of many states, the offices of doctors, dentists, and other highly trained professionals are not considered to be "places of public accommodation," meaning that these service providers may decide whom to have as clients or patients, free from any interference by antidiscrimination laws.[9] A California court, however, ruled that a lesbian could bring a claim of sexual-orientation discrimination under that state's law against an in vitro fertilization clinic that had denied her service.[10] Under the ADA, a federal law that protects people living with HIV and AIDS from discrimination because of their disease, these offices do count as public accommodations.[11]

Is it legal for a hotel, resort facility, or travel company to exclude LGBT travelers?

Unless you live in one of the states or cities that prohibit discrimination on the basis of sexual orientation or gender identity in public accommodations, it is legal for most business establishments to deny service to LGBT people. Historically, however, innkeepers and "common carriers" (e.g., trains) were thought to have a "duty to serve the public," meaning that they could not simply pick and choose their customers as other businesses were permitted to do, primarily because these businesses frequently enjoyed a monopoly in a local market. Therefore, an innkeeper or common carrier could only avoid its duty when it was able to demonstrate that serving a particular customer would conflict with other reasonable regulations adopted by the company, which were necessary to protect legitimate business interests.[12]

After Congress passed the 1964 federal public-accommodations statute, which codified and extended this "duty of service" to a broad range of businesses, people have rarely needed to rely on these common-law principles. For those groups not covered by Title II, however, these longstanding rules may offer some protection with regard to these specific types of businesses.

While visiting an area whose laws prohibit discrimination on the basis of sexual orientation or gender identity, I was refused service by a business owner because I am an LGBT person. I did not report it at the time—is there anything I can do?

Yes. You do not have to live in a location to be protected by its laws. If a store/company does business in a jurisdiction that prohibits discrimination on the basis of sexual orientation or gender identity, it must provide equal service to all customers, regardless of whether or not you are from the area. If you have suffered discriminatory treatment at the hands of a business owner, you should consider contacting an LGBT legal organization in that community about filing a complaint. Although you may need to come back to the area to testify, local lawyers can do the vast majority of the work on the case even though you have already returned home. You should also consider reporting the business to its local Better Business Bureau, which may take action against the company on your behalf.

May a bar or club throw out two people of the same sex for dancing together? For other displays of affection in public?

It may, unless the city or state in which it is located outlaws discrimination on the basis of sexual orientation. Disneyland, located in Anaheim, California, was sued successfully under the state's Unruh Civil Rights Act when it tried to stop gay couples from dancing. Later, Disneyland tried to prevent two men from dancing while holding one another, claiming that the previous case had only addressed "fast dancing." After a second lawsuit was filed, Disneyland agreed to let gay couples dance together however they choose, "fast" or "slow."[13] Similarly, if a club allows heterosexual couples to kiss or hold hands in public without hassling them, then a club may not single out same-sex couples for harassment in a jurisdiction that prohibits sexual-orientation discrimination.

In another case brought under California's Unruh Act, a California court of appeals found that a restaurant had unlawfully discriminated on the basis of sexual orientation by refusing to seat a lesbian couple in a semiprivate booth.[14] The restaurant's policy restricted seating in these booths to two people of the opposite sex and required all other patrons to eat in the main dining room of the restaurant. The court rejected the restaurant's argument that its policy was designed to shield other patrons from acts of intimacy by homosexuals, pointing out that by excluding gay and lesbian couples from dining in the semiprivate booths and forcing them to eat only in the main room, they were *more* likely to be observed by other patrons. Further undermining the restaurant's argument was the fact that couples with children were also prevented from eating at the booths under this policy. Finally, the court resoundingly rejected the suggestion that homosexual patrons would engage in unseemly and inappropriate conduct in a public place if permitted to eat in a booth that was partly hidden from public view.

I live in a state or city that prohibits sexual-orientation discrimination in public accommodations. When I attempted to donate blood/plasma at a local blood drive, however, I was turned away because I am a sexually active gay man. Is that legal?

Yes. The Federal Drug Administration has established certain standards for collecting blood and plasma,[15] and since 1983, the agency has disseminated criteria to blood and plasma centers designed to prevent the transmission of HIV and AIDS.[16] These criteria specify that any man who has had sex with even one man since 1977 is considered a high-risk donor who should not donate blood or plasma. Therefore, under the federal health regulations, sexually active gay men may be prohibited from donating blood. In *Johnson v. Plasma Alliance*,[17] the Minnesota Court of Appeals made clear, however, that the federal regulations did not provide a blood/plasma donation center with free reign to discriminate against homosexuals. The intake worker at Plasma Alliance refused to allow Johnson to donate after learning that he had had sex with another man since 1977. Johnson filed a discrimination claim against the center for discrimination based on "affectional preference," but his claims were ultimately rejected by the court, which determined, "This [was] not a case in which a heterosexual man was wrongly labeled because of his mannerisms, nor a case involving a celibate homosexual man who was not allowed to donate plasma because of his homosexuality. Johnson was not qualified to donate plasma because of his sexual activity, not because of his affectional preference. Neither his affectional preference nor his 'perceived' homosexuality, alone, would have disqualified Johnson from plasma donation."[18]

Soon after the manager of my health club learned that I was gay, he threatened to revoke my membership for "inappropriate behavior," but I haven't done anything wrong. What can I do?

If you live in an area that prohibits sexual-orientation discrimination in public accommodations, the health club manager will need to demonstrate that its rules regarding conduct at the facility are applied uniformly and without regard to a member's sexual orientation. In *Blanding v. Sports & Health Club*, the Minnesota Court of Appeals affirmed an award of damages against a club that tried to "crack down" on its homosexual members and enforced an unwritten "sodomite" rule preventing them from engaging in behavior that would have been acceptable when done by the club's straight members—in that case, dancing in the gym.[19] The court found that the health club's policies demonstrated that it "had different expectations for its heterosexual and homosexual members" and showed a "willful indifference to the rights of homosexuals" in violation of the state's public-accommodations law.[20]

May my health club or other membership group refuse to accept my partner and me for a "family" discount?

If you live in a city that prohibits discrimination on the basis of marital status or sexual orientation, the club should offer "family" discounts to gay and straight families alike. For example, the municipal pool in the Town of West Hartford offered family discounts to married couples and to step, legal, and adoptive parents, but it excluded gay and lesbian coparents, or someone who acts as a parent to the child of their nonmarital heterosexual partner. When LGBT rights attorneys filed a complaint, the city's Human Rights Commission determined that the pool's policy discriminated on the basis of sexual orientation and marital status.[21]

If the law in your area does not provide any protection, you should still consider lobbying the management of the health club to change their policy, perhaps in alliance with other nontraditional heterosexual families who are also affected.

May a company such as a brokerage firm refuse to open an account for me simply because I am gay?

Yes it may, unless the firm is located in an area with a public-accommodations law covering sexual orientation or unless you have been discriminated against for another prohibited reason. For example, in *Cheung v. Merrill Lynch, Pierce, Fenner & Smith, Inc.,*[22] Edmond Cheung and Paul Cheung, a father and son, were prevented from opening an investment account. The firm insisted that it could not open an account in Edmond's name because he had not been a citizen "long enough." However, Paul Cheung alleged that Merrill Lynch also rejected their business because, based on Paul's "appearance, mannerisms, and other factors, along with certain societal stereotypes regarding homosexuals," the brokerage firm knew that he was gay. Because sexual orientation was covered under New York City's public-accommodations law, the federal district court ruled that the Cheungs had stated a valid claim against Merrill Lynch. But the court also found that the Cheungs could bring other federal and state claims under the laws prohibiting race and national origin discrimination.[23] Therefore, if you feel as though you have been denied service for discriminatory reasons, it is best to contact an attorney to discuss the specific facts of your case.

Are big public events such as a parade included in the scope of "public accommodations"?

It depends on who is sponsoring the parade. When private individuals or groups host a parade, the Supreme Court has made clear that they have the right to invite or exclude whomever they wish. In *Hurley v. Irish-American Gay, Lesbian and Bisexual Group of Boston,* the Supreme Court held that the organizers of South Boston's St. Patrick's Day parade could not be forced to allow an LGBT Irish group to march along with the other participants, because doing so would amount to altering the organizer's message, in violation of their First Amendment rights.[24] In *Hurley,* the Supreme Court noted that even if the group could not articulate a specific message that it wanted to convey, it was entitled to exclude participants whose message was inconsistent with its own, whatever that "message" turned out to be.[25]

In reaching its decision in *Hurley,* however, the Supreme Court made clear that Boston's St. Patrick's Day parade was the speech of a private speaker.[26] When the government hosts a parade or any other type of civic celebration, on the other hand, not only must it comply with public-accommodations laws but it may also not exclude a class of citizens for irrational reasons.

What about organizations such as the Boy Scouts?

The supreme courts of various states have split on the issue of whether or not the Boy Scouts of America qualifies as a public accommodation.[27] Even if it is included within the definition of a public accommodation, however, the Supreme Court has determined that the Boy Scouts have a First Amendment defense to any charge of discrimination on the basis of sexual orientation.[28] While acknowledging that the Scout Oath and Law did not explicitly mention sexual orientation, the Boy Scouts argued to the Supreme Court that its philosophy, which states that scouts should be "morally straight" and "clean," precludes homosexuals from being Boy Scouts. In a 5-4 decision, the Court did not question the Boy Scouts' characterization of its own policy and mission, finding that "we must not be . . . guided by our views of whether the Boy Scouts' teachings with respect to homosexual conduct are right or wrong; public or judicial disapproval of a tenet of an organization's expression does not justify the State's effort to compel the organization to accept members where such acceptance would derogate from the organization's expressive message."[29]

As a result of the Boy Scouts' decision to espouse a policy that explicitly discriminates on the basis of sexual orientation, some states and localities, as well as religious and philanthropic organizations, have expressed their disapproval by severing their ties to the organization.[30] Therefore, public opinion may ultimately persuade the Boy Scouts to change their position. In the meantime, however, the Supreme Court has made clear that the Constitution protects the Boy Scouts' right to run their organization according to homophobic principles.

Is there any way to challenge discrimination, if my area does not have a law forbidding sexual-orientation discrimination in public accommodations?

If you believe that you have experienced discrimination, you should consult with an attorney. Even if the civil rights statute where you live does not cover sexual orientation, there are two possibilities to consider. First is whether another form of discrimination (e.g., race, sex, marital status, or religion) is at work. If that is the case, you may be protected by the corresponding provision of the statute. Second, if the entity discriminating against you is a government or other public agent, you may be able to prove a violation of your constitutional right to "equal protection of the laws," as guaranteed by the Fourteenth Amendment.

NOTES

1. 42 U.S.C. § 2000a(a) (2003).
2. Only Alabama, Arizona, Georgia, Mississippi, North Carolina, South Carolina, and Texas exclude sex/gender from protection under their public-accommodations laws, as does Puerto Rico. Nevada's public-accommodations law does not include sex, but Nevada Revised Statute § 233.010(1) makes clear that services in places of public accommodation must be offered without discrimination on the basis of sex. *See generally* Joseph William Singer, "No Right to Exclude: Public Accommodations and Private Property," 90

Nw. U.L. Rev. 1283, 1478–97 (1996) (collecting and classifying coverage of state public-accommodations statutes as they existed in 1996). The District of Columbia and twenty states—Alaska, Colorado, Connecticut, Delaware, Florida, Hawaii (limited to entities receiving state financial assistance), Illinois, Maryland, Michigan, Minnesota, Montana, New Hampshire, New Jersey, New York, North Dakota, Oregon, Pennsylvania, Tennessee (limited to innkeepers), Vermont, and Virginia—also prohibit marital-status discrimination. *See* Nan D. Hunter, "Accommodating the Public Sphere: Beyond the Market Model," 85 *Minn. L. Rev.* 1591, 1616 n.124 (2001).

3. *See generally* Robin Cheryl Miller, "Validity, Construction, and Application of State Enactment, Order, or Regulation Expressly Prohibiting Sexual Orientation Discrimination," 82 *A.L.R.*5th 1 (2000) (discussing specific types of public-accommodations litigation).

4. For example, the Supreme Court found that the Jaycees, despite its claims to be a private club, was a sufficiently public organization to justify government regulation. Therefore, the state of Minnesota could apply its state civil rights act to the group and compel the organization to admit women. *See Roberts v. United States Jaycees,* 468 U.S. 609 (1984).

5. 42 U.S.C. § 2000a (2003).

6. *See* Americans with Disabilities Act of 1990, 42 U.S.C. § 12101, *et seq.*; Rehabilitation Act of 1973, 29 U.S.C. § 701, *et seq.*

7. *See* Haw. Rev. Stat. § 368-1 (1993).

8. *See* 5 Me. Rev. Stat. Ann. § 4553(1)(G) (1999) ("'Unlawful discrimination' includes . . . [d]iscrimination in employment, housing, public accommodation and credit . . . on the basis of sexual orientation, except that a religious entity is exempt from these provisions with respect to discrimination based on sexual orientation.").

9. *See, e.g., Baksh v. Human Rights Comm'n,* 304 Ill. App. 3d 995, 711 N.E.2d 416 (1999).

10. *Benitez v. North Coast Women's Care Medical Group, Inc.,* 131 Cal. Rptr. 2d 364 (Cal. App. 4th Dist. 2003).

11. 42 U.S.C. § 12181(7)(F); *see also Bragdon v. Abbott,* 524 U.S. 624, 629 (1998).

12. *See* Singer, *supra* note 2, at 1291–92.

13. *See* 7 *Lambda Update* 10 (Winter 1990); *see also* Irving Wallace, et al., "Disney Heirs Run a Grumpy Kingdom," *S.F. Chronicle,* Dec. 20, 1989, at B4 ("Three homosexual men were stopped from slow-dancing by a Disneyland security guard who said that 'touch-dancing is reserved for heterosexual couples.' The men sued, claiming that their civil rights were violated, but dropped the case in 1989 when Disneyland reaffirmed that it has a policy against such discrimination. In 1980, another gay man had brought a successful suit against the Magic Kingdom for being prevented from fast-dancing.").

14. *See Rolon v. Kulwitzky,* 153 Cal. App. 3d 289, 200 Cal. Rptr. 217 (1984).

15. Blood and plasma centers are licensed by the U.S. Secretary of Health and Human Services and are subject to federal supervision under the Public Health Services Act, 42 U.S.C. § 262(a) (1998). The FDA has established minimum standards for the collection of blood and plasma, and for donor eligibility, 21 C.F.R. §§ 640.60–.76 (1998), as required by the Secretary for Health and Human Services. *See* 21 C.F.R. § 5.10(a)(5) (1998).

16. *See* General Biological Standards, Additional Standards for Human Blood and Blood Products, 51 Fed. Reg. 6362, 6362 (1986).

17. *See Johnson v. Plasma Alliance,* 2000 WL 665603 (Minn. Ct. App.).

18. *Id.* at *4.

19. *See Blanding v. Sports & Health Club,* 373 N.W.2d 784 (Minn. Ct. App. 1985), *aff'd,* 389 N.W.2d 205 (1986). For a similar case, see *Potter v. LaSalle Sports & Health Club,* 368 N.W.2d 413 (Minn. Ct. App. 1985), *aff'd,* 384 N.W.2d 873 (Minn. 1986). In that case, the Court of Appeals found that the health club's discriminatory treatment of Potter—namely, telling him to get on with his workout or leave—was not due to the "inappropriateness of Potter's conduct, but rather by the fact that Potter is a homosexual engaged in conversation with another homosexual." *Potter,* 368 N.W.2d at 417.

20. *Blanding, supra* note 19, at 792.

21. *See* Press Release, Gay & Lesbian Advocates & Defenders, "Marital Status and Sexual Orientation Discrimination at the Town Pool in West Hartford, Connecticut," available at <www.glad.org>.

22. *See Cheung v. Merrill Lynch, Pierce, Fenner & Smith, Inc.,* 913 F. Supp. 248 (S.D.N.Y. 1996).

23. *But see id.* at 252 (sustaining a federal claim for citizenship discrimination under § 1981 but rejecting plaintiff's state citizenship discrimination count because, under state law, national origin discrimination did not preclude unequal treatment based on citizenship).

24. *See Hurley v. Irish-American Gay, Lesbian and Bisexual Group of Boston,* 515 U.S. 557 (1995).

25. *See id.* at 569–70 ("[A] private speaker does not forfeit constitutional protection simply by combining multifarious voices, or by failing to edit their themes to isolate an exact message as the exclusive subject matter of the speech.").

26. *See id.* at 560–61 (noting that the city formally sponsored the parade until 1947 and allowed the parade organizers to use the city's official seal through 1992). Not all observers accept the Supreme Court's characterization of the Boston St. Patrick's Day parade as "private speech," including the Massachusetts Supreme Judicial Court, whose decision was overruled in *Hurley. See* Gretchen Van Ness, "Parades and Prejudice: The Incredible True Story of Boston's St. Patrick's Day Parade and the United States Supreme Court," 30 *New Eng. L. Rev.* 625 (1996).

27. *Compare Dale v. Boy Scouts of Am.,* 160 N.J. 562, 734 A.2d 1196 (1999) (finding that the Boy Scouts of America qualified as a public accommodation) *with Welsh v. Boy Scouts of Am.,* 993 F.2d 1267 (7th Cir. 1993); *Curran v. Mount Diablo Council of Boy Scouts of Am.,* 17 Cal.4th 670, 952 P.2d 218 (1998); *Seabourn v. Coronado Area Council, Boy Scouts of Am.,* 257 Kan. 178, 891 P.2d 385 (1995); *Quinnipiac Council, Boy Scouts of Am., Inc. v. Comm'n on Human Rights & Opportunities,* 204 Conn. 287, 528 A.2d 352 (1987); *Schwenk v. Boy Scouts of Am.,* 275 Or. 327, 551 P.2d 465 (1976) (coming to the opposite conclusion).

28. *Dale v. Boy Scouts of Am.,* 530 U.S. 640 (2000).

29. *Id.* at 661. Justice Stevens rejected the majority's position that the Court should simply accept the Boy Scouts' statement that homosexuality was antithetical to scouting principles, noting that the Boy Scouts' national leadership had only recently adopted any policy regarding homosexuality, and this position had not been universally adopted by Boy Scouts' councils. *See id.* at 663 (Stevens, J., dissenting).

30. *See, e.g.,* Audrey Hudson, "Reform Jewish Leaders Pressure Scouts on Homosexual Ban," *Wash. Times,* Jan. 11, 2001, at A3 ("Reform Jewish leaders want to force the Boy Scouts of America to include homosexuals and are calling on its members to renounce the organization and withdraw all financial support."); Pete Bowles, "City Schools to End Support of Boy Scouts," *Newsday,* Dec. 2, 2001, at A21 ("Saying its exclusion of gays as leaders is discriminatory, [New York City] Schools Chancellor Harold Levy Friday announced that the Boy Scouts of America would no longer have the support of the city Board of Education.").

PART 3
Families and Schools

IX

Relationships

On November 18, 2003, the highest court in Massachusetts became the first appellate court in the United States to hold that lesbian and gay couples cannot be excluded from civil marriage.[1] As of this writing, it is unclear what the impact of this decision will be in other states or federally. No other state currently allows lesbian and gay couples to marry. This is true regardless of how long the couples have been together or how committed they are to each other. In addition, as of June 2003, thirty-seven states and the federal government have statutes or constitutional provisions prohibiting marriages between two people of the same sex or explicitly providing that marriage can only be between one man and one woman.

In addition to being a visible symbol of the couple's commitment to each other, marriage confers more than one thousand federal rights, protections, and responsibilities, as well as hundreds of state conferred rights and responsibilities. While there are some steps lesbian and gay couples can take to protect their relationships and to mirror some of the benefits, protections, and responsibilities associated with civil marriage, many are difficult if not impossible to duplicate by other legal documents. The development of civil unions in Vermont marks a tremendous victory in the struggle for equal treatment and recognition of same-sex couples, but civil unions still fall far short of full equality. Civil unions are not recognized by the federal government, meaning, among other things, that civil union spouses are not recognized by the Social Security system, and that a civil union spouse cannot sponsor his or her partner as a spouse for immigration purposes. Moreover, there is no guarantee that civil unions will be recognized by states other than Vermont.

Domestic-partner and reciprocal-beneficiary benefits are also important but limited. Generally, domestic-partnership status confers many fewer benefits than those associated with marriage or civil unions. And like civil unions, it is likely that domestic partnerships will not be "portable": couples have to register and reregister with each new employer or each move to a different state or city.

This chapter will give an overview of the struggle for legal recognition of same-sex relationships, analyzing attempts to gain the freedom to marry and describing other means by which same-sex couples can protect themselves and/or obtain some of the benefits, protections, and responsibilities associated with civil marriage.

Does any state allow same-sex couples to marry?

On November 18, 2003, the highest court in Massachusetts became the first appellate court in the United States to hold that the rights and duties of marriage must be open to same-sex couples.[2] The court stated:

Limiting the protections, benefits, and obligations of civil marriage to opposite-sex couples violates the basic premises of individual liberty and equality under the law protected by the Massachusetts Constitution.[3]

The court delayed the date the decision takes effect for 180 days, so as of this writing, couples cannot yet marry in Massachusetts.[4] Challenges to the exclusion of same-sex couples from the right to marry date back to 1971. Until recently, courts have almost always upheld the exclusion of gay and lesbian couples from marriage, saying that marriage exists only for heterosexual couples.[5] In addition, Congress and the majority of state legislatures have enacted "defense of marriage" laws to further impede recognition of the right to marry by lesbians and gay men.

What are the arguments used most frequently in cases seeking the freedom to marry for same-sex couples?

There are three arguments that tend to arise in almost every case seeking the freedom to marry. Probably the most frequent argument against extending the freedom to marry is that marriage is, by definition, the union of one man and one woman, and therefore marriage statutes, even where not gender specific, do not include the union of two persons of the same sex. As one court wrote, "[M]arriage has always been considered as the union of a man and a woman and we have been presented with no authority to the contrary. . . . It appears to us that appellants are prevented from marrying, not by the statutes of Kentucky or the refusal of the County Court Clerk of Jefferson County to issue them a license, but rather by their own incapability of entering into a marriage as that term is defined."[6]

In holding that the state could not constitutionally prohibit marriage between two people of the same sex without a compelling reason, the Hawaii Supreme Court rejected this definitional argument, finding it "circular and unpersuasive."[7] The Hawaii Supreme Court recognized that this type of argument is strikingly similar to the arguments courts made forty or fifty years ago to uphold laws that prohibited white people from marrying people of color.[8] In upholding one such ban, a Virginia judge explained: "Almighty God created the races white, black, yellow, malay and red, and he placed them on separate continents. And but for the interference with his arrangement there would be no cause for such marriages. The fact that he separated the races shows that he did not intend for the races to mix."[9]

The U.S. Supreme Court rejected this reasoning of the Virginia trial judge in its 1967 decision in *Loving v. Virginia*,[10] and the Hawaii Supreme Court relied on the *Loving* Court's reasoning in analyzing the state's refusal to allow same-sex couples to marry:

The facts in *Loving* and the respective reasoning of the Virginia courts, on the one hand, and the United States Supreme Court, on the other, both . . . unmask the tautological and circular nature of [the state of Hawaii's] argument that [Hawaii's prohibition of same-sex marriage] does not implicate [the equal rights provision] of the Hawaii Constitution because same sex marriage is an innate impossibility . . . [C]onstitutional law may mandate, like it or not, that customs change with an evolving social order.[11]

A second frequent argument involves sex discrimination: LGBT advocates assert that current marriage laws discriminate based on sex because the sex of one's partner determines who one may marry. Opponents respond that such statutes do not discriminate on the basis of sex because they treat men and women equally, in that both men and women are prevented from marrying persons of the same sex.[12] Again, this response is similar to arguments made to justify bans on interracial marriage; arguments that were ultimately rejected by the U.S. Supreme Court. In rejecting this argument in the context of marriages between two people of the same sex, the Hawaii Supreme Court noted that it was expressly considered and rejected by the Supreme Court in *Loving,* in which the state had argued that "because the miscegenation statutes punish equally both the white and the Negro participants in an interracial marriage, these statutes, despite their reliance on racial classifications do not constitute an invidious discrimination based upon race."[13] "Substitution of 'sex' for 'race,'" the Hawaii Supreme Court explained, "yields the precise case before us together with the conclusion that we have reached," that the statute is premised on a sex-based classification.[14]

Third, opponents seek to justify the exclusion of same-sex couples from marriage by claiming that one male parent and one female parent is best for children. This was the primary argument relied on by the state of Hawaii to justify their refusal to grant marriage licenses to same-sex couples. On remand, however, the court held that the state had failed to support this claim. To the contrary, the evidence indicates that children are not harmed by having lesbian and gay parents, and that, on the whole, lesbian and gay couples are just as good as parents as heterosexual couples.[15] Moreover, as the Massachusetts court explained:

Excluding same-sex couples from civil marriage will not make children of opposite-sex marriages more secure, but it does prevent children of same-sex couples from enjoying the immeasurable advantages that flow from the assurance of "a stable family structure in which children will be reared, educated, and socialized."[16]

What are the other arguments used to challenge the exclusion of same-sex couples from marriage?

In addition to the arguments discussed above, prior challenges have also included arguments that the exclusion of same-sex couples from marriage infringes on the fundamental right to marry, freedom of association, and the right to privacy, and that it denies equal protection on the basis of sexual orientation.

For example, in Alaska, in addition to finding that the statute impermissibly discriminated on the basis of sex, a lower-court judge also held that the state's refusal to grant a marriage license to a same-sex couple infringed on their right to privacy under the state constitution. The court explained: "Government intrusion into the choice of a life partner encroaches on the intimate personal decisions of the individual. This the

Constitution does not allow unless the state can show a compelling interest."[17]

Other than Massachusetts, which states have gone the furthest toward granting marriage equality to same-sex couples?

In 1999, the Vermont Supreme Court declared that refusing to provide committed same-sex couples with the common benefits and privileges accorded to married couples violated the Vermont Constitution. The court instructed the state legislature either to amend the state's laws to allow same-sex couples to marry or to create a parallel system that gives same-sex couples all the benefits and responsibilities of marriage. The state legislature created "civil unions" for same-sex couples, which grants all of the state-conferred benefits and responsibilities of marriage and requires private entities to treat marriages and civil unions equally. However, the immediate benefits of this new system will probably go mainly to Vermonters while other governmental entities and private entities are deciding how to treat civil unions in other geographical areas. Moreover, even for Vermonters, civil unions do not confer any federal marital benefits.

In Hawaii, in 1993, the state supreme court was the first court to rule that denying same-sex couples the freedom to marry could violate the state constitution because it discriminated on the basis of sex.[18] That was not a final decision, though; the case was sent back to the trial court to decide whether the state could still supply a compelling reason to justify the discrimination. In 1996, after a trial, the lower court found that the state had failed to come up with a sufficient reason for limiting marriage to different-sex couples.[19] But in November 1998, while the Hawaii Supreme Court was considering this decision, the voters of Hawaii passed a state constitutional amendment allowing the state legislature to limit marriage to different-sex couples.[20] In 1999, the Hawaii Supreme Court dismissed the lawsuit, saying that the constitutional amendment made the restriction of marriage to different-sex couples valid.[21]

Should my partner and I travel to Vermont to get a civil union?

Maybe, but in making this decision, couples should be aware that the benefits and responsibilities that come with a civil union are guaranteed only if you live in Vermont. It may take years of litigation in every state before we know what the benefits and consequences of being in a civil union outside of Vermont are.

Another important consideration is that just as Vermont will not grant a divorce to a married couple unless they have lived in the state for a year, civil union divorces also require one party in the union to be a resident of Vermont for one year.[22] Because other states may not recognize the civil union, this may make it nearly impossible for couples residing in other states to divorce.[23]

If my partner and I get married in Massachusetts or enter into a civil union, may we sue to ensure that it is respected by other states and our employers?

We advise you to contact one of the LGBT legal organizations before filing suit, so your lawsuit can be evaluated for both the positive and negative consequences of initiating litigation to you and your partner as well as to the overall legal status of civil unions. Without careful strategy, uncoordinated lawsuits could make the law worse or cause a backlash of more anti-LGBT laws and policies. We expect and hope that states and private entities will recognize those in civil unions just as they do marriage. In the process of achieving that, however, recognition will be spotty.

Does any country recognize marriages between same-sex partners?

Yes. Same-sex couples can marry in the Netherlands,[24] Belgium,[25] and Canada.[26] Other countries have enacted laws allowing same-sex couples to obtain "registered partnerships" or an equivalent status, providing most of the legal benefits, protections, and responsibilities of civil marriage. These countries include Denmark (1989)[27] Norway (1993),[28] Greenland (1994),[29] Sweden (1995),[30] Iceland (1996),[31] France (1999),[32] Switzerland (2000),[33] Germany (2001),[34] Portugal (2001),[35] and Finland (2001).[36] Other countries also provide more limited protections. For example, Brazil's government recently announced it will recognize same-sex "stable unions" for retirement pension and inheritance rights.[37] In addition, Hungary's Constitutional Court held that same-sex spouses are entitled to the legal protections of common-law marriage.[38]

For purposes of immigration and/or residency, fifteen countries recognize same-sex partnerships: Australia, Belgium, Canada, Denmark, Finland, France, Germany, Iceland, Israel, the Netherlands, New Zealand,

Norway, Portugal, South Africa, Sweden, and the United Kingdom (see chapter 5).[39]

Is it illegal to perform a marriage ceremony between two women or two men?

Some states have laws forbidding any attempt to join in marriage two people who do not have a marriage license or who fail to meet the state's legal requirements for marriage.[40] But these statutes only cover *legal* marriage, as a way to prevent fraud. They do not apply to people performing or participating in same-sex holy unions or commitment ceremonies, probably even if the word *marriage* is used, as long as there is no attempt to claim the couple has legally married. Moreover, when such ceremonies are religious and do not attempt to convey any legal marital status, any effort to prosecute someone for holding the ceremony could be a violation of the right to free exercise of religion.

May my partner and I sue our state for the right to be allowed to marry?

Yes, but again we advise you to contact one of the LGBT legal organizations before filing suit.

What is the impact of the government's failure to allow same-sex couples to marry?

Although marriage is often thought of simply as the social recognition of a couple's lifelong commitment to one another, it also confers hundreds of important legal obligations and benefits. These include mutual obligations of financial support for one another,[41] automatic inheritance rights when one partner dies without leaving a will,[42] the right to sue for injuries to the other partner,[43] the right to petition for legal-immigration status for a spouse,[44] and other federal and state tax consequences.[45] Thus, the failure of the government to recognize the civil marriage of two persons of the same sex means that lesbian and gay couples are not entitled to benefit from these legal rights and protections.

In addition, private entities frequently extend benefits that favor married couples, including employment-related health benefits, sick and bereavement leave, survivorship rights to pension and insurance plans, and a host of others, from frequent-flyer miles to "family" discounts.

How does the fact that my partner and I are not married affect our tax status?

Married couples can file joint tax returns, thereby pooling their income, deductions, credits, gains, and losses. This can be advantageous for couples whose partners have very different levels of incomes, since it allows them more joint income than single individuals before they shift to a higher tax bracket. When the members of couple have similar incomes, getting married has caused a slight increase in taxes, but Congress recently amended this provision to end the "marriage penalty." Unmarried couples may not file jointly, no matter how long they have been living together. (The only exception is under Vermont state income-tax law, which treats same-sex couples in a civil union the same as married couples.)

Unmarried couples are also not entitled to the unlimited marital deduction under estate tax laws. When one member of a married couple dies, a surviving spouse does not have to pay any taxes on the estate that passes to him or her. An unmarried partner, on the other hand, has to pay estate tax on the full amount. Similarly, under federal gift tax laws, spouses may give each other any amount without being taxed; unmarried couples may only give up to $10,000 tax-free in any one year.

Another distinction concerns health benefits. Spousal health benefits paid to employees are not taxed as income to the employee, but domestic-partner benefits are taxed unless the employee can prove that the partner is dependent.[46]

What is the *Defense of Marriage Act?*

In 1996, Congress passed what it called the *Defense of Marriage Act,* or DOMA, purportedly because it expected that some state soon might recognize marriages of lesbian and gay couples.[47] DOMA says that no matter what the local state's law is, marriage is only a relationship between a man and a woman for purposes of federal law. It also says that states are free to refuse to recognize a civil marriage between members of the same sex, even if it is validly performed in another state.

Is the federal DOMA constitutional?

First, many people believe that the federal DOMA unconstitutionally violates the Full Faith and Credit Clause of the Constitution. "As a general rule, the Full Faith and Credit Clause of the United States Constitution requires that each state recognize laws and judgments that are valid under another state's laws."[48] At the same time, though, it has long been the practice that states may refuse to recognize an out-of-state marriage if it violates a strong public policy, such as an incestuous or polygamous marriage.[49] Second, the federal DOMA is also inconsistent with a long historical tradition of treating marriage and domestic relations as subjects within the exclusive control of the states, not the federal government.[50] Finally, the federal DOMA is also subject to challenge as a restriction on the constitutional right to travel,[51] an interference with the right to marry,[52] and discrimination on the basis of sexual orientation and gender in violation of the Equal Protection Clause.[53]

As of these questions will have to be resolved by the courts before we have an answer to the question of whether states will have to recognize the valid marriages of lesbian and gay couples that were entered in another state.

My state has its own DOMA law. How is that different?

As of June 2003, thirty-seven states have passed their own antimarriage laws or constitutional provisions banning same-sex marriage, which are often referred to as "state DOMAs" or "Baby DOMAs."[54] These laws vary, but typically they define marriage as only between one man and one woman, and many also provide that the state will not recognize a same-sex marriage validly entered into in another state.[55]

These state laws will also probably be challenged. One argument is that they violate the Equal Protection Clause of the federal Constitution because they single out same-sex couples and treat them differently from all other groups.[56] They also may violate the Constitution's Due Process Clause because they deny persons the fundamental right to marry. The U.S. Supreme Court has struck down other restrictions on marriage in the past, using these same theories. Until 1967, many states made marriages between the races illegal, and these states often refused to recognize a mixed-race marriage validly performed in another state. In 1967, the U.S. Supreme Court struck down these discriminatory laws and declared that the "freedom to marry" belongs to all Americans.[57] The Court described marriage as one of our "vital personal rights" that is "essential to the orderly pursuit of happiness by a free people."[58]

Can my partner and I get married in another state that allows same-sex couples to marry?

People from another state may go to any state and get married, as long as they meet the requirements for a valid marriage in that state. Some states impose residency requirements before a person can get married there. Once entered into, states usually recognize marriages validly entered into in other states. It is not clear, however, whether this will be true for marriages between same-sex partners, particularly in states that have enacted state DOMAs. Thus, respect may take years of litigation, as was true for recognition of interracial marriages.

Have courts ever recognized an LGBT couple in a common-law marriage, or given them other legal recognition?

No state has ever recognized an LGBT couple in a common-law marriage,[59] but courts have granted some legal recognition to LGBT relationships. In *Braschi v. Stahl Associates Co.*,[60] the New York Court of Appeals (New York's highest court) held that a gay man, who had been living with his lover in a rent-controlled apartment for eleven years prior to his lover's death, was protected under New York City rent and eviction laws that protected family members from eviction when a tenant in a rent-controlled apartment died. The court wrote:

[We] conclude that the term family . . . should not be rigidly restricted to those people who have formalized their relationship by obtaining, for instance, a marriage certificate or an adoption order. The intended protection against sudden eviction should not rest on fictitious legal distinctions or genetic history, but instead should find its foundation in the reality of family life. In the context of eviction, . . . family includes two adult lifetime partners whose relationship is long term and characterized by an emotional and financial commitment and interdependence.[61]

Courts in other places have treated lesbian and gay couples like spouses in some limited circumstances. *In Tanner v. Oregon Health Sciences University*,[62] three lesbian employees of the Oregon Health Science University challenged the university's denial of health and life insurance benefits to their unmarried domestic partners. The Oregon Court of Appeals held that the state university's denial of insurance benefits to its gay and lesbian employees' domestic partners violated the Oregon Constitution.[63] The court said that lesbian and gay couples could not be denied privileges and immunities of state employment unless the state could provide a justification based on "genuine differences," which the state could not do in *Tanner*. Oregon now offers domestic-partnership benefits to all state employees.

Similarly, in June 2001, the highest court in New York state unanimously ruled that university policies that require couples to be married to qualify for subsidized housing can be challenged as discrimination based on sexual orientation.[64]

In July 2001, a trial judge in California held that a surviving lesbian partner had the right to proceed as a spouse for purposes of her wrongful death suit. The judge explained: "Reading the wrongful death statute to exclude plaintiff would unduly punish her for her sexual orientation. Such a reading has no place in our system of government, which has as one of its basic tenets equal protection for all."[65] In 2003, a New York judge held that a surviving civil union partner had the right to sue as a surviving spouse under the New York wrongful death statute.[66]

What is a *domestic partnership?*

Domestic partnership refers to a committed relationship between two people who are not married. Domestic partnerships are recognized by dozens of cities and a handful of states that grant certain legal rights and protections to domestic partners.[67] To be eligible for domestic-partner benefits, unmarried couples typically must file a document confirming, for example, that they "have chosen to share one another's lives in an intimate and committed relationship of mutual caring, . . . live together, and . . . have agreed to be jointly responsible for basic living expenses incurred during the Domestic Partnership."[68]

Domestic-partner benefit coverage has been adopted for state government employees in 10 states (California, Connecticut, Iowa, Maine, New Mexico, New York, Oregon, Rhode Island, Vermont, and Washington) and more than 159 local governments and quasi-governmental agencies.[69] In addition, several thousand private employers extend benefits to the partners of unmarried employees, based on their internal domestic-partner policies. Common benefits of such plans include medical and life insurance coverage, family leave, and retirement benefits. The first private business to offer benefits was the *Village Voice* newspaper in 1982, and the first municipality in the United States was Berkeley, California, in 1984. (See chapters 3 and 6 for more discussion of employment-related systems.)

There also domestic-partner registrations systems that are open to the public. The rights that come with domestic-partner registration vary tremendously from locality to locality. Since January 1, 2002, California has provided some important protections to registered domestic partners, including, among other things, the right to sue for the wrongful death of a domestic partner, the right to adopt a partner's child using the stepparent adoption procedures, the right to make health-care decisions for a domestic partner, the right to use sick leave to attend the illness of a partner or a partner's child, the right to be appointed administrator to a partner's estate, and the right to make a claim for disability benefits for a partner who is unable to make the claim himself or herself.[70] Moreover, starting January 1, 2005, registered domestic partners in California will gain almost every state-conferred right, benefit, and responsibility of married spouses.[71]

Hawaii has a "reciprocal beneficiary" law providing that any two unmarried people, as long as they may not be married under Hawaii marriage law (such as same-sex couples or immediate family members), may confer health-care and other rights on one another.[72] Rights that go to reciprocal beneficiaries include inheritance rights and survivorship benefits; health-related rights such as hospital visitation, family and funeral leave, and motor vehicle insurance coverage; jointly held property rights such as tenancy in the entirety and public land leases; legal standing for wrongful death and crime victims rights; and other benefits related to the use of state facilities and state properties.

In many cities, the only benefit that registered couples receive is a registration certificate. In some localities, registered domestic partners are allowed hospital or jail visitation privileges that otherwise would be restricted to spouses or blood family.[73] In New York City, registered domestic partners do not have to pay tax on certain real estate transfers between the partners in a couple, just as spouses would not. Even in places where a domestic-partner registration gives no legal rights and amounts to a piece of paper, the fact that a couple has registered with the city is sometimes used by area employers to provide benefits or by a business to give "family" discounts.

How does domestic partnership compare to marriage?

While recognition of "domestic partnerships" is important, this status is different from civil marriage in several important ways. First, most importantly, domestic partnerships never provide the full extent of rights and responsibilities that accompany civil marriage. Second, to qualify, domestic partners often have to provide extensive documentation to prove their relationship. Third, different-sex marriages are automatically recognized by other jurisdictions, whereas domestic partnerships are recognized only by the employer and/or the city in which a couple is registered.

However, some persons may prefer domestic-partner status to marriage. Domestic-partner registration enables couples who do not want to undertake all the legal duties of marriage to secure recognition and certain rights. Additionally, it is usually far easier to end a domestic partnership than to end a marriage; generally, the former can be done by filing a certificate of termination, and the latter requires a divorce.

If marriage or domestic partnership is unavailable, are there other things my partner and I can do to secure our relationship?

It is possible to create contracts that will do some of the things that a marriage does automatically. For instance, unless you have executed a will and power of attorney, your partner probably has no right to inherit any of your property or any right to make an important medical decision on your behalf. When no documents are in place, courts generally turn to your biological family when you die or become incapacitated, no matter how long you and your partner have been together. But you can draft wills and powers of attorney to overcome many of these problems.[74]

In the past, courts were often reluctant to enforce agreements, either oral or written, between unmarried persons that imposed the same financial obligations on the couple that marriage entails—such as rights to support or property upon the dissolution of the relationship. The traditional reason for refusing to enforce such agreements was that they undermined support for marriage. Some judges even compared such agreements to prostitution, commenting that they formalized an arrangement in which sex was exchanged for financial or material benefits.

In 1976, the California Supreme Court departed dramatically from that prior judicial interpretation.[75] In *Marvin v. Marvin,* the court recognized that a woman in a heterosexual, unmarried relationship had a contractual right to support from her lover because she had given up the chance to work to support his career. Since the *Marvin* decision, the courts in almost every state have decided similar cases for heterosexuals, as long as sexual relations are not considered a necessary part of the contract.

For lesbian and gay couples at break-up, some courts have agreed to enforce oral or written contracts of mutual support, while others have refused.[76] When they do enforce these contracts, however, they rely on what the couple has actually agreed to and do not treat the couple as if they had been married. If you do enter into such a contract, it is important to make sure that sexual relations are not a part of the contract.[77] It is also very important not to rely on the existence of an oral contract. This is because the existence of an agreement is difficult to prove without something in writing, and even if an agreement is found, the exact terms of the agreement will also likely be in dispute. If there is no contract, or if a court does not want to recognize the relationship contract, courts may simply apply regular property rules.[78] Generally, this means property goes to the person who has title, as if the two parties are strangers. Sometimes, however, courts look to see if there was an oral agreement or contract between the parties about a specific piece of property and will apply property law governing oral agreements on property ownership.[79]

May I and my partner legally own property together?

Yes. Unmarried and unrelated persons may own property together. You can purchase property either as "joint tenants with rights of survivorship" or as "tenants in common." Joint tenants have an equal interest in one undivided property. When one dies, the property goes in full to the other without the need for a will. Tenants in common, on the other hand, own portions of the property, which need not be equal. If one dies, his or her portion does not necessarily go to the other; instead, it passes to whoever are his or her heirs. In every state, the law assumes that co-owners are tenants in common unless the title to the property clearly states otherwise. Unmarried partners seeking to own property as joint tenants should consult an attorney.

Does my partner have any right to inherit from me when I die?

Except for couples in formally recognized relationships in California, Hawaii, and Vermont, your partner does not have a right to inherit from you, unless you have a will making your partner the beneficiary of your estate. When a person dies without a will, his or her property is distributed according to the laws of the state in which he or she last had a permanent residence. These laws generally give property first to legal spouses, then to children, parents, siblings, and more distant relatives, with the remainder going to the state. And except for California residents in a registered domestic partnership,[80] Hawaii residents in a reciprocal beneficiary relationship,[81] and Vermont residents in a civil union,[82] same-sex partners are not recognized as legal heirs for purposes of intestate (without a will) succession.[83]

If you have a will, however, you can name your partner as the person who will inherit your estate. Generally, people are entitled to dispose of their property by will in any manner they wish, as long as it is not illegal or contrary to public policy.

Also, if you had previously titled the property as a joint tenancy naming each other as having the right of survivorship, then you are entitled to the property upon the death of your partner, irrespective of your partner's will or lack thereof.

May my relatives challenge it if I name my partner to inherit from me in my will?

Yes. A will may be challenged by anyone who would be an heir if the will did not exist. Reasons a will might be determined invalid include technical irregularities or questions about the circumstances under which it was written, including fraud, duress, or the mental competency of the individual when it was written. For lesbians and gay men, the most common challenge involves a claim that the partner exerted "undue influence," which is defined as physical coercion, threats, or mental duress that overpowered the will of the deceased.[84] A lawyer can advise you on ways to state your intentions that will minimize the likelihood of a successful challenge.

May I name my partner as beneficiary on my life insurance?

Probably. Typically, individuals may name anyone as the beneficiary of a life insurance policy or pension plan. However, some policies and some employers restrict beneficiaries to immediate family members or dependents. In addition, fearing excessive AIDS-related claims, some life insurance companies have refused to issue policies to adult males who name other unrelated adult males as beneficiaries. In 1986, responding to protests to such conduct, the National Association of Insurance Commissioners (NAIC) developed underwriting guidelines intended to preclude the use of sexual orientation in making determinations about the insurability of an applicant or in other underwriting decisions.[85] However, the NAIC guidelines are nonbinding, and even in those states in which the NAIC guidelines are adopted by legislative or administrative actions, effectively preventing offensive underwriting practices may prove to be difficult. In addition, if you live in a state that prohibits discrimination on the basis of sexual orientation in public accommodations, such policies may violate that law.

May I adopt my partner (and should I want to)?

Most states at least theoretically allow the adoption of an adult, as long as the person to be adopted and his or her natural parents (if alive and known) grant their consent. However, as with a child, the court must approve the adoption.

Some LGBT couples have attempted to legitimize their relationship and secure inheritance rights by having one partner adopt the other. Most of the reported cases dealing with this tactic have arisen in New York.[86] After lower courts in earlier cases divided on the legitimacy of such adoptions, the New York's highest court disallowed an adoption between two gay men, one fifty-seven and the other fifty years old, who had been living together twenty-five years.[87] The court held that the use of adoption to establish a family relationship between gay partners was "a cynical distortion of the adoption function,"[88] the purpose of which was to create a filial relationship to which "sexual intimacy is utterly repugnant."[89]

Even if a court accepts the legitimacy of adult adoptions between same-sex couples, the step of adopting another adult should be approached with great caution. The financial benefits of adoption are usually minimal. Many benefits generally available to parents apply only if the child is under eighteen or twenty-one, is disabled, or is actually economically dependent on the parent.

Moreover, the disadvantages of adult adoption may be substantial. An adoption is forever; it creates a virtually indissoluble legal link between "parent" and "child." The party who is being adopted may be cut off from any right to inherit from his or her natural parents.[90] Moreover, adoption may impose substantial financial liabilities on both parties. In some states, for example, an adopting parent is responsible for the financial support of the person adopted, at least under circumstances of extreme need; an adopted child may likewise be liable for the financial necessities of the parent. This is not an obligation that can be avoided if the relationship later ends. In addition, in some states, the parties may be guilty of incest if they engage in sexual relations with each other.

In most cases, estate-planning tools, such as wills, trusts, powers of attorney, and life insurance, together with a well-drafted "living together agreement" will prove a far better way to obtain the financial benefits while avoiding the downside of adult adoption.

Notes

1. *Goodridge v. Dept. of Public Health*, —N.E.2d—, 2003 WL 22710131 (Mass. 2003). This case was brought by Gay and Lesbian Advocates and Defenders (GLAD). For more information about *Goodridge*, see www.glad.org.

2. *Goodridge v. Dept. of Public Health*, — N.E.2d —, 2003 WL 22710131 (Mass. 2003).

3. *Id.* at *17.

4. There are appeals pending in three other cases challenging the exclusion of same-sex couples from the right to marry: *Lewis v. Harris*, Civ. No. MER-L-15-03 (N.J. Super. Ct.) (Nov. 5, 2003); *Standhardt v. Superior Court*, 77 P.3d 451 (Ariz. Ct. App. 2003); *Morrison v. Sadler*, Civ. No. 49A02-0305-CV-447 (Ind. Ct. App.).

5. *See, e.g., Dean v. District of Columbia*, 653 A.2d 307 (D.C. Ct. App. 1995); *Jones v. Hallahan*, 501 S.W.2d 588 (Ky. Ct. App. 1973); *Baker v. Nelson*, 191 N.W.2d 185 (Minn. 1971); *DeSanto v. Barnsley*, 476 A.2d 952 (Pa. Super. 1984) (declining to recognize same-sex common-law marriage); *Singer v. Hara*, 522 P.2d 1187 (Wash. Ct. App. 1974), *review denied*, 84 Wash. 2d 1008.

6. *Jones v. Hallahan, supra* note 1, at 589. *See also Baehr v. Lewin*, 852 P.2d 44, 61 (Hawaii 1993) (noting that the state had argued that "the right of persons of the same sex to marry one another does not exist because marriage, by definition and usage, means a special relationship between a man and a woman").

7. *Baehr v. Lewin, supra* note 2, at 60.

8. As of 1949, thirty of the forty-eight states banned interracial marriages by statute. *See Loving v. Virginia*, 388 U.S. at 6 n. 5.

9. *Loving, supra* note 4, at 3 (1967) (quoting the Virginia trial judge).

10. *See Baehr v. Lewin, supra* note 2, at 63 ("Analogously to Lewin's argument and the rationale of the *Jones* court, the Virginia courts declared that interracial marriage simply could not exist because the Deity had deemed such a union intrinsically unnatural, and, in effect, because it had theretofore never been the 'custom' of the state to recognize mixed marriages, marriage 'always' having been construed to presuppose a different configuration. With all due respect to the Virginia courts of a bygone era, we do not believe that trial judges are the ultimate authorities on the subject of Divine Will and, as *Loving* amply demonstrates, constitutional law may mandate, like it or not, that customs change with an evolving social order.").

11. *Id.*

12. *See id.* at 591, 71 (Heen, J., dissenting) ("HRS § 572-1 does not establish a 'suspect' classification based on gender because all males and females are treated alike. A male cannot obtain a license to marry another male, and a female cannot obtain a license to marry another female.").

13. *See id.* at 581, 68.

14. *Id. See also Brause v. Bureau of Vital Statistics*, 1998 WL 88743, at *6 (Alaska Super. Ct. 1998) ("That this is a sex-based classification can readily be demonstrated: if twins, one male and one female, both wished to marry a woman and otherwise met all the Code's requirements, only gender prevents the twin sister from marrying under the present law. Sex-based classifications can hardly be more obvious.").

15. *Baehr v. Miike*, 1996 WL 694235, at *21 (Hawaii Cir. Ct. 1996) ("As discussed hereinabove, Defendant has failed to present sufficient credible evidence which demonstrates that the public interest in the well-being of children and families, or the optimal development of children would be adversely affected by same-sex marriage. Nor has Defendant demonstrated how same-sex marriage would adversely affect the public fisc, the state interest in assuring recognition of Hawaii marriages in other states, the

institution of traditional marriage, or any other important public or governmental interest.")

16. *Goodridge*, 2003 WL 22701313, at *13 (citation omitted).

17. *Brause, supra* note 10, at *5.

18. This court determined that denying same-sex couples was sex discrimination because whether or not two persons were allowed to marry depended on the sex of the two applicants. *Baehr v. Lewin, supra* note 2, at 44 (finding sex discrimination and remanding to the lower court for evaluation of state's justification).

19. *Baehr v. Miike, supra* note 11 (finding no compelling reason to limit marriage to different-sex couples).

20. On November 3, 1998, the voters of Hawaii enacted House Bill 117, which amended the Hawaii Constitution to permit, although not require, the Hawaii legislature to restrict marriage to different-sex couples.

21. *Baehr v. Miike*, 92 Haw. 634, 994 P.2d 566 (1999) (finding that the legislature did not violate the state constitution by limiting marriages to different-sex couples because the newly amended constitution allowed the limitation).

22. One party to the union must live in Vermont for six months before applying for the dissolution and must stay for six months until the dissolution is complete.

23. *See, e.g., Rosengarten v. Downes*, 802 A.2d 170 (Conn. App. 2002), appeal dismissed as moot, 806 A.2d 1066 (Conn. 2002) (holding that Connecticut court did not have jurisdiction to dissolve a civil union). *See also* "Judge Dismisses Divorce Case Filed by Gay Texas Couple," *AP Newswires*, April 2, 2003 (noting that judge who had initially granted the couple a divorce then reversed himself and set aside his order after Texas attorney general intervened).

24. Same-sex marriages became legal in the Netherlands on April 1, 2001. Staatsblad 2001, nr. 9. An English translation of the law is available at <ruljis.leidenuniv.nl/user/cwaaldij/www/NHR/transl-marr.html>.

25. Belgium began granting marriage licenses to same-sex couples on January 30, 2003. *See* <http://www.wikipedia.org/wiki/same-sex_marriage>.

26. On June 10, 2003, the Ontario Court of Appeal held that denying the freedom to marry to same-sex couples violated the Canadian Constitution. *Halpern v. Attorney General*, Docket C39172 (Ontario Court of Appeal, June 10, 2003), available at <http://www. ontariocourts.on.ca/decisions/2003/june/halpernC39172.htm>.

Unlike two previous decisions—one from British Columbia and one from Quebec—which reached similar conclusions, the Ontario decision went into effect immediately, and same-sex couples began marrying within hours of the decision. On July 17, 2003, the Canadian government released draft legislation granting the freedom to marry to same-sex couples. The bill has been sent to the Canadian Supreme Court for a legal opinion.

27. In 1989, Denmark became the first country in the world to introduce a law on registered domestic partnerships for two persons of the same sex. See Act 372 of June 7, 1989, effective Oct. 1, 1989. The Act permits partnership registration for two persons of the same sex. Partnership registration has the same legal effect as marriage, except where otherwise provided by legislation, including that: a registered couple cannot adopt children, church weddings are impossible, and one of the partners must be a Danish citizen and live in Denmark. Apart from those exceptions, references to "marriage" or "spouse" in Danish law automatically include registered domestic partnerships. In 1999, several

changes were made to the Registered Partnership Law, including: (1) citizens from Norway, Sweden, and Iceland have the same rights as Danish citizens in relation to registered partnerships; (2) citizens of other countries having similar legislation as the partnership law can get the same rights; (3) two non-Danish citizens can entered into registered partnership if both partners have stayed in Denmark for at least two years; (4) a partner in a registered partnership can adopt the children of her/his partner unless the child is adopted from a foreign country. The remaining differences between registered partnership and marriage are: (1) no insemination by public health services for lesbians; (2) no adoption of foreign children; (3) no possibility of a church wedding, although blessings are possible; and (4) the two-year limitation for foreigners. See International Lesbian and Gay Association (ILGA), *World Legal Survey: Denmark,* available at <www.ilga.org/Information/legal_survey/europe/denmark.htm>.

28. Act of Registered Domestic Partnerships of April 30, 1993, No. 40, created a registration system similar to Denmark's, permitting partnership registration for two persons of the same sex. Under the law, registered partnerships are accorded the same legal obligations and rights as marriage except (1) adoption rights are excluded; (2) medically assisted conception is not available to lesbian couples; (3) a church wedding is not possible; and (4) one or both of the parties must be domiciled in Norway, and at least one of them must have a Norwegian nationality. Unlike the Danish legislation, a registered couple can share parental authority. See ILGA, *World Legal Survey: Norway,* available at <www.ilga.org/Information/legal_survey/europe/norway.htm>.

29. Greenland is a self-governing dependency of Denmark. Although most of the laws of Denmark apply, Greenland did not accept the 1989 Danish Registered Partnership Law until 1994. Such partnerships became effective in Greenland in 1996. See ILGA, *World Legal Survey: Greenland,* available at <www.ilga.org/Information/legal_survey/europe/greenland.htm.>.

30. On June 1, 1994, Sweden adopted the Registered Partnership Act. Lag 1994: 1117, Om Registrerat Partnerskap (adopted June 1, 1994, effective Jan. 1, 1995). The act provides for a registration procedure, whereby same-sex partners can obtain all the obligations and benefits of marriage except that registered couples cannot (1) adopt children; (2) have access to state-provided artificial insemination; or (3) have the benefit of certain state-provided benefits. See ILGA, *World Survey: Sweden,* available at <www.ilga.org/Information/legal_survey/europe/sweden.htm>.

31. In 1996, the Icelandic parliament adopted the Registered Partnership Law. Similar to that adopted by Denmark, Norway, and Sweden, the Icelandic law also gives lesbian and gay couples joint custody of the children either partner brings to the family. See ILGA, *World Survey: Iceland,* available at <www.ilga.org/Information/legal_survey/europe/iceland.htm>.

32. In 1998, France adopted legislation creating new pactes civiles de solidarite (Civil Solidarity Pacts) for same-sex couples. See Proposition de Loi Adoptee par L'Assemble Nacionale en Premi re Lecture, relative au pacte civil de solidarite, No. 207, 9 Dec. 1998, available at <www.senat.fr/leg/taan98-207>.

33. Registered partners may register for most benefits available to married couples. See "Partnerships Broadened in Switzerland," *Wash. Blade,* March 31, 2000.

34. On November 10, 2000, the German Parliament approved a bill (effective August 1, 2001) establishing registered "Life Partnerships" for same-sex couples, with some

of the benefits of marriage. Some of the benefits Life Partnerships do not entail include (1) the right to adopt children; (2) important financial provisions related to income and inheritance taxes; and (3) requirement to support an unemployed partner.

35. In March 2001, the Portuguese National Assembly, Portugal's parliament, passed a bill to allow same-sex couples who have lived together for more than two years the same rights as heterosexual couples in common-law marriages. *See Gay Couples Given Same Legal Rights As Heterosexuals in Portugal, available at <www.ananova.com/news/ story/sm 244161.htm>.*

36. Agence Fr. Presse, September 28, 2001, available at 2001 WL 25024366.

37. On June 8, 2000, retirement, death benefits, and joint tax filings were made available to same-sex couples in "stable unions." *See* Larry Rohter, "Brazil Grants Rights to Same-Sex Pairs," *Arizona Republic,* June 11, 2000, at A26.

38. In its decision 14/1995 regarding the legality of same sex partnerships, the Constitutional Court ruled that the state could refuse to recognize same-sex marriages but was required to recognize same-sex cohabiting relationships in the same manner that it recognizes different-sex cohabiting couples. In response, the Hungarian parliament enacted legislation to that effect in 1996. William Eskridge Jr., "Comparative Law and the Same-Sex Marriage Debate: A Step-By-Step Approach Toward State Recognition," 31 *McGeorge L. Rev.* 641, 666 (2000).

39. *See* IGLA, *World Legal Survey, Recognition of Immigration Rights for Same-Sex Partners,* available at <www.ilga.org/Information/legal_survey/Summary%20information/ recognition_of_im migration_right.htm>; *Israel Allows Partner Immigration,* available at <www.gaylawnet.com/news/2000/im2000.htm#israel_allows>; Lambda Legal Defense and Education Fund, *International Recognition of Same-Sex Partnerships,* available at <www.lambdalegal.org/cgi-bin/pages/documents/record?record=432>.

40. *See, e.g.,* Miss. Code Ann. § 93-1-13 (1990); N.C. Gen. State. 51-6 (1990).

41. *See, e.g.,* 21 Vt. Stat. Ann. § 471 (recognizing both the emotional ties spouses have to each other and the responsibilities that go with them by allowing a married person to take leave from work to care for a spouse who is seriously ill); 15 Vt. Stat. Ann. § 751 (directing courts to divide the property of the married couple equitably); Vt. Stat. Ann. § 752 (authorizing court to order maintenance payments, either rehabilitative or permanent when a spouse lacks sufficient income to provide for reasonable needs).

42. *See, e.g.,* 14 Vt. Stat. Ann. § 551(2) (establishing rules of intestate succession. In the situation of a married person who dies without issue, the spouse receives the entirety of a small estate and at least half of any larger estate).

43. *See, e.g.,* 12 Vt. Stat. Ann. § 5431 (providing that a married person may bring a suit for loss of consortium against a person who has wrongfully injured his or her spouse).

44. *See, e.g., Adams v. Howerton,* 673 F.2d 1036, 1040 (9th Cir. 1982) (holding that only marriages between two people of the same sex are not recognized for immigration purposes). The Permanent Partners Immigration Act (PPIA), H.R. 690, which would modify the federal Immigration and Nationality Act to allow U.S. citizens and permanent residents to sponsor their same-sex partners for immigration to the United States. The PPIA was first introduced in the House of Representatives on February 14, 2000, by Representative Jerrold Nadler (D-N.Y.). The bill garnered fifty-nine cosponsors during the 106th Congress and was reintroduced on February 14, 2001.

45. In 1996, the federal General Accounting Office (GAO) did a study of the federal laws in which benefits, rights, and privileges are contingent upon marital status. The GAO found 1,049 such federal laws. A copy of the report can be found at <www.buddybuddy.com/og97016.pdf>.

46. In an IRS private-letter ruling to companies, the IRS stated "that for an employee to exclude from income the cost of employer-provided health coverage for a domestic partner, the domestic partner generally must meet all the requirements for qualifying as the employee's dependent." IRS PLR 9231062 5/7/92.

47. Defense of Marriage Act, Pub. L. No. 104-199, (codified at 28 U.S.C. § 1738C and 1 U.S.C. § 7). The relevant text:

No state, territory or possession of the United States, or Indian tribe, shall be required to give effect to any public act, record, or judicial proceeding of any other State, territory, possession, or tribe respecting a relationship between persons of the same sex that is treated as a marriage under the laws of such other State, territory, possession, or tribe, or a right or claim arising from such relationship.

In determining the meaning of any Act of Congress, or of any ruling, regulation, or interpretation of the various administrative bureaus and agencies of the United States, the word "marriage" means only a legal union between one man and one woman as husband and wife, and the word "spouse" refers only to a person of the opposite sex who is a husband or a wife.

48. U.S. Const. art. IV, § 1; *Nevada v. Hall,* 440 U.S. 410, 421 (1979).

49. *See, e.g., Loughran v. Loughran,* 292 U.S. 216 (1934).

50. *See Ankenbrandt v. Richards.,* 504 U.S. 689 (1992) (holding that federal courts lack subject matter jurisdiction over domestic-relations cases); *see also In re Burrus,* 136 U.S. 586 (1890) ("The whole subject of domestic relations of husband and wife, parent and child, belongs to the laws of the States and not to the laws of the United States.").

51. *See Saenz v. Roe,* 526 U.S. 489 (1999) (holding that the Privileges and Immunities Clause of the Fourteenth Amendment protects "the right to be treated like other citizens of that State," a component of the right to travel). *See also Shapiro v. Thompson,* 394 U.S. 618, 629 (1969) (holding that it is unconstitutional to interfere with the right to migrate, resettle, find a new job, and start a new life).

52. *Turner v. Safley,* 482 U.S. 78, 94–95 (1987) ("[Petitioners] concede that the decision to marry is a fundamental right.") (citing *Zablocki v. Redhail,* 434 U.S. 374 (1978), and *Loving, supra* note 4).

53. *Romer v. Evans,* 517 U.S. 620 (1996).

54. These states include Alabama (1998); Alaska (by statute (1996) and by a state constitutional amendment (1998)); Arizona (1996); Arkansas (1997); California (2000); Colorado (2000); Delaware (1996); Florida (1997); Georgia (1996); Hawaii (state constitutional amendment gave the legislature authority to limit marriage by statute (1998)); Idaho (1996); Illinois (1996); Indiana (1997); Iowa (1998); Kansas (1996); Kentucky (1998); Louisiana (1999); Maine (1997); Michigan (1996); Minnesota (1997); Mississippi (1997); Missouri (2001); Montana (1997); Nebraska (2000); Nevada (2000); North Carolina (1996); North Dakota (1997); Oklahoma (1996); Pennsylvania (1996); South Caro-

lina (1996); South Dakota (1996); Tennessee (1996); Texas (1973); Utah (1995); Virginia (1997); Washington (1998); and West Virginia (2000). For more information, *see* <http://www.marriagewatch.org>.

55. *See, e.g.,* Md. Fam. Law Code Ann. § 2-201 (1984) ("Only a marriage between a man and a woman is valid in this State."); Tex. Fam. Code §2.001 (2000) (providing that a marriage "license may not be issued for the marriage of persons of the same sex"); Utah Code Ann. § 30-1-2 (1994) (providing that marriages between persons of the same sex are prohibited and void).

56. *See, e.g., Romer v. Evans.,* 517 U.S. 620, 633 (1996) ("A law declaring that in general it shall be more difficult for one group of citizens than for all others to seek aid from the government is itself a denial of equal protection of the laws in the most literal sense.").

57. *Loving, supra* note 4.

58. *Id.* at 12.

59. *Common-law marriage* is "[a] marriage that takes legal effect, without license or ceremony, when a couple live together as husband and wife, intend to be married, and hold themselves out to others as a married couple." *Black's Law Dictionary* (7th ed. 1999).

60. *Braschi v. Stahl Assoc. Co.,* 544 N.Y.S.2d 784, 543 N.E.2d 49 (N.Y. 1989).

61. *Id.* at 788–89, 53–54.

62. 157 Ore. App. 502, 971 P.2d 435 (Ore. 1998).

63. *Id.* at 523, 446 ("We therefore understand from the cases that the focus of suspect class definition is not necessarily the immutability of the common, class-defining characteristics, but instead the fact that such characteristics are historically regarded as defining distinct, socially-recognized groups that have been the subject of adverse social or political stereotyping or prejudice. If a law or government action fails to offer privileges and immunities to members of such a class on equal terms, the law or action is inherently suspect and . . . may be upheld only if the failure to make the privileges or immunities available to that class can be justified by genuine differences between the disparately treated class and those to whom the privileges and immunities are granted.").

64. *Levin v. Yeshiva University,* 96 N.Y.2d 484, 754 N.E.2d 1099, 730 N.Y.S.2d 15 (2001).

65. *Smith v. Knoller, et al.,* San Francisco Superior Court, Case No. 319532 (August 9, 2001).

66. *Langan v. St. Vincent's Hosp. of N.Y., N.Y.L.J.,* April 18, 2003, at 23 (N.Y. Sup. Ct. 2003).

67. As of early 2003, sixty-one states and municipalities had domestic-partner registries available to register couples. For more information, *see* Human Right's Campaign Worknet at <http://www.hrc.org/worknet/index.asp>.

68. San Francisco, Cal. Admin. Code ch. 62.

69. *See* Human Rights Campaign's WorkNet for the full list of jurisdictions, available at <www.hrc.org/worknet/index.asp>.

70. AB (Assembly Bill) 25 (Migden, Statutes of 2001) (effective January 1, 2002).

71. AB (Assembly Bill) 205 (Goldberg, 2003) (operative Jan. 1, 2005).

72. The Reciprocal Beneficiaries Law (Act 383, Session Laws of Hawaii 1997).

73. Christopher Elliott, "Gay, Lesbian Couples Get Partnered in San Francisco," *L.A. Times,* Feb. 15, 1991, at A3.

74. There are books and other resources available to help LGBT couples trying to create these documents to secure their relationships. Many local and national LGBT organizations also have information available. Also, a local LGBT bar association or organization may be able to refer you to a lawyer who has experience drafting these types of documents.

75. *Marvin v. Marvin,* 18 Cal. 3d 660, 557 P.2d 106 (1976).

76. *Crooke v. Gilden,* 262 Ga. 122, 414 S.E. 2d 645 (1992) (upholding a carefully written agreement between lesbians that did not include sexual relations); *Whorton v. Dillingham,* 248 Cal. Rptr. 405 (Ct. App. 1988) (enforcing a written agreement between two men, which included duties of chauffeur, bodyguard, and social and business services); *Jones v. Daly,* 176 Cal. Rptr. 130 (Ct. App. 1981) (not enforcing a written agreement between two males that included services as "lover"); *Ireland v. Flanagan,* 627 P.2d 496 (Or. Ct. App. 1981) (enforcing an oral agreement between two lesbians).

77. *Marvin, supra* note 69; *Jones v. Daly, supra* note 70 (not enforcing a written agreement between two males that included services as "lover").

78. *Seward v. Mentrup,* 87 Ohio App. 3d 601, 622 N.E.2d 756 (1993) (finding no agreement between two lesbians in an eight-year relationship and refusing to divide equally the property acquired during the relationship).

79. *Hanselman v. Shepardson,* No. 94 Civ. 4132, 1996 WL 99377 (S.D.N.Y. 1996) (seeking to enforce an agreement on the specific piece of property); *Bramlett v. Selman,* 268 Ark. 457, 597 S.W.2d 80 (1980) (evaluating an agreement concerning a specific piece of property owned under one partner's name).

80. Cal. Probate Code § 6401.

81. Haw. Rev. Stat. §§ 560:1-201; 560:2-102.

82. Vt. Stat. Ann., tit. 15 § 1204(e)(1).

83. *See Matter of Cooper,* 187 A.D.2d 128, 592 N.Y.S.2d 797 (1993) (holding gay male partner not entitled to be considered surviving "spouse" for purposes of intestate succession).

84. *Jackson v. Smith,* 679 So.2d 1123 (Ala. Civ. Ct. App. 1996) (finding undue influence in bequest of entire estate to surviving partner); *In re Bacot,* 502 So.2d 1118 (La. Ct. App. 1987) (honoring will to leave estate to surviving partner); *In re Will of Kaufman,* 247 N.Y.S.2d 664 (App. Div. 1964) (disregarding will due to "insidious, subtle and impalpable" undue influence of partner); *Evan v. May,* 923 S.W.2d 712 (Tex. Ct. App. 1996) (no undue influence by partner of thirty years).

85. *See* National Association of Insurance Commissioners, Medical/LifeStyle Questions and Underwriting Guidelines (1987). The standards also specify that an individual's marital status, living arrangements, beneficiary designation, zip code, or other territorial classification may not be employed to infer an applicant's sexual orientation.

86. Most recently, a Maryland court granted a petition allowing a gay man to adopt his partner. *See* Peter Freiberg, "Montgomery County Man Adopts Partner," *Wash. Blade,* June 1, 2001.

87. *In re Robert Paul P.,* 481 N.Y.S.2d 652, 471 N.E.2d 424 (New York 1984).

88. *Id.* at 655, 427.

89. *Id.* at 654, 426.

90. *See, e.g.,* N.Y. CLS Dom. Rel. Law § 117(b) (McKinney 1988).

X

Parenting

Since the 1970s, the legal environment for lesbian, gay, and bisexual parents has improved considerably. In many recent cases, judges faced with custody issues involving a lesbian or gay parent have shown an openmindedness that used to be almost nonexistent. In some states, however, anti-LGBT bias still strongly affects the law.

Legal issues regarding lesbian and gay parenthood usually arise in one of two contexts: in a divorce in which one of the divorcing parents is lesbian or gay or when a lesbian or gay couple separates.

When a legally married couple has or adopts a child, both people are automatically considered the "legal parents" of the child. A legal parent is a person who has the legal right to be with a child and make decisions about the child's health, education, and well-being and is obligated to support the child financially. When a married couple divorces, they both remain legal parents. A court's determination of custody and visitation upon divorce is generally governed by the "best interests of the child" standard. Fortunately, while previously more common, there remain only a few states in which simply being lesbian or gay is a sufficient basis for denying a parent custody of the child. In most states, a parent's sexual orientation is not considered relevant to a custody determination unless there is evidence of harm to the child.

Because no state currently allows same-sex couples to marry, automatic conferral of legal parental status is not available to lesbian and gay couples. The one exception is Vermont, where there is now an automatic presumption that a child born to a same-sex couple who has entered into a civil union has a legal parent-child relationship to both parents.[1] Otherwise, unless the couple has obtained a second-parent adoption or a parentage

138

decree, only one partner is a legal parent to their child. If the couple separates, the rights of the two coparents will be vastly different.

This chapter first addresses parenting rights in the context of disputes between a lesbian or gay parent and his or her former heterosexual spouse upon divorce. The second section discusses the emerging law on parenting rights and duties as they pertain to lesbian or gay coparents.

CHILDREN FROM A FORMER MARRIAGE

Will I lose custody of my child because of my sexual orientation?

Custody decisions must be determined according to the "best interests of the child." In nearly every state, the best interests of the child standard has been adopted as the law, sometimes with specific factors for judges to consider in determining a child's best interests.[2] Even so, application of this general rule varies greatly from state to state, and even from judge to judge.

In a few states, courts have decided that being gay or lesbian, by itself, is a good enough reason to deny custody to a parent, regardless of the parent's prior childrearing experience and relationship with the child. This is often referred to as the "per se" approach.[3]

The majority of states, however, have adopted the so-called nexus approach, which requires that the parent seeking custody show a connection between the other parent's sexual orientation and some harm to the child. Under this approach, in the absence of evidence that the other parent's sexual orientation is actually causing some harm to the child, the court should not consider sexual orientation in deciding a custody, visitation, or adoption dispute.[4] In practice, however, sometimes courts say that they are not considering the sexual orientation of a parent to be per se harmful to the child but, in reality, treat it as though it were.[5]

If I do not get custody of my child, do I have rights to visitation?

Yes. There is a heavy presumption in favor of allowing continued contact between parent and child. Although courts have sometimes placed restrictions on the visitation rights of lesbian or gay parents (see below), it would be very unusual for a court to deny all visitation on the basis of the parent's sexual orientation.[6] Moreover, after the Supreme Court's decision in *Lawrence v. Texas*,[7] imposing such a restriction in the absence of evidence of harm to the child would likely be held unconstitutional. As with custody, most states require proof of a nexus, or connection, between a parent's sexual orientation and some actual harm to the child before the court can consider the parent's sexual orientation in making a visitation order.

Boswell v. Boswell[8] is an example of how courts apply the nexus approach to visitation. In *Boswell*, two married parents separated after the husband told the wife that he was gay.[9] The court gave sole custody of the children to the mother and put severe restrictions on the father's visitation. The court prohibited any overnight visitation and visitation with the child in the presence of the father's same-sex partner or "anyone having homosexual tendencies or such persuasions, male or female, or with anyone that the father may be living with in a non-marital relationship."[10] The father appealed this decision. The Maryland Court of Appeals established the following rule: a court must have evidence that a parent's nonmarital relationship caused an adverse impact on the child before it can restrict or limit the parent's custody or visitation.[11] Applying that rule, the court reversed the limits set by the trial court on visitation in the presence of the father's boyfriend,[12] because the restriction was not backed up by any evidence of detriment or actual harm to the child.

May the court restrict my visitation with my child in any way?

Although increasingly uncommon in most states, it is not unheard-of for a court to impose restrictions on a lesbian or gay parent's visitation based on the court's disapproval of the parent's sexual orientation. These restrictions may be illegal, either because they are not supported by evidence of harm to the child, because they unconstitutionally discriminate on the basis of sexual orientation, or because they are an unconstitutional interference with a parent's right to determine the upbringing of the child.

Examples of restrictions that have been imposed on lesbian and gay parents in some cases include prohibitions on overnight visitation,[13] prohibitions on visitation in the presence of the parent's partner,[14] and prohibitions on visitation in the presence of any other lesbian or gay person.[15] Some courts have also ordered lesbian or gay parents to refrain from taking their children to gay-supportive places of worship or to places where other lesbian or gay people are "known to congregate."[16]

Legal challenges on these restrictions, though, are increasingly successful.[17] For example, in *Weigand v. Houghton*,[18] a gay father sought custody of his son when he learned that the mother's new husband was violent, drank heavily, and had past convictions for felony assault. The trial court found that the son had made a 911 call to report the assault of his mother and that he had been "greatly disturbed" by the domestic violence. The judge also found that the gay father was well bonded with his son and had a stable home. Despite these findings, however, the judge decided that custody should remain with the mother. He justified his decision by relying on the Mississippi sodomy law. The judge also barred visitation between the father and son in the presence of the father's male partner.

On appeal, the Mississippi Supreme Court left custody with the mother[19] but ordered that there should be no restriction on visitation with his gay father. The court wrote: "[E]ven if [the son] is embarrassed, or does not like the living arrangement of his father, this is not the type of harm that rises to the level necessary to place such restrictions on [the father's] visitation with his son."[20]

May I take my child to LGBT events or parades?

Yes. Unless a court has specifically restricted you from going to LGBT-related events with your child, you may take your child to LGBT events or parades. If you have a custody or visitation order that prohibits you from doing so, you should contact a lawyer before taking your child.

May my ex-spouse challenge my custody because I am lesbian or gay?

After you have been awarded custody, your ex-spouse may challenge your custody if he or she can show that there has been a substantial or important change in the living circumstances of the child since the original custody order was made.[21] Some states also require a showing of detriment to the child to justify a modification. Some parents have argued that discovering that the other parent is lesbian or gay, or that he or she is involved in a new same-sex relationship, is a substantial or important change in circumstances that should allow a change in custody.[22] Most courts have rejected these arguments.

May anyone else challenge my right to custody of my child?

In most states, a third party (nonparent) may not take custody away from a parent unless a judge finds that the parent is unfit or that the child is being harmed by living with the parent.[23] This includes challenges by grandparents and other relatives. While there have been cases in the past in which courts have awarded custody to grandparents or other third parties because the parent was lesbian or gay, they are increasingly rare.[24]

What should I do if my parental rights are challenged?

You should contact a lawyer immediately. Because few lawyers are familiar with the law concerning lesbian and gay parents, you may want to contact your local LGBT organization to see if they have lawyer referral lists. In addition, several national organizations provide advice and referral information (see list of groups in appendix A). If you cannot afford a lawyer, some courts will appoint one, or you can consult a local legal aid or legal services office or other community law project that offers free or inexpensive legal advice.

How can I prove that I am a good parent?

As in most custody hearings, the more expert testimony you present, the better. In addition to testimony by psychologists, teachers, clergy, and relatives familiar with both the parents and the children, lesbian and gay parents may need to present evidence that disproves some of the myths surrounding lesbian and gay adults as parents—including the myths that LGBT people are unfit to be parents and that the children of LGBT parents are harmed by their parent's sexual orientation.[25]

Is the court allowed to ask about the details of my sex life?

In custody cases, the court is entitled to have information regarding nearly all aspects of the parents' lives to decide what living situation is in the child's best interests. But even though a court has wide latitude to consider personal information, in the absence of a showing of how the parent's private sexual conduct directly affects the welfare of the child, a parent's right to privacy should limit such inquiries.

CHILDREN OF SAME-SEX PARTNERS

Am I considered a legal parent to our child?

A legal parent is a person who has the legal right to be with a child and make decisions about the child's health, education, and well-being. A legal parent is also financially obligated to support the child.

Generally speaking, a same-sex partner is not considered the legal parent unless he or she is the biological parent, has adopted the child, or has obtained a parentage decree (see below for more discussion about parentage decrees), or lives in Vermont and had a child while in a civil union with his or her partner. Generally, a person is not a legal parent simply because she or he is the partner of a legal parent, even if she or he planned and participated in the birth of the child together.

What does the fact that I am not a legal parent mean?

A person not recognized by the law as a parent does not have any automatic legal decision-making authority. This means that he or she may not be able to consent to medical care or even have the authority to approve things like school field trips. In addition, he or she may have no rights toward the child if something should happen to the biological parent, and probably no right to claim the child as a dependent for health insurance. In the absence of a will stating otherwise, the child has no right to inherit from that person.

When a legally married couple divorces and cannot agree on reasonable custody, visitation, and support issues, a court will resolve these issues. Because lesbian and gay couples cannot marry in the U.S., they do not have an automatic right to utilize these procedures. When couples have sought resolution in the courts, some judges have ruled that the nonlegal parent has no right to a continued relationship with the child of his or her former partner, even when he or she was an equal caretaker. These courts have treated the nonlegal parent as a stranger to the child, without rights to custody or visitation.[26]

How can I gain parental rights to our child?

The most common means by which lesbian or gay coparents establish a legal relationship with their child is through what is generally referred to as a "second-parent adoption." In most cases, people who allow their children to be adopted must give up their own parental rights. The most common exception to this rule is stepparent adoptions, which permit a second person (the stepparent) to adopt his or her spouse's child without terminating the spouse's parental rights. Similarly, a second-parent adoption allows a lesbian or gay parent to adopt his or her partner's child, without requiring the partner to give up her parental rights. This provides the child with two legal parents, both of whom have equal legal status in terms of their relationship to the child.[27]

As of June 2003, courts in at least twenty-two states and the District
of Columbia have granted these kinds of adoptions.[28] Appellate court
rulings in four states—Colorado, Nebraska, Ohio, and Wisconsin—however, provide that second-parent adoptions are not available on the ground
that they are not authorized by the adoption statutes in those states.[29]

While second-parent adoptions are currently the most common means
used to provide children in lesbian- and gay-parent families with a legally
protected relationship with both of their parents, an alternative method is
being used in California, Colorado, Massachusetts, and possibly other
states. This procedure is referred to as a "parentage action," "maternity
action," or "UPA (Uniform Parentage Act) action." It is based on the concept that when two people use reproductive technology to bring a child
into the world, both should be held legally accountable as parents.[30]

It has been used in cases in which a lesbian couple arrange for the birth
of a child together through donor insemination or in which a gay male
couple have a child together through the use of a gestational surrogate. In
these cases, the intended parents can petition the court to declare the nonbiological parent to be a legal parent to the child from the outset, without
the need for an adoption.

Finally, when a lesbian or gay couple who have entered into a civil
union have a child together in Vermont, both partners in the couple automatically become legal parents, and both parties have the same rights with
respect to the child "as those of a married couple."[31] This will also be true
for children born to registered domestic partners after AB 205 becomes
operational on January 1, 2005.

Is there anything else I can do to protect my relationship with my child?

If you live in a state that has not allowed same-sex couples to adopt or
obtain parentage decrees, you may want to draft a parenting agreement
with your partner, in consultation with an attorney. The agreement should
specify that although only one of you is the legal parent, you both consider
yourselves the parents of your child, with all of the rights and responsibilities that come with that position. Your agreement should include language
that clearly states whether you intend to continue to coparent even if your
relationship ends.

While coparenting agreements generally cannot be enforced in court,[32]
they can serve as strong evidence that the nonbiological parent acted as a

parent of the child and that both parents intended that relationship to continue. You may also want to draft other documents to protect the nonlegal parent's relationship with the child to the extent possible, such as a nomination of guardianship and an authorization for hospital visitation.

Do I have any right to custody or visitation of our child if we break up?

Unless you are a legal parent, you have no automatic right to custody or visitation. There are some states, however, in which a person who has played a parental role in a child's life may ask a court to determine whether it is in the child's best interests to maintain some contact with the person through court-ordered visitation or custody. In Massachusetts,[33] New Jersey,[34] New Mexico,[35] Pennsylvania,[36] Rhode Island,[37] and Wisconsin,[38] courts have recognized that when a same-sex partner participated in the day-to-day caretaking and developed a parentlike relationship with the child, then he or she is a "de facto" or "psychological" parent and should be permitted to request visitation with the child if the couple separates, even if the child's legal parent objects.

Recently, for example, the highest court in Massachusetts awarded visitation rights to a lesbian who had parented a child with her partner, the child's biological mother, who then attempted to prevent her former partner from having any contact with the child after the couple separated.[39] The court based its decision on the ground that the former partner was a de facto parent, which the court defined as "one who has no biological relation to the child, but has participated in the child's life as a member of the child's family. The de facto parent resides with the child and, with the consent and encouragement of the legal parent, performs a share of caretaking functions at least as great as the legal parent."[40]

In a similar decision from New Jersey,[41] the New Jersey Supreme Court outlined some of the factors to be considered when determining whether a person who is not a legal parent is nonetheless entitled to ask for visitation with a child: "the legal parent must consent to and foster the relationship between the third party and the child; the third party must have lived with the child; the third party must perform parental functions for the child to a significant degree; and most important, a parent-child bond must be forged."[42] If a court finds these factors are fulfilled, then it will order visitation if it is in the best interests of the child to do so.[43]

ADOPTIVE OR FOSTER CHILDREN
OF SAME-SEX PARENTS

Are there any restrictions on lesbians or gay men adopting children?

As of June 2003, three states exclude either lesbian and gay individuals or couples from adopting children. Two states—Utah and Mississippi—prohibit adoptions by lesbian and gay couples but not by single lesbians and gay men; Florida prohibits all adoptions by lesbian and gay people.[44] On the positive side, in April 1999, New Hampshire repealed its twelve-year-old ban on lesbian and gay adoption and foster parenting.

Even where there is no law prohibiting lesbian or gay adoptions, however, a court may sometimes deny a petition for adoption by a lesbian or gay men on its own accord. In 1990, for example, an Ohio trial court ruled: "It is not in the business of the government to encourage homosexuality. . . . [T]he so-called 'gay lifestyle' is patently incompatible with the manifest spirit, purpose and goals of adoption. Homosexuality negates procreation."[45] (The decision was reversed on appeal.)

This is also an area of law in which state officials and agencies are frequently altering their policies. In late 1999, for example, California governor Gray Davis eliminated a state policy—put in place in 1995 by then-governor Pete Wilson—of opposing adoptions by anyone other than a married couple.[46]

Are there any restrictions on lesbians or gay men being foster parents?

Currently, Arkansas is the only state in which lesbians and gay men are legally prohibited from becoming foster parents. In October 2000, pursuant to a decision by the state's Child Welfare Agency Review Board, the Arkansas Department of Human Services began asking prospective foster parents if they are gay or lesbian. Those who answer yes are denied the right to become foster parents.[47]

In Utah, the division cannot place a child in foster care with a lesbian or gay couple.[48]

Should I tell the adoption/foster care agency that I am lesbian or gay?

While it is never a good idea to lie about one's sexual orientation in response to a direct inquiry from an adoption or foster agency, there is also no particular reason to disclose it unless required to do so, given that being lesbian or gay has no direct relevance to one's parental ability. The consequences of disclosing or not disclosing one's identity as a lesbian or gay man varies greatly from state to state, community to community, and even agency to agency. In some cases, disclosing that one is lesbian or gay will expose a potential adoptive or foster parent to bias and prejudice; in others, it will make no difference. If confronted with this issue, you should contact an attorney knowledgeable about lesbian and gay custody issues in your state or locality.

NOTES

1. Vt. Stat. Ann. tit. 15, §1204(f).

2. *See, e.g.,* Alaska Stat. § 25.20.060 (Michie 1996) (directing the court to award the custody arrangement that is in the best interests of child); Ga. Code Ann. § 19-9-3(a)(2) (1999) (describing duty of the court to ascertain which parent will promote the best interests of the child); Mo. Rev. Stat. § 452.375(2) (Supp. 1998) (directing the court to determine custody in accordance with the best interests of the child and listing factors).

3. *Ex parte D. W.,* 717 So.2d 793 (Ala. 1993); *Larson v. Larson,* 902 S.W.2d (Ark. Ct. App. 1995); *Pulliam v. Smith,* 348 N.C. 616, 501 S.E.2d 898 (1998) (noting that mother did not have to prove detriment to children based on father's sexual orientation); *Roe v. Roe,* 228 Va. 722, 324 S.E.2d 691 (1985).

These cases are particularly vulnerable in light of the Supreme Court decision *Lawrence v. Texas,* 123 S. Ct. 2472 (2003), in which the Supreme Court held that moral disapproval is not a sufficient justification for infringing a person's liberty interests.

4. *See, e.g., Teegarden v. Teegarden,* 642 N.E.2d 1007 (Ind. Ct. App. 1994); *Fox v. Fox,* 904 P.2d 66 (Okla. 1995) (holding that trial court erred by ordering a change of custody from lesbian mother to heterosexual father when there was "no evidence that the mother's behavior has any adverse effect on the children"); *Blew v. Verta,* 420 Pa. Super. 528, 617 A.2d 31 (1992) (removing restrictions on lesbian mother's custody when "the trial court's conclusion that [the child] has been harmed by his mother's lesbian relationship is not supported by its own findings of fact"); *Stroman v. Williams,* 291 S.C. 376, 353 S.E.2d 704 (Ct. App. 1987) The District of Columbia is currently the only jurisdiction in the country that has a statute explicitly guaranteeing that sexual orientation cannot, in and of itself, be a conclusive factor in determining custody or visitation. *See* D.C. Code Ann. § 16-914(a)(1) ("With respect to matters of custody and visitation . . . sexual orientation, in and of itself, of a party, shall not be a conclusive consideration."). For further discussion of this issue, see generally, Karla J. Staff, "Adoption by Homosexuals: A Look at Differing State Court Opinions," 40 *Ariz. L. Rev.* 1497 (1998).

5. *See, e.g., S. v. S.,* 608 S.W.2d 64 (Ky. Ct. App. 1980), *cert. denied,* 451 U.S. 911 (1981) (relying on conjecture as to possible future harm as basis for custody determination); *Scott v. Scott,* 665 So.2d 760, 766 (La. Ct. App. 1995) (affirming *Lundin v. Lundin*

that while homosexuality in and of itself does not disqualify a parent for custody, "primary custody with the homosexual parent would rarely be held to be in the best interests of the child."); *J.A.D. v. F.J.D.,* 978 S.W.2d 336, 339 (Mo. Sup. Ct. 1998) (holding that "[a] homosexual parent is not ipso facto unfit for custody of his or her child, and no reported Missouri case has held otherwise. It is not error, however, to consider the impact of homosexual or heterosexual misconduct upon the children in making a custody determination.").

6. *But cf. Roberts v. Roberts,* 22 Ohio App. 3d 127, 129, 489 N.E.2d 1067, 1070 (Ohio App. 1985) (stating that the trial court might find that the only way to protect children from effects of father's "errant sexual behavior" would be to prohibit all visitation until children were old enough not to be harmed or influenced by father's lifestyle).

7. *Lawrence v. Texas,* 123 S. Ct. 2472 (2003).

8. *Boswell v. Boswell,* 352 Md. 204, 721 A.2d 662 (Md. Ct. App. 1998).

9. *Id.* at 210, 664.

10. *Id.* at 211, 665.

11. *Id.* at 237, 678. *See also id.* ("Therefore, before a trial court restricts the non-custodial parent's visitation, it must make specific factual findings based on sound evidence in the record. If the trial court does not make these factual findings, instead basing its ruling on personal bias or stereotypical beliefs, then such findings may be clearly erroneous and the order may be reversed. In addition, if a trial court relies on abstract presumptions, rather than sound principles of law, an abuse of discretion may be found.").

12. *Id.* at 237, 238, 721 A.2d at 678, 679.

13. *See, e.g., Irish v. Irish,* 102 Mich. App. 75, 300 N.W.2d 739 (Mich. App. 1980) (holding that children could not stay overnight with lesbian mother if the mother's lover was present); *H. v. P.,* 643 S.W.2d 865 (Mo. App. 1982) (upholding trial court's order denying gay father overnight visitation). For a more detailed summary of the cases regarding visitation rights of a gay or lesbian parent, see *Visitation Rights of Homosexual or Lesbian Parent,* 36 A.L.R.4th 997 (1999 Supp.).

14. *See, e.g., L. v. D.,* 630 S.W.2d 240 (Mo. App. 1982) (holding that it was proper to restrict lesbian mother's visitation by requiring that no female with whom the mother was living be present during the children's visits); *Ex parte D.W.W.,* 717 So.2d 793 (Ala. 1998), *on remand to,* 717 So.2d 799 (Ala. 1998) (holding that restriction prohibiting lesbian mother's partner from being around during visitation was reasonably drawn).

15. *See, e.g., Boswell, supra* note 8, at 211, 665 (noting that the trial court order prohibited any visitation with the children in the presence of the father's same-sex partner or "anyone having homosexual tendencies or such persuasions, male or female").

16. *See, e.g., H. v. P.,* 643 S.W.2d 865 (Mo. App. 1982) (upholding order requiring gay father's not to bring his children to gay political or social gatherings or to a gay-affirming church).

17. *See, e.g., Downey v. Muffley,* 767 N.E.2d 1014 (Ind. Ct. App. 2002) (holding there was no evidence to support order prohibiting ex-wife from cohabiting with same-sex partner while living with her children); *In re Marriage of Dorworth,* 2001 WL 987710 (Col. Ct. App. 2001) (holding that there was no evidence to support a trial court's order barring the bisexual father's having overnight guests during his visitation periods, nor could the court forbid him from bringing his daughter with him to church, on the ground that

attended a church with a "gay orientation"); *In re Marriage of Pleasant,* 256 Ill. App. 3d 742, 628 N.E.2d 633 (1993) (holding that trial court erred in restricting lesbian mother's visitation rights by requiring that visitation be supervised by heterosexual employees of state department of children and family services, by reducing her visitation, by eliminating overnight visitation, and by requiring that mother enroll in regular psychotherapy in a case in which the court made its order solely because mother's was openly involved in a lesbian relationship and there was no showing of inappropriate behavior in child's presence). *See also In re Marriage of Birdsall,* 197 Cal. App. 3d 1024 (1988); *Gottlieb v. Gottlieb,* 108 A.D.2d 120, 488 N.Y.S.2d 180 (N.Y. App. Div. 1985).

18. *Weigand v. Houghton,* 730 So.2d 581 (Miss. 1999).

19. To the extent the decision to deny custody to the father was based on the state sodomy statute, it is no longer good law after the Supreme Court's decision in *Lawrence v. Texas* holding sodomy laws unconstitutional as applied to private adult consensual sexual activity.

20. *Weigand, supra* note 18, at 587.

21. *See, e.g.,* Colo. Rev. Stat. § 14-10-13; Mo. Rev. Stat. § 452.410; Ohio Rev. Code Ann. § 3109.04. *See also* Unif. Marriage & Divorce Act § 409(b), 9 U.L. at 628.

22. *See, e.g., S., supra* note 5 (involving a motion to modify custody on the ground that father recently learned of his ex-wife's relationship with another woman).

23. *See, e.g., Albright v. Commonwealth ex rel. Fetters,* 491 Pa. 320, 323, 421 A.2d 157, 158 (1980) ("[T]he parent has a prima facie right to custody, which will be forfeited only if convincing reasons appear that the child's best interests will be served by an award to the third party.").

24. *See Chaffin v. Frye,* 45 Cal. App. 3d 39 (1975) (awarding custody to the maternal grandparents over lesbian mother); *Roberts v. Roberts,* 25 N.C. App. 198, 212 S.E.2d 410 (1975) (awarding custody to maternal aunt and uncle over lesbian mother). However, in 1995, Virginia removed a child from his mother and placed him with his grandmother. *See Bottoms v. Bottoms,* 249 Va. 410, 457 S.E.2d 102 (1995).

25. *See, e.g.,* Am. Psychological Ass'n, *Lesbian and Gay Parenting: A Resource for Psychologists* (1995); National Institute of Mental Health Task Force on Homosexuality, *Final Report and Background Paper* (1972); R. Green, "Sexual Identity of 37 Children Raised by Homosexual and Transsexual Parents," *Am. J. of Psychiatry* 692-697 (1978); Harris, "Gay and Lesbian Parents," 12 *J. Homosexuality* 101 (Winter 1985–86); Charlotte J. Patterson, "Children of Lesbian and Gay Parents," *Child Dev.* 1025–42 (1992); Fiona Tasker & Susan Golumbok, "Growing Up in a Lesbian Family," *Guilford Publ'ns* (1997).

26. *See, e.g., Alison D. v. Virginia M.,* 572 N.E.2d 27, 569 N.Y.S.2d 586 (1991); *Nancy S. v. Michele G.,* 228 Cal. App. 3d 831 (1991); *Curiale v. Reagan,* 222 Cal. App. 3d 1597 (1990).

27. The ability to do a second-parent adoption generally requires that there be no other legal biological parent (e.g., in the case of a lesbian couple, that the sperm donor does not have any parental rights, or in the case of a gay couple, that the surrogate does not have any parental rights). For additional information about this process, you should contact an attorney in your area familiar with this procedure or call one of the organizations in appendix A.

28. As of June 2003, second-parent adoptions have been approved by appellate courts

in seven states—California, Illinois, Indiana, Massachusetts, New York, New Jersey, and Pennsylvania—as well as in the District of Columbia. *See Sharon S. v. Superior Court*, 31 Cal. 4th 417, 73 P.3d 554 (2003); *In re Petition of K.M. & D.M.*, 274 Ill. App. 3d 189, 653 N.E.2d 888 (1995); *In re Adoption of M.M.G.C.*, 785 N.E.2d 267 (Ind. Ct. App. 2003); *In re Adoption of Tammy*, 416 Mass. 205, 619 N.E.2d 315 (1993); *In re Jacob, In re Dana*, 636 N.Y.S.2d 716, 660 N.E.2d 397 (1995); *In re the Adoption of Two Children by H.N.R.*, 285 N.J. Super. 1, 666 A.2d 535 (1995); *In re Adoption of R.B.F. & R.C.F.*, 803 A.2d 1195 (Pa. 2002); *In re M.M.D. v. B.H.M.*, 662 A.2d 837 (D.C. 1995). They are available by statute in three states—California, Connecticut, and Vermont. Cal. Fam. Code § 9000 (providing that registered domestic partners can use the stepparent adoption procedures); Conn. Gen. Stat. § 45a-724(3) (providing that "any parent of a minor child may agree in writing with one other person who shares parental responsibility for the child with such parent that the other person shall adopt or join in the adoption of the child"); 15A Vt. Stat. Ann. 1-102(b) (providing that if family unit consists of parent and parent's partner and adoption is in child's best interest, partner of parent may adopt child without terminating parent's rights). Finally, second-parent adoptions have been granted by lower courts and appear to be available in at least thirteen other states—Alabama, Alaska, Hawaii, Iowa, Louisiana, Maryland, Minnesota, Nevada, New Mexico, Oregon, Rhode Island, Texas, and Washington. *See* NCLR's *Second Parent Adoptions: An Information Fact Sheet*, available at <www.nclrights.org/publications/pubs_2ndparentadoptions.html>.

29. *In re Adoption of T.K.J.*, 931 P.2d 488 (Colo. 1996); *In re Adoption of Luke*, 263 Neb. 365 (2002); *In re Adoption of Doe*, 130 Ohio App. 3d 288, 719 N.E.2d 1071 (1998); *In re Angel Lace M.*, 84 Wis. 2d 492, 516 N.W.2d 678 (1994). A similar ruling in Connecticut—*In re Adoption of Baby Z.*, 247 Conn. 474, 724 A.2d 1035 (1999)—was superseded by a statute explicitly recognizing second-parent adoptions. *See supra* note 28.

30. *See* Shannon Minter & Kate Kendell, "Beyond Second-Parent Adoption: The Uniform Parentage Act and the 'Intended Parents'—A Model Brief," 2 *Geo. J. Gender & L.* 29 (2000).

31. Vt. Stat. Ann. tit. 15, §1204(f)

32. *See* Minter & Kendell, *supra* note 30.

33. *See E.N.O v. L.M.M.*, 429 Mass. 824, 711 N.E.2d 886 (1999) (holding that trial court had equity jurisdiction to grant visitation between former same-sex partner and child as the child's "de facto" parent).

34. *See V.C. v. J.M.B.*, 163 N.J. 200, 748 A.2d 539 (2000) (adopting the "psychological parent" theory).

35. *See A.C. v. C.B.*, 113 N.M. 581, 829 P.2d 660 (Ct. App. 1992) (holding that former same-sex partner had standing based on deprivation of right to maintain continuing relationship with child, and noting that the parties had a written agreement).

36. *See T.B. v. L.R.M.*, 786 A.2d 913 (Pa. 2001) (holding that mother's former same-sex partner could pursue visitation because she stood in loco parentis to child).

37. *See Rubano v. DiCenzo*, 759 A.2d 959 (R.I. 2000) (holding that the family court had the authority to grant parental rights to mother's former same-sex partner both on the ground that the former partner had a "de facto parent-child relationship" and on the basis of the state's Uniform Parentage Act).

38. *See Holtzman v. Knott*, 193 Wis. 2d 649, 533 N.W.2d 419 (1995) (holding that

former same-sex partner could seek visitation when she had parentlike relationship with child and significant triggering events justified state intervention in child's relationship with biological or adoptive parent).

39. *E.N.O., supra* note 33, at 829, 891.

40. *Id.*

41. *V.C., supra* note 34.

42. *Id.*

43. *Id.* ("When there is a conflict over custody and visitation between the legal parent and a psychological parent, the legal paradigm is that of two legal parents and the standard to be applied is the best interests of the child."). *See also E.N.O., supra* note 33 (holding that trial court had equity jurisdiction to grant visitation between former same-sex partner and child as the child's "de facto" parent).

44. Utah Code Ann. § 78-30-1(3)(b) ("A child may not be adopted by a person who is cohabitating in a relationship that is not a legally valid and binding marriage under the laws of this state. For purposes of this Subsection (3)(b), 'cohabitating' means residing with another person and being involved in a sexual relationship with that person."); Miss. Code Ann. § 93-17-3(2) ("Adoption by couples of the same gender is prohibited."); Fla. Stat. Ch. 63.042(3) ("No person eligible to adopt under this statute may adopt if that person is a homosexual."). The Florida statute was upheld by a federal trial court in August 2001. *Lofton v. Kearney,* 157 F. Supp. 2d 1372 (S.D. Fla. 2001), on appeal.

45. *In re Adoption of Charles B.,* 1988 Ohio App. LEXIS 4435, No. CA-3392 (1988), reversed by the Ohio Supreme Court in 552 N.E. 2d 884 (Ohio 1990).

46. *See* "Opposition Lifted on Adoption by Gays," *L.A. Times,* Nov. 23, 1999, at A34. The state sent letters to all California adoption agencies and county welfare directors advising them that licensed adoption agencies and the state "will no longer deny applications, withhold consent to an adoption petition, or recommend disapproval of an adoption petition based solely on the applicants' or petitioners' marital status." *Id.*

47. Child Welfare Agency Review Board, Minimum Licensing Standards § 230(2).

48. Utah Code Ann. 1953 § 62A-4a-602; Utah Code Ann. 1953 § 78-30-1.

XI

Youth

S chools and homes should be safe, supportive environments for all youth. Unfortunately, however, this is not true for many LGBT young people. A study released in 2001 by the Gay, Lesbian, Straight Education Network (GLSEN) revealed that over 80 percent of LGBT youth reported being verbally harassed because of their sexual orientation and that nearly 70 percent of LGBT youth reported feeling unsafe in school because of their sexual orientation.[1] Other studies have revealed that over 25 percent of LGBT youth are forced to leave their homes because of conflicts with their families over their sexual orientation.[2] In light of these conditions, it is particularly important for LGBT young people to have access to LGBT-supportive people and organizations.

Adolescence is a time when most young people begin to explore their own identity. Thus, it is a period when First Amendment rights—protecting the right to come out, to meet and associate with other LGBT people without fear of prosecution or harassment, to participate in a LGBT-supportive organization—are of particular importance. And while these rights are subject to some curtailment in school settings, a public school may not censor nondisruptive, nonvulgar speech merely to avoid discomfort or controversy. In addition to the First Amendment, several federal and state statutes protect the rights of LGBT students to speak about issues concerning sexual orientation and to form LGBT-supportive groups at school.

This chapter addresses some of the issues that impact LGBT youth, including issues related to their rights in the school contexts—public, private, high school, and college—as well as issues related to home environments.

If I come out as LGBT in my high school or middle school, may the school discipline me in any way?

As long as you come out in a way that respects the regular rules of the school about any student speech—in other words, you talk about your sexual orientation at appropriate times and places and follow whatever rules of conduct the school generally imposes—the school may not discipline you for it. While schools do retain the authority to prohibit speech and conduct that materially disrupts or substantially interferes with the operation of the school or the classroom,[3] disciplining you for others' uncomfortableness with your coming out would constitute a "heckler's veto."[4] The appropriate students to discipline would be those having an extreme reaction—not the students coming out.

If I talk to a school counselor about my sexual orientation or gender identity, can I be sure they won't tell my parents?

School counselors have an ethical obligation to maintain confidences and "secrets revealed to them by their clients."[5] These ethical standards, however, have not been adopted as a legal requirement by any state or agency. This means that although school counselors are under an ethical obligation to abide by the standards, the professional standards are not enforceable in court.[6]

You also have a constitutional right to privacy, which includes privacy about your sexual orientation.[7] If public-school officials disclose this private information to your parents without your consent, they may be violating your constitutional right to keep that information secret. However, your parents are allowed to see your school records under a federal law called the Family Educational Rights and Privacy Act (FERPA), and they may be allowed access to your medical records.[8]

Do my parents/guardians have access to my medical records?

Probably. In August 2002, the United States Department of Health and Human Services adopted final modifications to the Privacy Rule regulations implementing the Health Insurance Portability and Accountability Act (HIPAA). Under these regulations, parents or guardians generally have access to their minor children's medical records. There are three basic exceptions to this rule: (1) when state or other law does not require the consent of a parent before a minor can obtain a particular health-care service and the minor consents; (2) when a court determines or other law authorizes someone other than a parent to make treatment decisions for a minor; or (3) when a parent agrees to a confidential relationship between the minor and the physician.[9] Even in these three situations, however, if the state law is silent or unclear, the covered entity has discretion to provide access to the parent or guardian. Medical records can include information about a minor's sexual orientation or gender identity. More information about HIPAA and the Privacy Rule can be accessed at <www://www.hhs.gov/ocr/hipaa>.

My parents are abusing me because they think I'm LGBT, and I'm afraid they'll kick me out of the house. Do I have any rights?

Parents have enormous authority to direct the upbringing of their children, but those rights stop when it comes to abuse or neglect.[10] This means that if you are under eighteen, your parents or guardians can try to teach you their religious or political beliefs, or in many states they even may require you to see a psychiatrist against your will.[11] But they may not physically abuse, neglect, or abandon you. If they do, the state can step in and place you in foster care and may take away your parents' rights to decide your care.

You have some options if you are being abused by your family, but none of them promises a simple way out of the abuse. If you are experiencing violence or threats of violence, your first priority is to protect yourself. This may mean leaving the situation—for example, by going to the home of another relative or a friend. A supportive teacher or counselor at school might be a good person to talk to about your options. Another good resource may be an LGBT youth group. Local adult advisers for youth groups may be able to help you assess your situation. If you are under eighteen, you might want to call the local office of Child Protective or Child Welfare Services in your area.

You could leave your parents' home permanently and seek guardianship. Guardianship means that another adult agrees to become your legal custodian and must be approved by a judge.[12] You could also seek to be adopted by another adult. This is a difficult process, however—you and the adult adopting you would have to show a judge that your parents substantially abused you, neglected you, or abandoned you.[13]

Another option is to be "emancipated" from your parents. Emancipation means that a minor (anyone under eighteen) is freed from the custody and control of his or her parent(s) and is considered a legal adult. Nearly all states have laws that allow minors to terminate their legal relationship with their parents, if they can show that the parents "failed to provide for the child's well-being according to law."[14] Emancipation is a big decision, however, with heavy consequences. It ends any obligation on the part of your parents to support you and ends your eligibility for services like foster care from the state.[15] You are on your own as an adult, financially and emotionally.

My foster parents or the institution staff say it's a sin to be LGBT. What can I do?

In theory, foster children have a number of legal safeguards to protect them. Foster-care officials must protect the welfare of the children in their charge.[16] They must provide foster children with the basic necessities, including safety and protection from harm.[17] In a recent case challenging foster-care conditions in the District of Columbia, a federal court ruled that foster children have a right to services and planning necessary to protect them from harm, including psychological harm.[18]

States must provide court hearings every six months to review a child's placement in foster care and a full court review when a child has been in foster care for eighteen months.[19] Many states provide children in foster care with either a court-appointed lawyer or a court-appointed special advocate (CASA) to represent their interests in these hearings. The lawyers may also seek a hearing at any time during a child's placement in foster care to consider whether a child should be removed from a particular foster home.[20]

If you are in a placement where your foster parent or an institution staff member says that it is a sin to be LGBT, you should inform your advocate of the problem. Your institution may be violating the Constitution's prohibition on separation of church and state if it receives money from the state for your care, and/or the constitutional requirement of equal protection. Also, if the institution's message is inflicting psychological harm, a judge could require that you be placed in a more appropriate setting.

In addition, there may be state laws that provide some additional safeguards.[21]

I am being harassed and taunted at school because the other kids think I'm LGBT. Do I have any rights?

You have the right to be safe at school. Both federal laws and state laws require school officials to maintain a safe environment for students, and some of these laws may specifically require them to protect you from anti-LGBT abuse. Schools may not refuse to protect students because they are LGBT.

Several federal provisions have helped to force school officials to address anti-LGBT harassment. Title IX of the Education Amendments of 1972[22] requires any school that receives federal money—and nearly all of them do, even if they are private—to ensure that students are not sexually harassed. Under Title IX, a school district can be held liable if officials knew about sexual harassment of a student by other students and failed to do enough to stop it.[23] Although Title IX does *not* prohibit discrimination on the basis of sexual orientation, it does prohibit sexual harassment directed against an LGBT student.[24] Moreover, Title IX also prohibits gender-based harassment, including harassment on the basis of a student's failure to conform to stereotyped notions of masculinity or femininity.[25]

A public school also has a duty under the Equal Protection Clause to protect LGBT students from harassment in the same way they would protect any other student from harassment.[26] If the school failed to take action against anti-LGBT harassment because officials believed that LGBT students should expect to be harassed, because they thought the student invited it simply by being LGBT, or because the officials did not like openly LGBT students, then the school failed to provide equal protection to the student.[27] Likewise, if the school failed to provide the same level of protection for boys as it did for girls—for example, doing nothing when students threaten or beat up a gay boy, call him names, or make harassing advances toward him, while it would have acted quickly if boys had harassed a girl the same way—then the school district may be liable.[28]

In addition, there may be state laws that provide protection against sexual-orientation-based harassment. As of 2003, nine jurisdictions— California,[29] Connecticut,[30] Massachusetts,[31] Minnesota,[32] New Jersey,[33] Vermont,[34] Washington,[35] Wisconsin,[36] and the District of Columbia[37]— have laws that prohibit discrimination or harassment against students on the basis of sexual orientation. Of these, three states—California, Minnesota, and New Jersey—also explicitly prohibit harassment or discrimination on the basis of gender identity. Several other states, including Alaska and Florida, have language in their statewide ethical codes for teachers that requires them to take reasonable efforts to assure that students are not discriminated against on the basis of sexual orientation.[38] In addition, many local school districts all over the county have adopted antiharassment polices that prohibit harassment and discrimination on the basis of real or perceived sexual orientation and/or gender identity.

Finally, students and their parents or guardians may also be able to file criminal charges against harassers for assault, battery, sexual assault, and other crimes. Some of these offenses may fall under the state's definition of hate crimes and be eligible for stricter penalties.

What should I do to get my school to stop the harassment?

First, you should notify someone in authority about the incidents—at least a teacher, but preferably the principal or assistant principal. Second, you should keep records of the harassment, including the date, time, and place of each event, the names of the individuals involved if you know them, and a description of what happened. Finally, if the school has not responded adequately and the harassment continues, take the problem to the school board or the superintendent. You could write a letter or make an appointment to meet. Under some theories of liability, a school district can only be held responsible if someone with authority to respond had knowledge of and failed to respond to the harassment.[39] Accordingly, if possible, it is a good idea to tell people such as the principal, vice-principal, Title IX coordinator, or superintendent about the harassment.

If your school takes no action, or if its actions are not enough to make the harassment stop, depending on the circumstances you or your parents may have a right to file a complaint with the U.S. Department of Education through its Office of Civil Rights (OCR). The OCR is the agency that enforces Title IX, the federal law prohibiting sex discrimination in schools. Title IX requires school districts to have a "compliance officer" who oversees the complaint process.[40] You may ask that person for forms and file the appropriate complaints. When the OCR receives your complaint, it will investigate. If it finds that the school violated Title IX, it may work with you to require the school to change its practices. Finally, you can consider filing a lawsuit against the school in state or federal court. At any of these stages, however, it is wise to confer with a lawyer.

Does a transgender student have a right to dress in accordance with his or her gender identity?

A transgender student's right to dress in accordance with his or her gender identity may be protected under the First Amendment and the Equal Protection and Due Process Clauses of the U.S. Constitution, as well as similar state constitutional provisions and statutory law. The First Amendment limits the right of school officials to censor a student's speech or expression.[41] Students also have a protected liberty interest under the Due Process Clause in their personal appearance.[42] In addition, a transgender student has a right under the Equal Protection Clause to be treated similarly to other students of the same gender identity. If the school treats the student differently from the way it would treat other students of the same gender identity, then the school is applying rules in a sex discriminatory way.[43] Finally, the student may have a right to wear clothing consistent with his or her gender identity under the state statute prohibiting discrimination on the basis of disability.[44]

Do I have the right to start a Gay-Straight Alliance (GSA) in my high school or middle school?

If you are in a public middle or high school and the school permits other noncurricular student clubs, the answer is yes. Under the Equal Access Act,[45] a federal law passed in 1984 that applies to all public secondary schools that receive federal funding, a school that allows at least one student-initiated non-curriculum-related club to meet on campus during noninstructional time (such as during lunch or after school) *must* allow all other non-curriculum-related student groups, including GSAs, even if the club represents an unpopular viewpoint.[46]

Whether a club is curriculum-related or not for purposes of the act is a fact-based inquiry based on the connection between the subject matter of the club and the school's courses. The Supreme Court has defined a curriculum-related group as one "that has more than just a tangential or attenuated relationship to courses offered by the school."[47] "[A] student group directly relates to a school's curriculum if the subject matter of the group is actually taught, or will soon be taught, in a regularly offered course; if the subject matter of the group concerns the body of courses as a whole; if participation in the group is required for a particular course; or if participation in the group results in academic credit."[48] Examples of groups likely to be curriculum-related include the French Club, student government, and the school band. The Supreme Court has defined a "non-curriculum related student group," on the other hand, as a group "that does not directly relate to the body of courses offered by the school."[49] Examples of groups likely to be non-curriculum-related include the Chess Club, the Key Club, the Bowling Club, and the Future Business Leaders of America.[50]

Does the school have to give our GSA the same privileges as other clubs?

Yes. The Equal Access Act requires that schools provide all non-curriculum-related student clubs with the same privileges. This means that the school has to allow the club to meet in classrooms if it allows that for other groups, has to allow a picture in the yearbook if it allows that to other groups, has to give the GSA bulletin-board space or access to the public-address system if that is what it does for other groups, and so on.[51]

Can we require the school library to have books on LGBT issues? Can we make sure they keep the books they already have?

You probably will not be able to legally force the school library to have books on LGBT issues. Buying a book for the library is considered a very different thing, legally, from removing a book that is already on the shelves, and it is harder to force a school to buy a book than it is to stop them from removing one that is already there.

Schools have no obligation to purchase a particular book.[52] Courts have given schools broad leeway in deciding how to stock their libraries so that they can fulfill the traditional role of inculcating local values. Courts generally defer those kinds of community-value judgments to school boards, and so they give the boards the discretion to make decisions about which books to make available to students and what subjects they will include in their library holdings.

Court intervention may be justified, however, if a school board were to select books that espoused only one particular ideological perspective, barring a variety of viewpoints on some issue.[53] Thus, it might be a First Amendment violation if the school refused to include any LGBT-positive books while at the same time acquiring books with an anti-LGBT message, in the hopes of censoring gay-positive material.

You have a better chance of preventing the removal of books that are already in school library. Courts have held that once a book is on the shelf, it may not be removed just because the local authorities disagreed with the ideological or religious viewpoint of the book[54] or, in the case of a public library, because a large number of patrons petitioned to have gay-positive books removed from the children's section of the library.[55]

May a teacher refuse to let me talk about LGBT issues in class?

This question has not yet been answered clearly by courts, but some recent decisions suggest that as long as your speech is appropriate to the subject matter of the class, teachers may not bar your speech just because of its LGBT-positive viewpoint.[56] A teacher may restrict a student's speech if it would interfere with the work of the class, impinge on the rights of other students,[57] or if the speech is "vulgar" or "lewd."[58] Also, schools and teachers have substantial rights to control what gets taught in the classroom and what is a part of the curriculum.[59] But as long as your speech is obviously *your* speech and not sponsored or endorsed by the school *and* it is appropriate for the subject matter of the class, a teacher may not suppress it just because he or she disagrees with its viewpoint.

May the school prevent me from writing about LGBT issues in the school newspaper?

It depends. School officials have much broader authority to restrict speech in the context of school-sponsored activities, such as a school newspaper or a school forum, or other activities that people might reasonably think have the approval of the school.[60] In this context, "educators do not offend the First Amendment by exercising editorial control over the style and content of student speech in school-sponsored expressive activities so long as their actions are reasonably related to legitimate pedagogical concerns."[61] In other words, the school may censor the content of the newspaper if it can present a reasonable educational justification.[62]

Even in the context of school-sponsored activities, however, the censorship generally has to be "viewpoint neutral"; that is, most courts have held that officials may not censor speech simply because they disagree with the particular side of an issue.[63] In addition, some states have "high school free expression" laws that give students more rights than the Supreme Court has required.[64]

May I go to the prom with a same-sex date?

Almost certainly. In a 1979 case in Rhode Island, a federal judge decided that a gay male student had the right to bring a male date to the senior prom and that the school had to provide enough security to make it safe for them to attend together. The court characterized the student's decision to bring a male date as "symbolic speech" that had a strong political and social message and ruled that his speech was protected under the First Amendment.[65] Even though the decision is binding only in Rhode Island, no other court has contradicted it, and school officials would have a weak argument that same-sex prom dates would cause serious disruption of the event if it is properly supervised.

Is the law any different in private schools?

Unless the private school is in a state or city that has a civil rights statute that prohibits discrimination on the basis of sexual orientation, the law is very different in private schools. The U.S. Constitution and many federal laws do not apply in private schools. For that reason, absent some other provision of law, private schools are free to prohibit GSAs from meeting on campus.[66] Constitutional guarantees of free speech and equal protection apply only to public schools, so students in private school may have no right to be openly gay without retaliation or to equal treatment regardless of sexual orientation.

If the state or city has a law that prohibits discrimination in public accommodations on the basis of sexual orientation, however, that law may apply to private schools and may require the school not to discriminate against gay students and to provide equal benefits to a gay student group.[67]

Also, with the exception of some religious schools, all schools that receive federal funding have a duty under Title IX, a federal law, not to discriminate against students on the basis of sex. Most private schools are covered under this law. If a school covered by Title IX is aware of sexual harassment of a student, it has a duty to make the harassment stop, even when the harassers are also other students.[68] And regardless of whether it is a public or private school, all schools have a duty to keep students safe.

Does my college have to recognize a LGBT campus organization?

Yes, it must if it is a public institution, and perhaps, if it is a private institution. The Constitution applies only to public schools, and private schools are generally free to discriminate unless some other local law prohibits sexual-orientation discrimination.

If you attend a public college or university, then your school may not discriminate against an LGBT student group based on the content or viewpoint of the group's message. Under the First Amendment, if a state university has a system for funding student groups, it may not discriminate in its funding decisions on the basis of the viewpoint of the group applying.[69]

If you attend a private institution, it may be covered by state and local public-accommodations statutes.[70] Some of these statutes prohibit sexual-orientation discrimination. If your school is covered by a state or local statute, it must recognize and grant benefits to an LGBT campus group on the same terms that it recognizes other groups. Additionally, many private colleges have adopted internal antidiscrimination policies that include sexual orientation.

If you attend a religiously affiliated college or university, courts will protect the rights that it has as an institution to not endorse views contrary to the tenets of the religion, but courts may nonetheless order the school not to discriminate in its policies concerning material benefits if a state or local antidiscrimination law prohibits sexual-orientation discrimination.[71]

NOTES

1. *See* GLSEN's *2001 National School Climate Survey: The School Related Experiences of Our Nation's Lesbian, Gay, Bisexual, and Transgender Youth*, available at <http://www.glsen.org>.
2. G. Remafedi, "Male Homosexuality: The Adolescent's Perspective," 79 *Pediatrics* 326 (1987); National Gay and Lesbian Task Force, *Anti-Gay/Lesbian Victimization* (1984).
3. *Hazelwood v. Kuhlmeier*, 484 U.S. 260 (1988).
4. *See Doe v. Yunits*, 2000 WL 33162199, at *5 (Mass. Super.), *aff'd sub nom, Doe v. Brockton Sch. Comm.*, No. 2000-J-638 (Mass. App. 2000) ("To rule in defendants' favor in this regard, however, would grant those contentious students a 'heckler's veto.'") (citing *Fricke v. Lynch*, 491 F. Supp. 381, 387 (D.R.I. 1980)).
5. Steven R. Smith, "Privacy, Dangerousness and Counselors," 15 *J.L. & Educ.* 121, 123 (1986). More specifically, the American Association for Counseling and Development, Ethical Standards § B(2) (Mar. 1988) provides: "The counseling relationship and information resulting therefrom are to be kept confidential, consistent with the obligations of the member as a professional person." The American School Counselor Association, Ethical Standards for School Counselors § A(8) (May 1984) protects "the confidentiality of information received in the counseling process as specified by law and ethical standards." *See also* The American School Counselor Association, *Position Statement, The School Counselor and Confidentiality* (1986) (noting that "confidentiality assures that disclosures made will not be divulged to others except when authorized by the student").
6. Stephen R. Ripps, Martin H. Ritchie & Mary Kathryn Chaffee, "To Disclose or

Not to Disclose: The Dilemma of the School Counselor," 13 *Miss. C.L. Rev.* 323, 327 (1993).

7. *See Sterling v. Borough of Minersville,* 232 F.3d 190 (3d Cir. 2000) (holding that individuals have a constitutional right to maintain privacy concerning their sexual orientation, and public officials may not violate that privacy right through unwarranted disclosure).

8. 20 U.S.C. § 1232g.

9. 1 45 C.F.R. 164.502(g).

10. *See, e.g., Santosky v. Kramer,* 455 U.S. 745, 753 (1982) (holding that parents have a fundamental liberty interest in the care, custody, and management of their child); *Pierce v. Society of Sisters,* 268 U.S. 510 (1925) (holding that parents have a right to send their children to a religious school).

11. Most states have statutes that empower parents to commit their children to psychiatric hospitalization. *See generally* James W. Ellis, "Volunteering Children: Parental Commitment of Minors to Mental Institutions," 62 *Cal. L. Rev.* 840 (1974). *See, e.g.,* Wash. Rev. Stat. 71.34.030(2) ("A minor may be admitted to an evaluation and treatment facility in accordance with the following requirements: (a) A minor may be voluntarily admitted by application of the parent. The consent of the minor is not required for the minor to be evaluated and admitted as appropriate.").

12. The procedure for obtaining legal guardianship varies from state to state, but generally, each state has laws allowing a court to appoint a guardian for a child whenever such action is "necessary or convenient." Cal. Probate Code § 1514. If the parent(s) do(es) not consent, the court must find (1) that custody with the parent(s) would be detrimental to the minor, and (2) that it would be in the best interest of the child to live with the proposed guardian. Cal. Fam. Code § 3040. Unlike Juvenile Court dependency proceedings, in guardianship proceedings, the court does not need to find the parent unfit.

13. Abby Abinati, "Legal Challenges Facing Lesbian and Gay Youth," in *Helping Gay and Lesbian Youth: New Policies, New Programs, New Practice* 149, 153 (Teresa DeCrescenzo ed., 1994).

14. Sonia Renee Martin, "A Child's Right to Be Gay: Addressing the Emotional Maltreatment of Queer Youth", 48 *Hastings L.J.* 167, 194 (1996).

15. *See id.* at 195.

16. *Taylor v. Ledbetter,* 818 F.2d 791 (11th Cir. 1987); *cert. denied,* 489 U.S. 1065 (1989); *L.J. v. Massinga,* 838 F.2d 118 (4th Cir. 1988), *cert. denied,* 488 U.S. 1018 (1989).

17. *Taylor, supra* note 16, at 797 (holding that state officials can be held liable where it can be shown that the state officials were deliberately indifferent to the welfare of the child).

18. *LaShawn A. v. Dixon,* 762 F. Supp. 959 (D.D.C. 1991), *aff'd in part, rev'd in part,* 990 F.2d 1319 (D.C. Cir. 1993). *See also* Maureen S. Duggan, *Failure of State or Local Government Entity to Protect Child Abuse Victim as Violation of Federal Constitutional Rights,* 79 A.L.R. Fed. 514 (Supp. 1994).

19. 42 U.S.C. § 675(5)(B) & (C).

20. *In re Jamie "YY",* 575 N.Y.S.2d 172 (App. Div. 1991); *Little Flower Children's Servs. v. Andrew C.,* 545 N.Y.S.2d 444 (Fam. Ct. 1989).

21. For example, in 2003, California passed a law prohibiting discrimination on the

basis of sexual orientation and gender identity in foster care. AB (Assembly Bill) 458 (Chu, 2003).

22. 20 U.S.C. § 1681(a). Title IX provides, in relevant part: "No person in the United States shall, on the basis of sex, be excluded from participation in, be denied the benefits of, or be subjected to discrimination under any education program or activity receiving Federal financial assistance."

23. *Davis v. Monroe County Sch. Dist.*, 526 U.S. 629, 646–647 (1999).

24. Revised Sexual Harassment Guidance: Sexual Harassment by School Employees, Other Students, or Third Parties, 66 Fed. Reg. 5,512 (Jan. 19, 2001), available at <http://www.ed.gov/ocv/shguide> (OCR Revised Guidance) ("Although Title IX does not prohibit discrimination on the basis of sexual orientation, sexual harassment directed at gay or lesbian students that is sufficiently serious to limit or deny a student's ability to participate in or benefit from the school's program constitutes sexual harassment prohibited by Title IX under circumstances described in this guidance. For example, if a male student or group of male students targets a gay student for sexual advances, serious enough to deny or limit the victim's ability to participate in or benefit from the school's program, the school would need to respond promptly and effectively, as described in this guidance, just as it would if the victim were heterosexual.").

25. *See id.* ("Though beyond the scope of this guidance, gender-based harassment, which may include acts of verbal, nonverbal, or physical aggression, intimidation, or hostility based on sex or sex-stereotyping, but not involving conduct of a sexual nature, is also a form of sex discrimination to which a school must respond, if it rises to the level that denies or limits a student's ability to participate in or benefit from the educational program. . . . A school must respond to such harassment in accordance with the standards and procedures described in this guidance.") (citing *Price Waterhouse v. Hopkins*, 490 U.S. 228, 251 (1989) (holding sex stereotyping is a form of sex discrimination prohibited by Title VII)). *See also Montgomery v. Independent Sch. Dist. No. 709*, 109 F. Supp. 2d 1081, 1092 (D. Minn. 2000) ("The Court for these reasons concludes that by pleading facts from which a reasonable fact-finder could infer that he suffered harassment due to his failure to meet masculine stereotypes, plaintiff has stated a cognizable claim under Title IX.").

26. *See Flores v. Morgan Hill Unified Sch. Dist.*, 324 F.3d 1130 (9th Cir. 2003) (holding that the Equal Protection Clause requires school officials to investigate and remedy incidents of peer sexual-orientation harassment); *Nabozny v. Podlesny*, 92 F.3d 446, 458 (7th Cir. 1996) (holding gay student could maintain claims alleging discrimination on the basis of gender and sexual orientation under the Equal Protection Clause when school district failed to protect the student because of the student's gender and sexual orientation, explaining "We are unable to garner any rational basis for permitting one student to assault another based on the victim's sexual orientation, and the defendants do not offer us one."). In the *Nabozny* case, after reporting incidents of physical violence to the appropriate school administrator, the administrator told the student and his parents that such acts should be expected because the student was openly gay and failed to take any protective actions. *Id.* at 451. *See also Montgomery, supra* note 24, at 1089 (citing *Nabozny*).

27. *See Nabozny, supra* note 25.

28. *Id.*

29. Cal. Educ. Code § 220.

30. Conn. Gen. Stat. § 10-15c.

31. Mass. Gen. Laws Chp. 76, § 5.

32. Minn. Stat. § 363.03, subd. 5.

33. N.J. Stat. 10:5-12f(1); N.J. Stat. 10:5-5(1); N.J. Stat. 18A: 37-13.

34. 16 Vt. Stat. § 11(a)(26); 16 Vt. Stat. § 565.

35. Wash. Rev. Code §§ 28.A.600.

36. Wis. Stat. 118.13.

37. D.C. Code 1981 § 1-2520.

38. State of Alaska Code of Ethics of the Education Profession, AAC 20.10.020, provides, "In fulfilling obligations to students, an educator . . . may not harass, discriminate against, or grant a discriminatory advantage to a student on the grounds of race, color, creed, sex, national origin, marital status, or cultural background, or sexual orientation; shall make reasonable effort to assure that a student is protected from harassment or discrimination on these grounds; and may not engage in a course of conduct that would encourage a reasonable student to develop a prejudice on these grounds." The Florida State Board of Education Rule 6B-1.006 provides, "Obligation to the student requires that the individual . . . [s]hall not harass or discriminate against any student on the basis of race, color, religion, sex, age, national or ethnic origin, political beliefs, marital status, handicapping condition, sexual orientation or social and family background and shall make reasonable effort to assure that each student is protected from harassment or discrimination." Violations of these ethical codes can jeopardize the professional licenses of educators.

39. *Gebser v. Lago Vista Indep. Sch. Dist.*, 524 U.S. 274, 290 (1998) (holding that school district could be held liable under Title IX only if a school official with the authority to take corrective action had knowledge of and failed to respond to the alleged harassment). *See also Davis, supra* note 22, at 640 (applying the same theory of liability to peer-peer sex-based harassment).

40. 34 C.F.R. 106.8(a).

41. *See Yunits, supra* note 4, at *3–4 (finding transgender student's "feminine" clothing and accessories were symbolic expressions of her female gender identity that were understood by those perceiving it and that the school officials' rule prohibiting the student from wearing such clothing was likely meant to suppress the student's speech).

42. *See id.* at *6 (holding transgender student had a liberty interest in her personal appearance).

43. *See id.* (explaining that, with respect to the plaintiff's sex discrimination claim, because "plaintiff identifies with the female gender, the right question is whether a female student would be disciplined for wearing items of clothes plaintiff chooses to wear. If the answer to that question is no, plaintiff is being discriminated against on the basis of her sex, which is biologically male.").

44. *See Doe v. Bell*, 754 N.Y.S.2d 846 (N.Y. Sup. Ct. 2003) (holding transgender youth had right to wear clothing consistent with her gender identity under state law prohibiting discrimination on the basis of disability); *Doe v. Yunits*, 2001 WL 664947 (Mass. Super. 2001) (same).

45. 20 U.S.C. §§ 4071–74.

46. *Board of Educ. of Westside Community Schs. v. Mergens*, 496 U.S. 226 (1990); *Colin v. Orange Unified Sch. Dist.*, 83 F.Supp.2d 1135 (C.D. Cal. 2000) (holding that school had to allow GSA to meet).

47. *Id.* at 238.

48. *Id.* at 239–40.

49. *Id.* at 239.

50. *Id.*

51. *See id.* (holding that school that permitted Christian club to meet informally after school but did not allow it to be part of student activities program, which would carry with it access to school newspaper, bulletin boards, public-address system, and annual club fair, was not giving the Christian club equal access with other clubs as required by the Equal Access Act).

52. *See, e.g., Minarcini v. Strongsville City Sch. Dist.,* 541 F.2d 577, 582 (6th Cir. 1976); *Right to Read Defense Comm. v. School Comm.,* 454 F. Supp. 703, 712 (D. Mass. 1978).

53. *See Zykan v. Warsaw Community Sch. Corp.,* 631 F.2d 1300, 1308 (7th Cir. 1980).

54. *See, e.g., Board of Educ. v. Pico,* 457 U.S. 853, 872 (1982) (plurality) (school boards could not remove books from school libraries merely because "they dislike the ideas contained in the books," and thus "seek by their removal to 'prescribe what shall be orthodoxy in politics, nationalism, religion, or other matters of opinion,'"); *Pratt v. Independent Sch. Dist.,* 670 F.2d 771, 776 (8th Cir. 1982); *Bicknell v. Vergennes Union High Sch. Bd.,* 638 F.2d 438 (2nd Cir. 1980) (dicta); *Cary v. Board of Educ.,* 598 F.2d 535 (10th Cir. 1979) (dicta); *Right to Read Defense Comm. of Chelsea v. School Comm. of Chelsea,* 454 F. Supp. 703, 712 (D. Mass. 1978).

55. *Sund v. City of Wichita Falls,* 121 F. Supp. 2d 530 (N.D. Tex. 2000).

56. *East High Gay/Straight Alliance v. Board of Educ. of Salt Lake City Sch. Dist.,* 81 F. Supp. 2d 1199 (D. Utah 1999).

57. *Tinker v. Des Moines School Dist.,* 393 U.S. 503, 509 (1969).

58. *Bethel Sch. Dist. v. Fraser,* 478 U.S. 675, 685 (1986).

59. *Hazelwood, supra* note 3, at 266 (1988) (holding that a school "need not tolerate student speech that is inconsistent with its 'basic educational mission'").

60. *See id.* at 271.

61. *Id.* at 273.

62. For example, in *Hazelwood,* the U.S. Supreme Court upheld the right of public-school officials to censor stories about teen pregnancy and the effects of divorce on children from a school-sponsored newspaper. In upholding the censorship, the Court found it was "not unreasonable" for the principal to have concluded that "frank talk" by the students about their sexual history and use of birth control, even though the comments were not graphic, was "inappropriate in a school-sponsored publication distributed to 14 year-old freshmen." *Id.* at 274.

63. *See Downs v. Los Angeles Unified Sch. Dist.,* 228 F.3d 1003 (9th Cir. 2000); *Kincaid v. Gibson,* 236 F.3d 342, 355 (6th Cir. 2001) (en banc) ("Although the government may act to preserve a nonpublic forum for its intended purposes, its regulation of speech must nonetheless be reasonable, and it must not attempt to suppress expression based on the speaker's viewpoint."); *Planned Parenthood of So. Nev. v. Clark County Sch. Dist.,* 941 F.2d 817, 829 (9th Cir. 1991); *Searcey v. Harris,* 888 F.2d 1314, 1319 & n.7 (11th Cir. 1989). *But see C.H. v. Oliva,* 195 F.3d 167, 172 (3d Cir.), *reh'g en banc granted, opinion vacated,* 197 F.3d 63 (1999) (holding public-school educators may impose non-viewpoint-neutral restrictions on the content of students' speech in school-sponsored expressive activi-

ties), *aff'd in part on other grounds,* 226 F.3d 198 (3d Cir. 2000) (en banc), *cert. denied sub nom, Hood v. Medford Township Bd. of Educ.,* 121 S. Ct. 2519 (2001); *Ward v. Hickey,* 996 F.2d 448, 454 (1st Cir. 1993) (same).

64. *See, e.g.,* Ark. Code Ann. § 6-18-1202; Cal. Educ. Code § 48907; Colo. Rev. Stat. § 22-1-120; Iowa Code § 280.22; Kan. Stat. Ann. § 72-1506; Mass. Gen. Laws ch. 71, § 82.

65. *Fricke v. Lynch,* 491 F. Supp. 381 (D.R.I. 1980).

66. *See Gay Rights Coalition of Georgetown Univ. Law Ctr. v. Georgetown Univ.,* 536 A.2d 1, 20 n.15 (D.C. Cir. 1987)(en banc).

67. *See, e.g., id.*

68. *Davis, supra* note 22, at 646–47.

69. *Board of Regents v. Southworth,* 529 U.S. 217, 233 (2000).

70. *Gay Rights Coalition, supra* note 65, at 27–29.

71. *Id.* at 38–39.

PART 4
Specialized Issues

XII

Transgender People

Transgender people often face severe discrimination in virtually every aspect of their lives—in employment, housing, public accommodations, credit, marriage, parenting, and law enforcement, among others. Despite these circumstances, until very recently, most courts have held that transgender people are excluded from basic civil rights protections.

Fortunately, however, over the past decade, transgender activists have been increasingly successful in their efforts to obtain explicit civil rights protections. In 1975, Minneapolis, Minnesota, became the first municipality to pass a local ordinance explicitly prohibiting discrimination against transgender people. By 1990, only a handful of additional cities had followed suit. By the summer of 2003, however, fifty-nine cities and counties and four states had passed laws protecting transgender people. In addition, many schools and employers have recently amended their nondiscrimination policies to include explicit protections for transgender people.

With these legislative and advocacy successes have come judicial victories. Several recent decisions, on both the state and federal level, have repudiated the older case law and have held that transgender people are protected under provisions prohibiting discrimination on the basis of sex and/or disability.

This chapter will review the current status of protection for transgender people under civil rights laws and ordinances. It will also provide a basic overview of the law with respect to modifying government documents, as well as a discussion of family law, health care, and immigration issues that may be of particular concern to transgender people. Finally, the chapter will address the treatment of transgender prisoners.

What do the terms *transsexual* **and** *transgender* **mean?**

Most people experience their gender identity as correlating to, or in line with, their physical sex. That is, most people who are born with female bodies also have a female gender identity, and most people who are born with male bodies have a male gender identity. For a transsexual person, however, a conflict exists between one's physical sex and one's gender identity as a man or woman. Female-to-male transsexual (FTM) people are born with female bodies but have a predominantly male gender identity. Male-to-female transsexual (MTF) people are born with male bodies but have a female gender identity. Many, but not all, transsexual people undergo medical treatment to change their physical sex through hormone therapy and/or sex-reassignment surgery (SRS).

Gender Identity Disorder (GID) is a diagnosable condition that is evidenced by a "strong and persistent cross-gender identification, which is the desire to be, or the insistence that one is, of the other sex."[1] GID is accompanied by a "persistent discomfort about one's assigned sex or a sense of inappropriateness in the gender role of that sex."[2]

Transgender is an umbrella term used to describe a range of identities and experiences, including but not limited to preoperative, postoperative, and nonoperative transsexual people; male and female cross-dressers; intersex individuals; and men and woman, regardless of their sexual orientation, whose appearance, behavior, or characteristics are perceived to be different than that stereotypically associated with their sex assigned at birth. In the broadest sense, transgender encompasses anyone whose identity or behavior falls outside of stereotypical gender norms. That includes people who do not self-identify as transgender but who are perceived as such. Other current terms used as synonyms for *transgender* include *gender variant,* and *gender nonconforming.*

Are there laws that explicitly prohibit discrimination against transgender people?

Yes. In 1993, Minnesota became the first state to enact an antidiscrimination statute that expressly prohibits discrimination against transsexual and transgender people in the areas of employment, housing, education, and public accommodations.[3] On July 17, 2001, Rhode Island became the second state to have such protections,[4] and New Mexico became the third state on April 9, 2003.[5]

Establishing important, but more limited, protection in 1999, California passed legislation prohibiting discrimination against transgender teachers and other public-school employees.[6] In 2003, California passed legislation prohibiting discrimination on the basis of gender identity in all areas of employment and housing.[7] Also in 2003, the Governors of Kentucky and Pennsylvania issued executive orders prohibiting discrimination in state government employment based on gender identity.[8]

In addition to these state protections, a growing number of cities and municipalities prohibit discrimination against transgender people. The first jurisdiction to provide this kind of protection was the city of Minneapolis, Minnesota, which established the protection in 1975. As of June 2003, fifty-seven cities and counties have added protections for transgender people, including, among others, Phoenix, Arizona; Tucson, Arizona; San Francisco, California; Santa Cruz, California; West Hollywood, California; Iowa City, Iowa; Atlanta, Georgia; Evanston, Illinois; Louisville, Kentucky; New Orleans, Louisiana; Cambridge, Massachusetts; Ann Arbor, Michigan; Ypsilanti, Michigan; St. Paul, Minnesota; Toledo, Ohio; Benton County, Oregon; Pittsburgh, Pennsylvania; York, Pennsylvania; Olympia, Washington; and Seattle, Washington.[9]

Are there laws that prohibit hate crimes against transgender people?

Yes. In 1998, California[10] became the second state (following Minnesota[11] in 1993) to amend its state hate-crimes law to include protection for transgender and transsexual people. Since then, five additional states, Hawaii,[12] Missouri,[13] New Mexico,[14] Pennsylvania,[15] and Vermont,[16] have followed suit by amending their state hate-crimes statutes to include transgender people.

Do laws that prohibit sexual-orientation discrimination protect transgender people?

It depends. Courts addressing this issue have said that gender identity is not the same as sexual orientation.[17] Sexual orientation refers to whether a person is homosexual, bisexual, or heterosexual. Gender refers to characteristics that are stereotypically perceived to be masculine or feminine. Thus, discrimination directed at a person because of that person's transgender status or because that person is perceived not to conform to stereotypical notions of masculinity or femininity is not ordinarily prohibited by a statute that prohibits discrimination on the basis of sexual orientation.[18]

If, however, anti-LGBT harassment—such as calling someone homophobic slurs—is directed at a transgender person either because that person is LGBT or he or she is perceived to be LGBT, that form of harassment would be prohibited by statutes or ordinances that prohibit discrimination on the basis of sexual orientation.

Do laws that prohibit sex discrimination protect transgender people?

Until the late 1990s, federal courts uniformly held that transsexual people are not protected under Title VII's[19] prohibition of sex discrimination, on the ground that Congress did not intend the term *sex* to include transsexualism.[20] Since then, however, several federal courts have repudiated these older decisions and have held that transsexual people are protected from discrimination under Title VII and other sex discrimination statutes.[21]

Similar to the federal trend, the older employment-discrimination cases brought under *state* laws prohibiting sex discrimination were unsuccessful,[22] but more recently, some state courts have interpreted state and local sex-discrimination laws to prohibit discrimination against transsexual people.[23]

Do laws that prohibit disability discrimination protect transgender people?

Transsexual people are not protected under federal laws that prohibit discrimination on the basis of handicap or disability. Although transsexualism has been recognized as a medical condition for many years and is included as a psychiatric disorder in the Diagnostic and Statistical Manual (DSM) IV under the rubric of "gender identity disorder," both the federal Rehabilitation Act of 1973 (Rehabilitation Act) and the federal Americans with Disabilities Act (ADA) explicitly *exclude* "transsexualism" and "gender identity disorders not resulting from physical impairments" from protection under either act.[24]

Most states and the District of Columbia have state laws prohibiting employment discrimination against people with disabilities. Several of the states follow the Rehabilitation Act and the ADA, and expressly exclude transsexual people. These states include Indiana, Iowa, Louisiana, Nebraska, Ohio, Oklahoma, Oregon, Texas, and Virginia. Even in the absence of a specific exclusion, some courts in other states have held that transsexualism is not a protected disability.[25] In a more positive development, California recently amended its state disability law to *remove* the exclusions for transsexualism and gender dysphoria.[26]

As of June 2003, courts in five states—Massachusetts, New Hampshire, New Jersey, New York, and Washington—have ruled that transsexual people may be protected under the relevant state disability laws.[27] In addition, in the spring of 2001, a Massachusetts trial court denied a motion to dismiss a disability claim brought by a transgender youth under the Massachusetts disability statute.[28]

At the administrative level, state agencies responsible for enforcing state disability-protection laws have issued favorable rulings for transsexual plaintiffs in at least four states.[29]

Are transgender students protected from discrimination?

Minnesota,[30] California,[31] and New Jersey[32] have laws explicitly prohibiting discrimination or harassment against transgender students.

In addition to these explicit state law protections, Title IX of the Education Amendment Acts of 1972[33] prohibits discrimination based on sex in education programs and activities receiving federal financial assistance. Sexual harassment directed at a transgender student is prohibited by Title IX if it is sufficiently severe and pervasive.[34] Title IX also prohibits gender-based harassment, including harassment on the basis of a student's failure to conform to stereotyped notions of masculinity and femininity.[35]

In addition, if the student attends a public school, he or she may be protected under various constitutional provisions, as discussed in more detail below.

Do any other laws or constitutional provisions protect transsexual people from discrimination?

If a transgender or transsexual person is discriminated against by a government actor, that person's right to dress in accordance with his or her gender identity may also be protected under the First Amendment and the Equal Protection and Due Process Clauses of the U.S. Constitution.

The First Amendment limits the right of government officials to censor a person's speech or expression. Dressing in clothing and accessories consistent with one's gender identity is a form of symbolic expression of one's identity. Thus, prohibiting a person from wearing clothing consistent with his or her gender identity may violate the person's First Amendment rights.[36] People also may have a protected liberty interest (under the Due Process Clause) in their personal appearance.[37]

The Equal Protection Clause requires that the government treat similarly situated persons similarly. If, for example, a government employer treats an employee differently than it would treat other employees of the same gender identity (i.e., if it imposes a dress code on an MTF transsexual that is different than the dress code that is applied to biological females), then that employer is applying rules in a way that discriminates on the basis of sex (i.e., it is applying the code differently based on the employee's biological sex).[38]

May a transsexual person use the restroom consistent with his or her gender identity?

The right to use the restroom corresponding to one's gender identity is one of the most basic aspects of nondiscrimination for a transgender person. Thus, while there is very little case law on this issue, it stands to reason that if you are in a jurisdiction that provides protections for transgender people—either under sex, disability, or a transgender specific law—you should have that right. In practice, however, the right to use the appropriate restroom is one of the most uncertain and untested areas of the law.

There is only one decision on this issue from a state's highest court, and it held that Minnesota's antidiscrimination law does not prohibit employers from requiring a transgender person to alter her biological sex before being permitted to use the restroom consistent with her gender identity.[39] A better approach has been developed by the San Francisco Human Rights Commission, which requires businesses and places of public accommodation to allow all persons to use the restroom consistent with their gender identity so long as they have at least one piece of current identification with the requisite sex.[40]

May a transsexual person be arrested for cross-dressing?

Although most cross-dressing statutes have been struck down or repealed, some still exist and where they do, you could be arrested for cross-dressing. However, you might be able to successfully challenge the law's constitutionality.

A so-called cross-dressing statute generally prohibits "impersonating," being "disguised as," or "masquerading" as a member of the opposite sex. Although these were not initially enacted for the purpose of targeting cross-dressers, police regularly used these statutes and ordinances as a means to harass and arrest cross-dressers, transsexuals, and gender-nonconforming people.

One of the first decisions striking down a cross-dressing ordinance was *City of Columbus v. Rogers*,[41] which found the statute "void for vagueness." The court reasoned that clothing sold for both sexes was so similar that it was not uncommon for people to wear "clothes of the opposite" sex.[42] "The terms of the ordinance, 'dress not belonging to his or her sex,' when considered in the light of contemporary dress habits, make it so vague that men of common intelligence must necessarily guess at its meaning and differ as to its application."[43] This reasoning was adopted by other courts in striking down similar ordinances.[44]

In addition, several other courts have held cross-dressing statutes to be invalid as applied to transsexual people. For example, in *Doe v. McConn*,[45] the court declared a city ordinance, making it illegal to appear in public areas "dressed with the designed intent to disguise his or her true sex as that of the opposite sex," unconstitutional as applied to the transsexual plaintiffs. The court noted that an integral part of the presurgery process was a requirement that the person dress consistent with their gender identity, and the court, therefore, found that the ordinance directly interfered with their plaintiffs' treatment.

May a transgender person change his or her name to reflect his or her gender identity?

In most states, transgender people may change their name simply by using a new name—this method is called a common-law name change.[46]

The other method available is a court-ordered name change. While in a few cases, courts have required a preoperative transsexual to present evidence that he or she wanted to live permanently as a member of the opposite sex before the name change would be granted, imposing such requirements is generally not consistent with the statutes or case law, and such results are increasingly rare.[47] As a general rule, most courts will grant a name change "so long as there is no intent to defraud creditors or deceive others and the applicant has acted in good faith."[48]

May a person change his or her gender on his or her birth certificate?

Most states now have statutes or policies that allow transsexual people who have undergone SRS to amend or be issued a new birth certificate that indicates their new sex.[49] In most of these states, to change your gender on your birth certificate, you must present an original letter from a sex-reassignment surgeon and an original or certified copy of the court order of your name change.

Moreover, a denial of a transsexual person's request for a change of sex on his or her birth certificate may violate the Equal Protection Clause.[50]

At what point in the transition process is one's sex legally changed; that is, is surgery required?

What constitutes a legal change of sex is not entirely clear. Courts may find that your sex is legally changed for some purposes but not for others.

As described above, in most states, to change your sex on your birth certificate, you must provide evidence of SRS. It is important to be aware, however, that SRS encompasses a range of procedures and that these statutes do not necessarily contemplate any particular one.

Unfortunately, however, some cases have been decided that make it clear that just because you have changed your sex on your birth certificate (and possibly other official documents as well) does not necessarily mean that a court will deem you to be of that sex for purposes of determining the validity of your marriage.[51]

One possible solution to this problem may be to obtain a court order declaring your legal change of gender. Because this is a court judgment, even a court in another state will have to accord the judgment full faith and credit, which is not true of a driver's license or birth certificate.

If one spouse in a marriage transitions, is the couple still legally married?

There are no published decisions on this issue. So long as both spouses want to stay in the marriage and continue to live as a married couple, many "same-sex married couples" in this situation have avoided legal problems, in large part because there are relatively few situations in which anyone other than one of the spouses has legal standing to challenge the validity of a marriage. Legal problems may arise when one spouse dies and the other attempts to collect survivorship benefits or to claim inheritance or other tax benefits that are restricted to married couples. Alternatively, an employer may challenge the validity of the marriage in the context of trying to exclude the spouse from an employer-provided health plan.

If challenged, will a court hold that a transsexual person's marriage is valid?

There are only a handful of cases involving postoperative transsexual marriages, and the holdings are mixed. Courts in California,[52] Florida,[53] and New Jersey[54] have held that an individual is considered to be their postoperative sex for purposes of determining the validity of marriage, whereas courts in Kansas,[55] New York,[56] Ohio,[57] and Texas[58] have held that the individual is considered to be their sex assigned at birth, following an older English case, *Corbett v. Corbett.*[59]

What about parental rights?

If you and your spouse had children by means of assisted reproductive technology, the answer to this question may depend on whether you had children with your spouse prior to or subsequent to your transition. If you had children with your spouse prior to your transition, your transition should have no affect on your parental rights. If you had children with your spouse subsequent to your transition *and* you are the biological parent to your children, then your parental rights should also be secure.

If, however, you had children with your spouse subsequent to your transition and you are *not* the biological parent to your children, your legal status as a parent is uncertain. Under these circumstances, if your marriage is held to be void, then your parental rights might be jeopardized.

Will my transgender status affect my child custody or visitation rights?

Transgender and transsexual parents face tremendous discrimination in the child custody area, as evidenced by most of the published decisions.

At least one court has terminated a transsexual parent's parental rights because of the parent's transsexuality.[60] Several other courts have granted custody to transgender or transsexual parents only when the parent agreed to hide his or her transgender or transsexual status.[61]

There are some positive cases in this area, however. For example, in *Kantaras v. Kantaras,*[62] after finding that Michael Kantaras, an FTM, was legally male and that his marriage to Linda was valid, a Florida court awarded Michael primary custody of the two children he and his former wife raised during their marriage. In an older case, *Christian v. Randall,*[63] the court held that the fact that the mother who had been awarded custody of four girls was transitioning, had changed his name, and had married a woman, did not justify a change of custody to the father in light of the evidence that the mother was providing a high-quality home environment for the children, and in the absence of a showing that the mother's relationship with his children had been adversely affected or that the children's emotional development had been impaired.

In addition, there have been several additional positive trial court decisions that are not published decisions.

Will the cost of SRS be covered by a private health insurance or by a public program like Medicaid?

The overwhelming majority of transsexual people must pay for any surgeries on their own. As a result, many (perhaps even most) transsexual people are never able to obtain genital surgeries.

Medicare[64] does not pay for SRS.[65] SRS is also excluded from the Civilian Health and Medical Program of the Uniformed Services.[66]

Under Medicaid,[67] despite some favorable court decisions holding that states cannot categorically exclude SRS from Medicaid coverage,[68] many states do just that. States have excluded SRS from coverage, both by explicit categorical rules and by case-by-case denials.[69] As a practical matter, it is extremely difficult to obtain Medicaid reimbursement for SRS.

Private insurance is largely governed by contract law. In the absence of an explicit contractual provision specifying that the insurance company will not pay for SRS treatment, some transsexual people have won claims requiring the company to pay for surgeries.[70] Today, most insurance contracts specify that medical services related to SRS are excluded from coverage.

Transsexual people who have completed sex reassignment are also frequently denied routine medical treatments that are sex-linked, such as the denial of gynecological care for transsexual men who may still have some female reproductive organs. There may also be unfair denials of coverage for conditions that have nothing to do with sex reassignment, such as cancer or high blood pressure, due to the mistaken assumption that any illness or condition is "caused by" having undergone sex reassignment. In the first published decision to address health insurance discrimination, the Superior Court of Massachusetts held that a transsexual woman who had undergone sex reassignment over twenty-five years earlier could not be denied medically necessary breast reconstruction surgery simply because she is transsexual.[71]

Do transgender prisoners have a right to be housed in a cellblock consistent with their gender identity?

Transgender and transsexual people who have not had genital surgery are classified according to their birth sex for purposes of prison housing, regardless of the extent of their nongenital transition[72]—a situation that puts MTF transsexuals at great risk of sexual violence.

Particularly for transsexual prisoners who have not had genital surgery, one "solution" utilized by some prisons is to segregate the transgender and transsexual prisoners. This segregation may provide greater protection for the prisoner. Segregation also results, however, in the exclusion of the prisoner from full access to things such as recreation, educational and occupational opportunities, and associational rights.[73]

Do transsexual prisoners have a right to obtain hormone therapy while in prison?

Transsexual prisoners should be allowed to maintain their hormone treatment in prison.[74] The policy of the U.S. Bureau of Prisons is to provide hormones at the level that was maintained prior to incarceration. Specifically, the policy provides:

It is the policy of the Bureau of Prisons to maintain the transsexual inmate at the level of change existing upon admission to the Bureau. Should responsible medical staff determine that either progressive or regressive treatment changes are indicated, these changes must be approved by the [Bureau of Prisons] Medical Director prior to implementation. The use of hormones to maintain secondary sexual characteristics may be continued at approximately the same levels as prior to incarceration, but such use must be approved by the Medical Director.[75]

Even if the prison does provide hormones, however, there is no guarantee that they will be provided at the appropriate levels and with the necessary physical and psychological support services.[76]

The issue of whether a transsexual person is entitled to hormone therapy while in prison has been litigated extensively, based on the established constitutional principle that it is a violation of the Eighth Amendment prohibition on cruel and unusual punishment for prison officials to exhibit "deliberate indifference" to a prisoner's "serious medical needs." Until the last several years, in almost every case, courts have ruled in favor of prison officials.[77] More recently, however, prisoners have had more success.[78]

Can a transsexual person receive asylum based on his or her transsexual status?

Neither the Immigration and Naturalization Service nor the Board of Immigration Appeals has recognized transsexual people as "a particular social group" for the purposes of asylum. Nonetheless, some individuals who have been persecuted on the basis of their transgender or transsexual status have received asylum in the past few years, under the rubric of persecution on the basis of sexual orientation and/or gender.[79]

In a groundbreaking decision, the U.S. Court of Appeals for the Ninth Circuit recently held that Geovanni Hernandez-Montiel, a transgender gay man from Mexico who was repeatedly beaten, kidnapped, and raped by police officers was entitled to asylum.[80] The Board of Immigration Appeals had denied his claim, holding that he was persecuted because of his effeminate appearance rather than his sexual orientation and that he should try to alter his appearance to be more masculine. The Ninth Circuit rejected that rationale, which the court described as "offensive."[81]

NOTES

1. *Diagnostic and Statistical Manual of Mental Disorders* (DSM-IV), at 532 (4th ed. 1994).

2. *Id.*

3. *See* Minn. Stat. § 363.01(45).

4. R.I. Stat. § 28-5-7.

5. N.M. Stat. § 28-1-7 (as amended by S.B. 28 (2003)).

6. Cal. Educ. Code § 220 (prohibiting discrimination against all persons in public schools on the same bases used in the Hate Crimes Statute, which had been previously amended to extend protection to transgender people).

7. AB (Assembly Bill) 196 (Leno, 2003).

8. Kentucky Executive Order 2003-533 (May 29, 2003), Pennsylvania Executive Order 2003–10 (July 28, 2003).

9. For an updated list, *see* <http://transgenderlaw.org>. For an overview of legislation protecting transgender people, *see* Paisley Currah & Shannon Minter, *Transgender Equality: A Handbook for Activists and Policymakers* (2000), available at <www.nclrights.org/pubs/transeq.pdf>.

10. Cal. Penal Code §§ 422.6 & 422.76 (defining *gender* to mean "the victim's actual sex or the defendant's perception of the victim's sex, and includes the defendant's perception of the victim's identity, appearance, or behavior, whether or not that identity, appear-

ance, or behavior is different from that traditionally associated with the victim's sex at birth).

11. Minn. Stat. Ann. § 611A.29 (incorporating the transgender inclusive definition of sexual orientation as defined in Minn Stat. Ann. § 363.01(45)).

12. Haw. Rev. Stat. § 846-51 (as amended by S.B. 616 (2003)).

13. Mo. Stat. § 557.035.

14. S.B. 38 (N.M. 2003).

15. Pa. Stat. Ann., tit. 18, § 2710.

16. 13 Vt. Stat. §§ 1455 & 1458.

17. *See Conway v. City of Hartford*, 1997 Conn. Super. LEXIS 282 (1997) (refusing to dismiss transsexual plaintiff's claim of sexual-orientation discrimination but noting that "[h]ad the plaintiff failed to allege specifically discrimination based on sexual orientation, but rather merely referenced his transsexualism as a basis for discrimination based on sexual orientation, the . . . claim would have been legally insufficient"); *Maffei v. Kolaeton Indus., Inc.*, 626 N.Y.S. 2d 391 (Sup. Ct. 1995) (holding that the definition of *sexual orientation* in New York City ordinance does not include transsexualism); *Underwood v. Archer Mgmt. Servs., Inc.*, 857 F. Supp. 96 (D.D.C. 1994) (holding that "a conclusory statement that [transsexual plaintiff] was discharged on the basis of transsexuality . . . does not constitute a claim for relief on the basis of . . . sexual orientation").

18. This is true unless, however, the definition of *sexual orientation* encompasses gender identity, as is true of the Minnesota statute, which defines the term as follows: "'Sexual orientation' means having or being perceived as having an emotional, physical, or sexual attachment to another person without regard to the sex of that person or having or being perceived as having an orientation for such attachment, *or having or being perceived as having a self-image or identity not traditionally associated with one's biological maleness or femaleness*." Minn. Stat. § 363.01(45) (emphasis added).

19. Title VII of the Civil Rights Act of 1964, 42 U.S.C. §§ 2000e *et seq.*, is the federal law that prohibits employment discrimination on the basis of sex, among other bases.

20. *See Ulane v. Eastern Airlines, Inc.*, 742 F.2d 1081 (7th Cir. 1984), *cert. denied*, 471 U.S. 1017 (1985) (holding that "the words of Title VII do not outlaw discrimination against a person who has a sexual identity disorder, *i.e.*, . . . a person born with a female body who believes herself to be a male"); *Somers v. Budget Marketing*, 667 F.2d 748 (8th Cir. 1982) (same); *Holloway v. Arthur Andersen & Co.*, 566 F.2d 659 (9th Cir. 1977) (same); *James v. Ranch Mart Hardware, Inc.*, 881 F. Supp. 478 (D. Kan. 1995) (same); *Powell v. Read's, Inc.*, 436 F. Supp. 369 (D. Md. 1977) (same); *Voyles v. Ralph K. Davies Medical Center*, 403 F. Supp. 456 (N.D. Cal. 1975) (same).

21. *See, e.g., Nichols v. Azteca Rest. Enters.*, 256 F.3d 864 (9th Cir. 2001) (holding harassment on the basis of gender stereotypes violates Title VII and the Washington Law Against Discrimination); *Schwenk v. Hartford*, 204 F.3d 1187 (9th Cir. 2000) (holding that the "initial judicial approach taken in cases such as *Holloway* has been overruled by the logic and language of *Price Waterhouse*"). *See also Rosa v. Park West Bank & Trust Co.*, 214 F.3d 213 (1st Cir. 2000) (reinstating Equal Credit Opportunity Act claim on behalf of biologically male plaintiff who alleged that he was denied an opportunity to apply for a loan because he was not dressed in "masculine attire"); *Miles v. New York Univ.*, 979

F. Supp. 248, 249 (S.D.N.Y. 1997) (holding Title IX prohibits sexual harassment of a transsexual woman). *See also Price Waterhouse v. Hopkins,* 490 U.S. 228 (1989) (holding that harassment directed at a person because that person does not conform to traditional sex stereotypes is covered by Title VII);

22. *See Conway, supra* note 16 (dismissing sex-discrimination claim alleging violations of Connecticut Fair Employment Practice Act); *Underwood, supra* note 16 (dismissing sex-discrimination claim alleging violations of the D.C. Human Rights Act); *Dobre v. National R.R. Passenger Corp. (AMTRAK),* 850 F. Supp. 284 (E.D. Pa. 1993) (dismissing claim brought under sex-discrimination provision of Pennsylvania Human Rights Act); *Kirkpatrick v. Seligman,* 636 F.2d 1047 (5th Cir. 1981) (no violation under state law prohibiting sex discrimination when employer fired plaintiff after plaintiff notified employer of her intent to undergo sex reassignment, began living and dressing as a female, and refused to comply with employer's requirement that she must wear male clothing to work).

23. *See Lie v. Sky Publishing Corp.,* 15 Mass. L. Rptr. 412 (Mass. Super. 2002) (holding that transsexual plaintiff had established prima facie case of discrimination based on sex and disability under state nondiscrimination law); *Enriquez v. West Jersey Health Sys.,* 342 N.J. Super 501, 777 A.2d 365 (N.J. Super. 2001) (concluding that state law prohibiting sex discrimination in employment protects transsexual people); *Maffei, supra* note 16 (holding that city ordinance prohibiting "gender" discrimination protects transsexuals and disagreeing with the reasoning of federal cases that hold that Title VII does not protect transsexuals); *Rentos v. OCE-Office Sys.,* 1996 U.S. Dist. LEXIS 19060 (S.D.N.Y. 1996) (refusing to dismiss transsexual woman's claim that she had been discriminated against on the basis of sex in violation of the New York State Human Rights Law and the New York City Human Rights Law). *See also Declaratory Ruling on Behalf of John/Jane Doe* (Conn. Human Rights Comm'n 2000) (relying on *Price Waterhouse, Schwenk, Rosa,* and other recent federal court decisions in holding that the Connecticut state statute prohibiting discrimination on the basis of sex encompasses discrimination against transgender individuals); *Doe v. Yunits,* 2000 WL 33162199, at *3–4 (Mass. Super.), *aff'd sub nom Doe v. Brockton Sch. Comm.,* No. 2000-J-638 (Mass. App. 2000) (explaining that, with respect to the plaintiff's sex-discrimination claim, because "plaintiff identifies with the female gender, the right question is whether a female student would be disciplined for wearing items of clothes plaintiff chooses to wear. If the answer to that question is no, plaintiff is being discriminated against on the basis of her sex, which is biologically male."). *See also Millett v. Lutco, Inc.,* 2001 Mass. Comm. Discrim. LEXIS 52 (Mass. Comm. Discrim. 2001) (administrative agency decision holding that discrimination on the basis of one's transsexual status is discrimination on the basis of sex).

24. *See* Rehabilitation Act, 29 U.S.C. §706(8)(F)(i) (1997); Americans with Disabilities Act, 42 U.S.C. §12211(b)(1) (1997). Prior to these amendments, two courts had refused to dismiss claims brought under the Rehabilitation Act by persons suffering from gender identity disorders. *See Blackwell v. United States Dep't of Treasury,* 639 F. Supp. 289 (D.D.C. 1986) (finding plaintiff had stated a claim under the Rehabilitation Act either because his gender identity disorder was a physical or mental impairment that substantially limited his ability to function, or because he was regarded as having such an impairment); *Doe v. United States Postal Service,* 1985 WL 9446 (D.D.C. 1985) (same).

25. *See Holt v. Northwest Pa. Training P'ship Consortium, Inc.,* 694 A.2d 1134 (Pa. Commw. 1997) (holding that transsexualism is not a protected disability under the Penn-

sylvania Human Rights Act); *Dobre, supra* note 21 (same); *Somers v. Iowa Civil Rights Comm'n,* 337 N.W.2d 470 (Iowa 1983) (holding that transsexualism not a protected disability under Iowa Civil Rights Act).

26. A.B. 2222 (Cal. 2000).

27. *Lie v. Sky Publishing Corp.,* 15 Mass. L. Rptr. 412, 2002 WL 31492397 (Mass. Super. 2002) (holding that transsexual plaintiff had established a prima facie case of discrimination based on sex and disability under state law prohibiting employment discrimination); *Doe v. Yunits,* 2001 WL 664947 (Mass. Super. 2001) (holding that a transgender student had stated a viable disability discrimination claim); *Jane Doe v. Electro-Craft Corporation,* No. 87-B-132 (N.H. Sup. Ct. 1988) (holding that transsexualism is a disability within the meaning of the state employment discrimination statute); *Enriquez v. West Jersey Health Systems,* 342 N.J. Super. 501, 777 A.2d 365 (N.J. Super.), cert. denied, 170 N.J. 211, 785 A.2d 439 (N.J. 2001) (concluding that transsexual people are protected by state law prohibitions against sex and disability discrimination); *Jean Doe v. Bell,* New York Supreme Court, 754 N.Y.S.2d 846 (N.Y. Sup. Ct. 2003) (holding that transsexual foster youth protected by state law prohibiting discrimination on the basis of disability in housing); *Doe v. Boeing Co.,* 6 P.2d 531, 536 (Wash. 1993) (holding that gender dysphoria "is a medically cognizable condition with a prescribed course of treatment," but that the plaintiff (an MTF transsexual) had failed to prove that she was discriminated against because of her transsexualism).

In addition, many courts have recognized that gender identity disorder is a serious medical condition. *See, e.g., Wolfe v. Horn,* 130 F. Supp. 2d 650, 652 (E.D. Pa. 2001) (noting that courts have consistently considered transsexualism a "serious medical need" for purposes of the Eighth Amendment); *G.B. v. Lackner,* 80 Cal. App. 3d 64 (1978) (describing that seriousness of transsexualism as a medical condition).

28. *Yunits, supra* note 22.

29. *See Jette v. Honey Farms Mini Market,* 2001 Mass. Comm. Discrim. LEXIS 50 (Mass. Comm. Discrim. 2001) (holding transsexuality is not excluded under the state law barring discrimination on the basis of disability); *Evans v. Hamburger Hamlet & Forncrook,* 1996 WL 941676 (Chi. Comm'n. Hum. Rel. 1996) (denying motion to dismiss disability claim brought by transsexual plaintiff); *Smith v. City of Jacksonville Corr. Inst.,* 1991 WL 833882 (Fla. Div. Admin. Hrgs. 1991) (holding that an individual with gender dysphoria is within the disability coverage of the Florida Human Rights Act, as well as the portions of the Act prohibiting discrimination based on perceived disability). In a decision issued on Oct. 9, 1996, the Oregon Bureau of Labor and Industry ruled that a transsexual woman who was fired from her job as a result of her transition was protected from employment discrimination under the Oregon state disability law. Unfortunately, the Oregon Legislature responded to this decision in 1997 by amending the state law to state that "an employer may not be found to have engaged in an unlawful employment practice solely because the employer fails to provide reasonable accommodation to a person with a disability arising out of transsexualism." Ore. Rev. Stats. § 659.439(2) (1997).

30. Minn. Stat. Ann. § 363.01, subd. 15 & subd. 45; *id.* at § 363.03, subd. 5.

31. Cal. Educ. Code § 220; Cal. Penal Code § 422.6.

32. N.J. Stat. 18A: 37-13.

33. 20 U.S.C. § 1681(a). Title IX provides, in relevant part: "No person in the United States shall, on the basis of sex, be excluded from participation in, be denied the benefits

of, or be subjected to discrimination under any education program or activity receiving Federal financial assistance."

34. *See* Revised Sexual Harassment Guidance: Sexual Harassment by School Employees, Other Students, or Third Parties, 66 Fed. Reg. 5,512 (Jan. 19, 2001), available at <http://www.ed.gov/ocv/shguide> (OCR Revised Guidance) ("Although Title IX does not prohibit discrimination on the basis of sexual orientation, sexual harassment directed at gay or lesbian students that is sufficiently serious to limit or deny a student's ability to participate in or benefit from the school's program constitutes sexual harassment prohibited by Title IX under circumstances described in this guidance. For example, if a male student or a group of male students target a gay student for physical sexual advances, serious enough to deny or limit the victim's ability to participate in or benefit from the school's program, the school would need to respond promptly and effectively, as described in this guidance, just as it would if the victim were heterosexual."). *See also Montgomery v. Local Sch. Dist. No. 709,* 109 F. Supp. 2d 1081 (D. Minn. 2000).

35. *See* OCR Revised Guidance, *supra* note 33, at § III ("Though beyond the scope of this guidance, *gender-based harassment,* which may include acts of verbal, nonverbal, or physical aggression, intimidation, or hostility based on sex or sex-stereotyping, but not involving conduct of a sexual nature, *is also a form of sex discrimination to which a school must respond,* if it rises to the level that denies or limits a student's ability to participate in or benefit from the educational program. . . . A school must respond to such harassment in accordance with the standards and procedures described in this guidance. In assessing all related circumstances to determine whether a hostile environment exists, incidents of gender-based harassment combined with incidents of sexual harassment could create a hostile environment, even if neither the gender-based harassment alone nor the sexual harassment alone would be sufficient to do so.") (citing *Hopkins, supra* note 20, at 251 (holding sex-stereotyping is a form of sex discrimination prohibited by Title VII) (emphasis added). *See also Montgomery, supra* note 33; *Miles, supra* note 20.

36. *See Yunits, supra* note 22, at *3 ("Plaintiff in this case is likely to establish that, by dressing in clothing and accessories traditionally associated with the female gender, she is expressing her identification with that gender. In addition, plaintiff's ability to express herself and her gender identity through dress is important to her health and well-being, as attested to by her treating therapist. Therefore, plaintiff's expression is not merely a personal preference but a necessary symbol of her very identity.").

37. *See id.* at *6 ("Given that plaintiff has a likelihood of success in proving that her attire is not distracting, as discussed above, she is likely to prove that defendants' interests do not overcome the recognized liberty interest in appearance.").

38. *See id.* ("Defendants' argument does not frame the issue properly. Since plaintiff identifies with the female gender, the right question is whether a female student would be disciplined for wearing items of clothes plaintiff chooses to wear. If the answer to that question is no, plaintiff is being discriminated against on the basis of her sex, which is biologically male.")

39. *Goins v. West Group,* 635 N.W.2d 717 (Minn. 2001) (in this case, the plaintiff argued only that her biological sex should not be relevant to the question of whether she could use the appropriate restroom. The plaintiff did not argue that she should be considered biologically female based on having undergone hormone therapy. Therefore, the court

did not consider how much medical treatment a person must undergo before being considered a member of his or her reassigned sex).

40. San Francisco Human Rights Commission, Compliance Guidelines to Prohibit Gender Identity Discrimination § IV (available at www.ci.sf.ca.us/sfhumanrights/lg_info.htm). This standard assumes that transsexual persons, including those who have not undergone any medical treatment, can readily obtain a driver's license or other documents reflecting their gender identity. In jurisdictions in which this is not true, it would not be appropriate to have the standard tied to a piece of current identification.

41. *City of Columbus v. Rogers,* 324 N.E.2d 563, 41 Ohio St. 161 (1975).

42. *Id.* at 565.

43. *Id.* (quoting *Connally v. General Constr. Co.,* 269 U.S.85, 391 (1926)).

44. *See, e.g., D.C. v. City of St. Louis,* 795 F.2d 652 (8th Cir. 1986); *City of Chicago v. Wilson,* 75 Ill.2d 525, 389 N.E.2d 522 (1978); *City of Cincinnati v. Adams,* 330 N.E.2d 463 (Ohio Mun. Ct. 1974).

45. *Doe v. McCann,* 489 F. Supp. 76 (S.D. Tex. 1980). *See also Wilson, supra* note 43.

46. *See, e.g., In the Matter of Marley,* 1996 WL 1581132 (Del. Com. Pl. 1996) ("Rather than abrogating the substantive common law, these statutes merely serve to assist the common law by establishing a record of the name change."); *In the Matter of Eck,* 245 N.J. Super. 220, 223, 584 A.2d 859, 860 (1991) ("At common law, any adult or emancipated person is free to adopt any name, except for a fraudulent, criminal or other illegitimate purpose.") (citations omitted); *In re Anonymous,* 582 N.Y.S.2d 941, 941, 153 Misc.2d 893, 894 (Civ. Ct. 1992) (recognizing that the New York name-change statute supplemented but did not replace the common-law method of name change by usage).

47. *See, e.g., In the Matter of Anonymous,* 57 Misc. 2d 813, 293 N.Y.S.2d 834 (Civ. Ct. 1968) (holding that a name change should only be granted transsexuals "only in those cases where physiological orientation is complete").

48. *In re Ladrach,* 513 N.E.2d 828, 829 (Ohio Prob. 1987). *See also Eck, supra* note 45, at 223, 860–61 ("Absent fraud or other improper purpose a person has a right to a name change whether he or she has undergone or intends to undergo a sex change through surgery, has received hormonal injections to induce physical change, is a transvestite, or simply wants to change from a traditional 'male' first name to one traditionally 'female,' or vice versa."); *But see* "Judge Denies Plea for New Name Court Turns Down Request by Man Awaiting Sex-Change Operation to Legally Be Called Heather Jeanine," *Augusta Chronicle,* Jan. 22, 2000, at D5.

49. *See, e.g.,* Ala. Code § 22-9A-19 (1997); Ariz. Rev. Stat. Ann. § 36-326(a)(4) (West 1993); Colo. Rev. Stat. Ann. § 25-2-115(4) (West 1990); D.C. Code Ann. § 6-217(d) (1995); Ga. Code Ann. § 31-10-23(e) (Harrison 1998); 10 Guam Code Ann. § 3222 (1998); Haw. Rev. Stat. § 338-17.7(4)(b) (1993); 410 Ill. Comp. Stat. Ann. § 535(d)17 (West 1997); Iowa Code Ann. § 144.23.3 (West 1997); La. Rev. Stat. § 40:62 (West 1992); Md. Code Ann. Health-Gen. I, § 4-214(b)(5) (1999); Mass. Gen. Laws Ann. Ch. 46 § 13(e) (West 1993); Mich. Comp. Laws § 333.2891(9)(a) (1998); Mo. Ann. Stat. § 193.215(9) (West Supp. 1999); Neb. Rev. Stat. § 71-604.01 (1999); N.J. Stat. Ann. § 26:8-40.12 (West 1999); N.M. Stat. Ann. § 24-14-25(D) (Michie 1997); N.C. Gen. Stat. § 130A-118(b)(4) (1997); Or. Rev. Stat. § 432.235(4) (1997); Utah Code Ann. § 26-2-11 (Supp. 1998); Wis. Stat. Ann. § 69.15(1)(a) (West 1990). It appears that

Idaho, Ohio, and Tennessee will not allow transsexual people to change their sex on their birth certificates. For more information, *see* <http://www.drbecky.com/birthcert.html>.

50. *See Darnell v. Lloyd,* 395 F. Supp. 1210 (D. Conn. 1975) (holding that plaintiff's complaint alleging that the state commissioner of health had violated equal protection in selective approval of requests for birth certificate changes stated a cause of action, and noting that the Commission must demonstrate some substantial state interest to justify its refusal to change birth certificates to reflect current sex).

51. *See Littleton v. Prange,* 9 S.W.3d 223 (Tex. Ct. App. 1999), *cert. denied,* 531 U.S. 872 (2000) (holding MTF transsexual person to be a male for purposes of determining the validity of her marriage, despite the fact that she had amended her birth certificate to change her name and sex); *In re: Estate of Gardiner,* 42 P.3d 120 (Kan. 2002), *cert. denied sub. nom Gardiner v. Gardiner,* 123 S. Ct. 113 (2002) (same).

52. *See* Stuart Pfeifer, "Transsexual Can Sue for Custody," *Orange Co. Reg.,* Nov. 26, 1997, at B1 (discussing the unreported case of *Vecchione v. Vecchione*).

53. *Kantaras v. Kantaras,* Case No. 98-5375CA (Fla. Cir. Ct. 2003), available at <http://www.nclrights.org>.

54. *See M.T. v. J.T.,* 140 N.J. Super. 77, 355 A.2d 204, *cert. denied,* 71 N.J. 345, 364 A.2d 1076 (1976) (upholding validity of a marriage involving a "post-operative" transsexual woman).

55. *In re Estate of Gardiner,* 42 P.3d 120 (Kan. 2002), *cert. denied* sub. nom. *Gardiner v. Gardiner,* 123 S.Ct. 113 (2002).

56. *See Anonymous v. Anonymous,* 325 N.Y.S.2d 499, 500 (Sup. Ct. 1971) (nullifying marriage involving an FTM in which spouse alleged that he had defrauded her by not informing her of his transsexual status prior to marriage).

57. *See In re Ladrach,* 32 Ohio Misc.2d 6, 10 513 N.E.2d 828, 832 (Prob. Ct. 1987) (concluding that "there is no authority in Ohio for the issuance of a marriage license to consummate a marriage between a post-operative male to female transsexual person and a male person").

58. *See Littleton, supra* note 50, at 231.

59. *Corbett v. Corbett,* 2 All E.R.33 (P. 1970) (U.K.).

60. *Daly v. Daly,* 102 Nev. 66, 71, 715 P.2d 56, 59 (1986) (characterizing MTF transsexual parent as "selfish" and holding that "[i]t was strictly Tim Daly's choice to discard his fatherhood and assume the role of a female who could never be either mother or sister to his daughter"). *See also In re Darnell,* 49 Or. App. 561, 619 P.2d 1349 (1980) (terminating mother's parental rights on the ground that the mother's continued relationship with her former husband, a FTM transsexual, was detrimental to the best interests of the child; an earlier proceeding had terminated the parental rights of the father).

61. *See In re V.H.,* 412 N.W.2d 389 (Minn. Ct. App. 1987) (granting custody to cross-dressing father on condition that father never cross-dress in front of daughter or have any literature relating to transvestism in his home); *In re D.F.D. and D.G.D.,* 261 Mont. 186 (1993) (awarding custody to cross-dressing father after expert testimony that father no longer cross-dressed and would not do so in the future); *In re T.J.,* Minn. App. LEXIS 144 (1988) (awarding custody to "gender dysphoric" father in which father agreed to undergo therapy and "to maintain his male identity" and in which there was no evidence that the

child manifested any gender "atypical" behaviors or gender-identity problems). *See also J.L.S. v. D.K.S.,* 1997 Mo. App. LEXIS 377 (March 11, 1997) (reversing a trial court order that had awarded joint legal, but not physical, custody to a MTF parent and imposing an indefinite moratorium on visitation, based on finding that it would be emotionally confusing for the children to see their father as a woman); *Cisek v. Cisek,* Docket No. 80 CA 113 (Ohio, 7th Appellate Dist. 1982) (holding that in case in which psychiatric testimony established that the continued contact with the father, a MTF transsexual, would be detrimental to the children, the mother had produced sufficient evidence of a substantial change in circumstances to warrant a denial of visitation rights to the father).

62. *Kantaras, supra* note 52.

63. *Christian v. Randall,* 33 Colo. App. 129, 516 P.2d 132 (1973).

64. Medicare is a federal health insurance program for people sixty-five years of age or older, certain people with disabilities, and people with end-stage renal disease (ESRD). Medicare has two parts—Part A, which is hospital insurance, and Part B, which is medical insurance.

65. Medicare Program: National Coverage Decisions, 54 Fed. Reg. 34555, 34572 (Aug. 21, 1989).

66. 32 C.F.R. § 199.4(e)(7).

67. Medicaid is a health insurance program for certain low-income people. It covers children, the aged, the blind and disabled, and people who are eligible to receive other federal assistance.

68. *See, e.g., Pinneke v. Preisser,* 623 F.2d 546, 549 (8th Cir. 1980) ("We find that a state plan absolutely excluding the only available treatment known at this stage of the art for a particular condition must be considered an arbitrary denial of benefits based solely on the 'diagnosis, type of illness, or condition.'"); *Doe v. State,* 257 N.W.2d 816, 820 (Minn. 1977) (noting that SRS was "the only surgical treatment which, if recommended by a physician and related to a patient's heath is not covered by the [Minnesota Medicaid] program."); *J.D. v. Lackner,* 80 Cal. App. 3d 90 (Cal. Ct. App. 1978).

69. *See, e.g.,* Alaska Admin. Code tit. 7, § 43.385(a)(1); Ill. Admin. Code tit. 89 § 140.6(1); 55 Pa. Code § 1163.59(a)(1); *Smith v. Rasmussen,* 249 F.3d 755 (8th Cir. 2001) (reversing district court's ruling and holding that Iowa's rule denying coverage for SRS was not arbitrary or inconsistent with the Medicaid Act); *Rush v. Parham,* 625 F.2d 1150 (5th Cir. 1980) (reversing district court's ruling that Georgia's Medicaid program could not categorically deny coverage for SRS); *Denise R. v. Lavine,* 39 N.Y.2d 279, 347 N.E.2d 893 (1976) (holding New York's Medicaid agency's denial of coverage for SRS was not "arbitrary or capricious," given conflicting evidence as to medical necessity).

70. *See, e.g., Davidson v. Aetna Life & Casualty Ins. Co.,* 420 N.Y.S. 2d 450 (N.Y. Sup. Ct. 1979).

71. *Beger v. Division of Med. Assistance,* 2000 Mass. Super. LEXIS 126 (2000).

72. *See Farmer v. Brennan,* 511 U.S. 825, 829 (1994); *Farmer v. Haas,* 990 F.2d 319, 320 (7th Cir. 1993).

73. *See* Darren Rosenblum, "'Trapped' in Sing Sing: Transgendered Prisoners Caught in the Gender Binarism," 6 *Mich. J. Gender & L.* 499, 530 (2000).

74. *See* Dennis Duggan, "Is Treatment for Sex Change a Prison Perk?" *Newsday,*

Dec. 13, 1994, at A14 (noting that, at the time of the article, there were seventy prisoners on hormone treatments in New York state prisons and seventeen in the New York City prisons).

75. Bureau of Prisons Health Services Manual, Program Statement 6000.3, § 6803.

76. *See* Rosenblum, *supra* note 72, at 545.

77. *See Maggert v. Hanks,* 131 F.3d 670 (7th Cir. 1997) (recognizing that SRS is the only effective treatment for transsexual prisoners but holding that it is permissible to withhold treatment from transsexual prisoners in light of fact that neither public nor private health insurance programs will pay for sex reassignment); *Long v. Nix,* 86 F.3d 761 (8th Cir. 1996) (holding that prisoner diagnosed with gender identity disorder had no right to cross-dress or to estrogen therapy); *Brown v. Zavaras,* 63 F.3d 967 (10th Cir. 1995) (rejecting equal protection claim brought by preoperative MTF transsexual based on evidence that Colorado provided hormone therapy to nontranssexual prisoners with low hormone levels and to postoperative MTF transsexuals); *White v. Farrier,* 849 F.2d 322 (8th Cir. 1988) (holding that MTF transsexual prisoner is not entitled to cross-dress or wear cosmetics and does not have a constitutional right to hormone therapy); *Meriwether v. Faulkner,* 821 F.2d 408 (7th Cir. 1987), *cert. denied,* 484 U.S. 935 (1987) (holding that transsexual prisoner is constitutionally entitled to some type of medical treatment for diagnosed condition of transsexualism, but she "does not have a right to any particular type of treatment, such as estrogen therapy"); *Jones v. Flannigan,* 1991 U.S. App. LEXIS 29606 (7th Cir. 1991) (same); *Supre v. Ricketts,* 792 F.2d 958 (10th Cir. 1986) (same); *Lamb v. Maschner,* 633 F. Supp. 351 (D. Kan. 1986) (holding that transsexual prisoner had no right to hormone therapy). *See also Cuoco v. Mortisugo,* 222 F.3d 99 (2d Cir. 2000) (holding officials entitled to immunity against claim by transsexual pretrial detainee who was denied hormones).

78. *See Kosilek v. Maloney,* 221 F. Supp.2d 156 (D. Mass. 2002) (holding that if determined to be medically necessary, prison officials had to provide treatment, including hormone therapy and possibly SRS to transsexual inmate); *South v. Gomez,* 211 F.3d 1275 (9th Cir. 2000) (finding Eighth Amendment violation when a prisoner's course of hormone treatment was abruptly cut off after being transferred to a new prison). *Cf. Wolfe v. Horn,* 130 F. Supp. 2d 648 (E.D. Pa. 2001) (noting that abrupt termination of prescribed hormonal treatment by a prison official with no understanding of Wolfe's condition and failure to treat her severe withdrawal symptoms or aftereffects could constitute "deliberate indifference"). *See also Phillips v. Michigan Dep't of Corr.,* 731 F. Supp. 792 (W.D. Mich. 1990), *aff'd,* 932 F.2d 969 (6th Cir. 1991) (granting preliminary injunction directing prison officials to provide estrogen therapy to a preoperative transsexual woman who had been taking estrogen for several years prior to her transfer to a new prison and distinguishing failure "to provide an inmate with care that would improve his or her medical state, such as refusing to provide sex reassignment surgery" from "[t]aking measures which actually reverse the effects of years of healing medical treatment").

79. *See, e.g.,* Law Office of Robert Jobe, Press Release, "Six More Gays Receive Asylum as Window of Opportunity Closes in April 1997," Feb. 25, 1997 (San Francisco, CA) (describing a 1997 decision granting asylum to an intersexed FTM from Pakistan who was raised as a woman and persecuted as a woman and another 1997 decision granting asylum to a MTF transsexual from Peru who "was harassed throughout her childhood for being

effeminate and gay," "taunted, humiliated, and physically attacked by her family, class-mates, teachers, and strangers on the street," and "arrested and detained . . . [by the Peruvian police] for being a gay man"). *Cf. Miranda v. INS,* 51 F.3d 767 (8th Cir. 1995) (holding that MTF transsexual from Honduras was not entitled to suspension of deportation based on hardship due to absence of comprehensive medical care for transsexual people in Honduras, where she had already undergone SRS, and there was no evidence that she would be unable to obtain necessary care to maintain her health in Honduras).

80. *Hernandez-Montiel v. INS,* 225 F.3d 1084 (9th Cir. 2000).

81. *Id.* at 1098.

XIII

People with HIV/AIDS

Nothing has been as tragic in its impact on LGBT persons as AIDS. First reported in 1981, AIDS had killed 467,910 Americans by December 2001; almost half of all reported cases were men who had sex with men.[1] The legal response to the disease was decidedly mixed: it led to both new civil rights laws and new civil liberties violations.

The twenty-first century began with substantial, although incomplete, advances in treatment. Unfortunately, it also began with clear signs that the disease is not going away. The U.S. Centers for Disease Control and Prevention (CDC) reported in 2001 that the sharp annual decreases in the number of reported cases that had occurred in the early 1990s had stopped in 1998, and the numbers had since leveled off.[2] Moreover, men of color within the LGBT community appeared to be at heightened risk. According to CDC data, of all men who have sex with men diagnosed with AIDS in 2001, 35.5 percent were African American and 18.5 percent were Hispanic—rates far in excess of their percentages of the U.S. population.[3] A CDC study of young gay men in seven cities found the annual infection rate to be 14.7 percent among African Americans, 3.5 percent among Hispanics and 2.5 percent among whites.[4]

The intricacies of law that relate to every aspect of living with AIDS or HIV are beyond the scope of this chapter. Indeed, there is a separate book in the ACLU series on that very topic: *The Rights of People Who Are HIV Positive*.[5] What follows is an overview of the law pertaining to discrimination and privacy.

EMPLOYMENT DISCRIMINATION

In general, what kinds of laws protect people with HIV against discrimination?

Both state and federal laws prohibit medically unjustified discrimination against persons with disabilities. All of the federal laws that cover disability discrimination include HIV disease as a disability and thus prohibit that form of discrimination as well. Most states have antidiscrimination laws as well, and most of these have been invoked to protect people with HIV disease. The state laws tend to provide less powerful remedies than the federal laws.

The primary federal law that protects people with HIV disease is the Americans with Disabilities Act (ADA).[6] The ADA prohibits employment discrimination by most employers, public or private, where fifteen or more persons are employed. Another federal law, Section 504 of the Rehabilitation Act,[7] prohibits employment discrimination by the federal government and by all entities that receive federal funds; this includes all private businesses that have federal contracts. In addition, a number of states have laws that protect against job discrimination based on handicap, including HIV disease.

Is asymptomatic HIV infection considered to be a disability for purposes of the antidiscrimination laws?

Yes. In *Bragdon v. Abbott,* a person with HIV brought an action under the ADA against a dentist who refused to treat her in his office.[8] The Supreme Court held that the patient's HIV status was a disability under the ADA even though her infection had not yet progressed to the symptomatic phase. The Court found in *Bragdon* that HIV was an impairment under the ADA from the moment the plaintiff had been infected. Although the person must demonstrate that some major life activity has been impaired in order to meet the statute's requirements, it is not necessary to prove that the individual's HIV-infected status impaired his or her ability to work. In *Bragdon,* the Court found that the impairment to the plaintiff's reproductive capacity satisfied the "major life activity" requirement. Future courts will consider whether other nonwork activities satisfy that requirement.

May job applicants be required under the ADA or Section 504 to take an HIV test before an employer offers them a job?

Job applicants can be required to undergo a medical examination, including an HIV test, if two critically important conditions are met. First, an employer must offer the applicant the job, conditional on results of the exam, *before* the examination. This ensures that the employer cannot later claim that there was another reason for not hiring the applicant if the HIV test comes back positive; if the offer is withdrawn, the employer then must prove that not being HIV-infected is a legitimate qualification for the job. Second, the employer must require all applicants to take medical examinations; particular individuals cannot be singled out for testing.[9]

May an employer make employees take an HIV test as a condition of continued employment?

An employer may not require an HIV test of an individual already employed unless the employer can prove the test is necessary for the job.[10] In *EEOC v. Prevo's Family Market, Inc.,* the U.S. Court of Appeals for the Sixth Circuit held that the ADA permits medical examinations of employees, but only under limited circumstances.[11] The court found that a "legitimate business purpose" had been met where the HIV-infected employee used sharp knives to cut produce at a grocery store before it was put out for sale.

May a person be fired or hired because the employer fears that HIV can be transmitted to coworkers or others?

No. A mere fear of contagiousness cannot justify a discriminatory action. The Supreme Court ruled on this very question in 1987, in a case involving a school teacher with tuberculosis. The Court held that one major purpose of the federal law against disability discrimination was to protect individuals from myths and stereotypes—including a fear of contagion that is not justified by objective knowledge about a disease.[12]

Of course, if the fear is justified—if there really is a risk of transmission—the employer would be justified in taking action. In the same 1987 case, the Supreme Court adopted the prevailing standard: a person who poses "a significant risk" of transmission will not be qualified for a job, unless use of reasonable accommodations (such as protective gloves or other devices) will eliminate the risk.[13] The "significant risk" standard has now been formally adopted by Congress as part of the ADA and Section 504.[14] Because HIV cannot be transmitted by normal workplace conduct, however, there is virtually no situation in which discrimination based on a risk of harm would be permitted.

Does the law prohibit discrimination against persons who are suspected of having the disease?

Yes. Both the ADA and Section 504 cover persons who are "regarded as" having a disability.[15] Regulations have defined "regarded as" to mean a person who: "(1) has a physical or mental impairment that does not substantially limit major life activities but is treated by a covered entity as constituting such limitation; (2) has a physical or mental impairment that substantially limits major life activities only as a result of the attitudes of others toward such impairment; or (3) has none of the impairments defined in paragraphs (1) or (2) of this section but is treated by a covered entity as having a substantially limiting impairment."[16]

Does the ADA protect friends, family, and caregivers of HIV-infected people?

Yes, the ADA covers persons who associate with HIV-infected persons, including those who live with, care for, or provide services to those with HIV disease.[17] For example, a federal district court in Oklahoma awarded back pay to a gay waiter who was fired for having discussed the health condition of his partner, who had AIDS, with customers who had inquired about it.[18] The court ruled that the plaintiff's "relationship and association with a person with a disability was a motivating factor" in his discharge.[19]

Does the ADA require that an employer's health insurance policy cover HIV-related expenses?

The law concerning health insurance benefits is extremely complex. In addition to the ADA, there are other federal laws and some state laws that may apply, depending in part on whether the employer is self-insured or purchases group coverage from an insurance company. For answers to questions on this topic, an attorney experienced in insurance law should be consulted.

Each case will depend on the facts of the specific situation. The ADA specifically allows employers to offer health insurance policies that include limited coverage for certain expenses as long as certain conditions are met. Limitations on coverage must be based on legitimate actuarial principles or a bona fide classification of risks. A health insurance plan may not deny all coverage to a person with a disability or charge a different rate for the same coverage because of an individual's disability, independent of actuarial classification. Although limitations or caps may be placed on reimbursement for a specific procedure or the types of procedures or drugs covered, that limitation must apply to all persons with or without disabilities.[20]

In *McGann v. H & H Music Co.*,[21] the U.S. Court of Appeals for the Fifth Circuit held that an employer did not unlawfully discriminate against an employee when it reduced the benefits payable under its group medical plan for AIDS-related claims to $5,000 from $1 million, although the employer had been informed of an employee's AIDS diagnosis at the time the benefits payable was reduced. The court stated that because the reduction in payable benefits would apply equally to all employees filing AIDS-related claims the effect of reduction would not necessarily be felt only by the employee.

May an employer refuse to hire a person with asymptomatic HIV disease because he or she might get sick in the future?

In enacting the ADA, Congress intended to prohibit an employer from using the fact that a person might become too sick to work in the future as an excuse for not hiring or for firing him or her.[22] However, there has been no definitive case law on this point since the ADA was enacted.[23]

What if an employee is already so ill that she or he cannot continue to work?

This presents a different question. Under both the ADA and Section 504, discrimination is prohibited only against *qualified* persons with a disability.[24] To be qualified, a person must be able to perform all the essential functions of the job, despite the HIV disease,[25] which includes being well enough to go to work and to perform the job properly. Most courts have held that the ADA ceases to cover a person who has become too ill to work.[26]

May an employee be fired if symptoms cause him or her to have to leave work early occasionally because of fatigue or to receive treatment?

Under both the ADA and Section 504, an employer must make reasonable accommodations for workers with disabilities.[27] If the employee can perform the essential functions of the job but needs help in overcoming the impact of the disability, the law places a duty on the employer to make accommodations that do not cause an undue hardship (in expense or management) for the business. Establishing a flexible work schedule or allowing time off for treatment could qualify as reasonable accommodations. In its ADA Technical Assistance Manual, the Equal Employment Opportunity Commission includes people with AIDS among the groups who could qualify for modified work schedules as a reasonable accommodation.[28]

Do I have any recourse if I am being harassed at work?

Yes. If you are being harassed because you have AIDS or HIV disease, you can obtain relief under the ADA. Although the ADA does not specifically mention harassment in its text, at least one court has ruled that the ADA covers disability-based harassment as a form of employment discrimination.[29] (For more about workplace harassment generally, see chapter 6.)

What are the rules for health-care workers with HIV disease?

In 1991, the Centers for Disease Control published recommendations concerning the question of whether HIV-infected health-care workers (HCWs) should be subject to special work restrictions. The recommendations stated in part:

> • "Infected HCWs who adhere to universal precautions and who do not perform invasive procedures pose no risk for transmitting HIV or HBV [hepatitis virus] to patients."
> • "Currently available data provide no basis for recommendations to restrict the practice of HCWs infected with HIV or HBV who perform invasive procedures not identified as exposure-prone," provided that the workers comply with what are known as "universal precautions"

for infection control (such as using gloves and complying with standards for sterilization and disinfection).

- "HCWs who perform exposure-prone procedures should know their HIV antibody status. . . . HCWs who are infected with HIV . . . should not perform exposure-prone procedures unless they have sought counsel from an expert review panel and been advised under what circumstances, if any, they may continue to perform these procedures. Such circumstances should include notifying prospective patients of the HCW's seropositivity before they undergo exposure-prone invasive procedures."[30]

Under these guidelines, which have not been altered since 1991, HCWs who do not perform exposure-prone invasive procedures should not be subject to restrictions, so long as they observe the proper safety precautions. However, different states and medical authorities may define differently which, if any, procedures are exposure prone; the CDC guidelines do not have the force of law. In practice, courts have tended to enforce testing and disclosure requirements imposed on HIV-positive HCWs.[31]

ACCESS TO HEALTH CARE

May a health-care provider discriminate against a person with HIV disease?

No. As with employment-related law, there are three possible sources of a legal right against discrimination by a health-care provider: the ADA, Section 504, and state antidiscrimination laws. The ADA provides powerful protection because it defines providers of health-care services to fall within the category of "public accommodations," entities that are forbidden to discriminate on the basis of disability.[32] It was this provision of the ADA that formed the basis for the successful suit against a dentist in *Bragdon v. Abbott.*[33] Most state laws are less protective, although a few (California, New Jersey, and New York) provide stronger remedies than the ADA.

What kinds of health-care providers are covered?

The ADA includes a variety of providers: doctors, dentists, hospitals, nursing homes, ambulance companies, paramedic services, and other health-care providers are all considered "public accommodations" under the ADA.[34] Section 504 covers any provider of health-care and individual physicians that receive federal financial assistance.[35] Federal financial assistance includes grants, loans, contracts, and most significantly, receipt of Medicaid or Medicare payments.

Housing Discrimination

Is there a federal law that prohibits housing discrimination against people with HIV disease?

Yes. Since 1989, the Fair Housing Act (FHA) has prohibited discrimination on the basis of disability (as well as race, sex, religion, and national origin).[36] The regulations implementing the law specify that HIV infection is one of the conditions included within the meaning of disability or handicap.[37] The act outlaws discrimination in the sale, rental, or financing of virtually all housing in the United States; only buildings with four or fewer units where the landlord lives on the premises are excluded from coverage under the act.

Does the FHA cover lovers or roommates of HIV patients?

Yes. It is unlawful to threaten, intimidate, or interfere with persons in the enjoyment of their dwelling because of their handicap or because of the handicap of their visitors or associates.[38] This includes situations in which the partner of a person with AIDS is perceived to be infected because of the relationship.[39]

How can rights be enforced under the FHA?

A lawsuit can be filed in court, or a complaint can be filed with the federal Department of Housing and Urban Development (HUD). An agency complaint can be filed by calling the nearest HUD office and asking for assistance.

Confidentiality

Are there laws protecting the confidentiality of medical records pertaining to HIV-related condition(s)?

In April 2001, federal regulations took effect that created national standards for ensuring the privacy of medical records.[40] These regulations cover doctors' offices, hospitals, managed-care organizations, health insurance companies, and a number of other entities that handle such records. The regulations are quite lengthy and complex. In general terms, they require patient consent before medical information can be disclosed in most instances, and they require those holding the information to disclose only the minimum necessary for the particular purpose, for example, billing. You may be able to obtain more detailed consumer guides to these regulations either from an AIDS service provider or from the U.S. Department of Health and Human Services, which is responsible for their implementation.[41]

State laws also cover this area. Nearly every state has enacted some form of confidentiality law specifically concerning HIV-related medical records. The strength of these laws varies enormously from state to state. In addition, personal injury law might provide a cause of action if records are wrongfully disclosed.[42]

If an individual tests HIV positive, will his or her name be reported to the state health department?

This depends on where the test is conducted. In some states, all HIV testing is "anonymous," which means that no name is reported to a health department. In most states, testing is "confidential," which means that the names of persons who test positive are reported to the state health department.[43] However, there may be particular sites offering "anonymous" testing within states that have "confidential" reporting systems. If you wish to receive anonymous testing, you should inquire whether your state is one of those which offers that service, or you may want to consider traveling to a state that does allow anonymous testing.

May testing for HIV be done without the knowledge and consent of the subject?

In most states, nonconsensual HIV testing is against the law in almost all situations. Surreptitious testing violates the patient's right to insist that informed consent precede any procedure carrying serious ramifications, social and psychological as well as physical.[44] Some statutes reinforce this principle: in Texas a person who requires another to undergo an HIV test when not otherwise permitted by statute is guilty of a Class A misdemeanor.[45]

There are exceptions, however. Many states require or authorize mandatory testing for persons convicted of sexually related crimes. Those states include Arizona,[46] California,[47] Colorado,[48] Delaware,[49] Illinois,[50] Indiana,[51] North Carolina,[52] Rhode Island,[53] South Carolina,[54] and Washington.[55] Additionally, insurance companies often require an HIV test when persons apply for an individual (rather than a group) policy. Thus, despite the right to consent to or to refuse an HIV test in that situation, the insurance company can make consent a condition of selling the policy.

Must a person with HIV inform sexual partners about the infection?

Most states have partner-notification laws that provide for notification of sexual (or drug-using) partners of a person who has tested HIV positive. In general, such laws provide that health department personnel will do the notification without disclosing the name of the infected person, although that individual's identity may be obvious to the person being informed. A person with HIV may also voluntarily request that health department staff notify partners. Some states merely authorize physicians or health department staff to do such notification; other states require that it be done. A lawyer or a local AIDS service provider should be consulted to determine which procedures have been established in any particular state.

In addition to partner-notification laws and general ethical obligations, the law related to personal injuries establishes that a person can be liable for money damages for knowing transmission of an infectious disease.

In any case, the practice of safer sex should begin immediately. Legal liability—either for money damages or for prosecution—begins only if a person fails to practice safer sex after learning that he or she is HIV-infected.

Is it a crime to transmit HIV or to engage in acts which could transmit HIV?

In approximately half the states, it is a crime for persons with HIV who know they are infected to have intercourse if their partners are not informed, regardless of whether transmission occurs.[56] The seriousness of the offense varies. In Maryland, for example, knowing transmission of HIV is a misdemeanor.[57] However, it is a felony in many states.

The details of criminal responsibility vary widely, and anyone with questions about a particular state's law should consult a local attorney. For example, California requires proof of specific intent to infect the other person and allows a defendant to attempt to prove that the activity took place between two consenting adults as a defense.[58] Colorado law has felony penalties for sexual activity by an HIV-infected prostitute or by an HIV-infected person who patronizes a prostitute.[59] Kentucky makes it a Class D felony for any person infected with HIV to donate organs, skin, or other tissues when the person knows he or she is HIV positive and may communicate it through such donation.[60] Louisiana law enhances penalties for knowing HIV transmission when the victim is a police officer.[61] Washington law provides increased penalties for serious sex crimes by up to five years if there was knowing HIV transmission.[62] A person who has engaged in sexual conduct that could transmit HIV—knowing the possibility of transmission—should consult an attorney for advice.

NOTES

1. U.S. Centers for Disease Control and Prevention, *HIV-AIDS Surveillance Report,* Vol. 13, No. 2 (Year-end edition, December 2000), table 20 at 29; U.S. Centers for Disease Control and Prevention, *Basic Statistics* (2001), available at <http://www.cdc.gov/hiv/stats.htm cumaids>.

2. Susan Okie, "Sharp Drop in AIDS Toll May Be Over," *Wash. Post,* Aug. 14, 2001, p. A1, col. 6.

3. *HIV-AIDS Surveillance Report, supra* note 1, table 22, at 31. Data from the 2000 census indicated that African Americans comprise 12.3 per cent of the population, while 12.5 per cent of Americans identify as Hispanic or Latino <http://www.census.gov/prod/2001pubs/c2kkbr001>.

4. U.S. Centers for Disease Control and Prevention, "HIV Incidences among Young Men Who Have Sex with Men—Seven U.S. Cities, 1994–2000," 50 *Mortality and Morbidity Weekly Report* 440 (2001).

5. William B. Rubenstein, Ruth Eisenberg & Lawrence O. Gostin, *The Rights of People Who Are HIV Positive* (1996), available for purchase at <http://www.aclu.org>.

6. 42 U.S.C. § 12101 (1994 and Supp. III 1997).

7. 29 U.S.C. § 794 (1982).

8. *Bragdon v. Abbott,* 524 U.S. 624 (1998).

9. 42 U.S.C. § 12112(d)(3).

10. *Id.*

11. *EEOC v. Prevo's Family Market, Inc.,* 135 F.3d 1089 (6th Cir. 1998).

12. *School Bd. of Nassau County v. Arline,* 480 U.S. 273, 282-6 (1987).

13. *Id.* at 287 n. 16.

14. 42 U.S.C. §§ 12111(3), 12113(b); 29 U.S.C. § 706(8)(D) (1985 and Supp.).

15. 42 U.S.C. § 12102(2)(c); 29 U.S.C. § 706(8)(B).

16. 29 C.F.R. §1630.2(l).

17. 42 U.S.C. § 12112(b)(4).

18. *Saladin v. Turner,* 936 F. Supp. 1571 (N.D. Okla. 1996).

19. *Id.* at 1581.

20. H.R. Rep. No. 485, at 38, 71; 1990 U.S. Code Cong. and Admin. News 460–61, 494.

21. *McGann v. H & H Music Co.,* 946 F.2d 401 (5th Cir. 1991).

22. H.R. Rep. No. 485, at 34; 1990 U.S. Code Cong. and Admin. News 456.

23. *See generally* Bryan P. Neal, "The Proper Standard for Risk of Future Injury under the Americans with Disabilities Act: Risk to Self or Risk to Others," 46 *S.M.U. L. Rev.* 483 (1992).

24. 42 U.S.C. § 12112(a).

25. 42 U.S.C. § 12111(8).

26. *See, e.g., Gonzales v. Garner Food Serv., Inc.,* 89 F.3d 1523 (11th Cir. 1996).

27. 42 U.S.C. § 12111(9), § 12112(b)(5); 45 C.F.R. § 84.3(k)(1).

28. ADA Title I EEOC Technical Assistance Manual, § I-3.10(3) in Ruth Colker & Bonnie Poitras Tucker, *The Law of Disability Discrimination Handbook: Statutory and Regulatory Guidance* 66 (3d ed. 2000).

29. *Flowers v. Southern Regional Physician Services, Inc.,* 247 F.3d 229 (5th Cir. 2001).

30. U.S. Centers for Disease Control, "Recommendations for Preventing Transmission of Human Immunodeficiency Virus and Hepatitis-B Virus to Patients During Exposure-Prone Invasive Procedures," 40 *Mortality and Morbidity Weekly Report,* No. RR-8, July 12, 1991.

31. *See, e.g., Estate of Mauro v. Borgess Med. Ctr.,* 137 F.3d 398 (6th Cir. 1998); *Doe v. University of Maryland Med. Sys. Corp.,* 50 F.3d 1261 (4th Cir. 1995); *Bradley v. University of Texas M.D. Anderson Cancer Ctr.,* 3 F.3d 922 (5th Cir. 1993); *Leckelt v. Board of Comm'rs of Hosp. Dist. No. 1,* 909 F.2d 820 (5th Cir. 1990).

32. 42 U.S.C. § 12181(7)(f).

33. *Bragdon, supra* note 8.

34. 42 U.S.C. § 12181(7)(F).

35. 45 C.F.R. § 84.3(h) (1988); *United States v. Baylor Univ. Med. Ctr.,* 736 F.2d 1039 (5th Cir. 1984), *cert. denied* 469 U.S. 1189 (1984).

36. 42 U.S.C. § 3601 *et seq.* (1982 and Supp. 1991).

37. 54 Fed. Reg. 32345 (Jan. 23, 1989). See *Baxter v. City of Belleville,* 720 F. Supp. 720 (S.D. Ill. 1989).

38. § 100.400(c)(1)-(2) of the regulations, 54 Fed. Reg. 3291 (Jan. 23, 1989).

39. *Neithamer v. Brenneman Prop. Servs., Inc.,* 81 F. Supp. 2d 1 (D.D.C. 1999).

40. 45 C.F.R. §§ 160, 164.

41. The HHS Web site address for information about the privacy regulations is <www.hhs.gov/ocr/hipaa>.

42. *See, e.g., Jeffrey H. v. Imai, Tadlock & Keeney,* 101 Cal. Rptr. 2d 916 (Ct. App. 2001); *Biddle v. Warren Gen. Hosp.,* 86 Ohio St. 395, 715 N.E.2d 518 (1999).

43. Names are routinely reported to public health departments from test sites in the following states: Alabama, Alaska, Arizona, Arkansas, Colorado, Florida, Idaho, Indiana,

Iowa, Kansas, Louisiana, Michigan, Minnesota, Mississippi, Missouri, Nebraska, Nevada, New Jersey, New Mexico, North Carolina, North Dakota, Ohio, Oklahoma, South Carolina, South Dakota, Tennessee, Texas, Utah, Virginia, West Virginia, Wisconsin, and Wyoming. *HIV-AIDS Surveillance Report, supra* note 1, table 3, at 9.

44. *See, e.g., People v. Khonsavanh S.,* 79 Cal. Rptr.2d 80 (Ct. App.1998) (person convicted of felony could not be tested absent a specific statutory basis authorizing the test).

45. Texas Health and Safety Code § 81.102.

46. The survivor of a sexual offense or other crime involving a significant exposure may request that the arrested person submit to an HIV test and consent to release of the test result to the survivor. *See* Ariz. Rev. Stat. Ann. §13-1415.

47. California Penal Code § 1202.1 (persons convicted of a sexual offense) and California Penal Code §1202.6 (persons convicted of prostitution).

48. *See* Colo. Rev. Stat. § 18-3-415 (any adult or juvenile who is bound over for trial for any sexual offense involving sexual penetration).

49. *See* Del. Code Ann. 10, §1076 and 11, § 3911 (the survivor of a sexual assault can request the court to order an HIV test on the accused).

50. *See* Ill Ann. Stat. Ch. 720, § 5/12-18 (same as Delaware).

51. *See* Ind. Code Ann. § 35-38-2-2.3 (requirement of an HIV test as a condition of probation if the person had been convicted of a sex crime or an offense relating to controlled substances).

52. *See* N.C. Gen. Stat. §15A ("If, in an initial appearance hearing, a judicial official finds probable cause that an individual was exposed to a defendant in a manner that poses a significant risk of transmission of the AIDS virus by the defendant, the judicial official shall order the defendant be detained for a period not to exceed twenty-four hours for an investigation and AIDS testing, if required by public health officials.")

53. *See* R.I. Gen. Laws §11-34-10, 21-28-4.2, 42-56-37, 11-37-17, 23-11-12 ("[a]ny person convicted of prostitution or lewdness," "any person convicted of possession of a hypodermic instrument associated with intravenous drug use," "every person committed to an adult correctional institution," and any admitted or convicted sexual offenders. The state also makes it a misdemeanor for a person suspected of transmission of sexually transmitted disease to refuse to submit to an examination).

54. *See* S.C. Code Ann. § 16-15-255 (persons convicted of prostitution).

55. *See* Wash. Rev. Code Ann. §§ 70.24.350 (same as South Carolina).

56. States with criminal laws are Alabama, Arkansas, California, Colorado, Florida, Georgia, Idaho, Illinois, Indiana, Kansas, Kentucky, Louisiana, Maryland, Michigan, Missouri, Montana, Nevada, New Jersey, North Dakota, Ohio, Oklahoma, Pennsylvania, South Carolina, Tennessee, Utah, and Virginia. Wisconsin allows sentence enhancement for punishment of certain sex crimes if the defendant knew that he or she was HIV positive. See further details at <http://aclu.org/issues/aids/HIV_criminalization.html>.

57. *See* Maryland Health-Gen. § 18-601.1.

58. *See* California Health and Safety Code §120291.

59. *See* Colo. Rev. Stat. §18-7-201.7, 205.7.

60. *See* Ky. Rev. Stat. Ann § 311.990.

61. *See* La. Rev. Stat. §14:43.5.

62. *See* Wash. Stat. Ann. §939.622.

APPENDIX A
National and Regional LGBT Legal Groups

APPENDIX B
An Introduction to Law and
the Legal System

INDEX

APPENDIX A

National and Regional LGBT Legal Groups

ACLU Lesbian and Gay Rights Project and AIDS Project

www.aclu.org/issues/gay/hmgl.html
125 Broad Street
New York, NY 10004
Phone: (212) 549-2627
Fax: (212) 549-2650
ACLU state affiliates—see Web site:
http://www.aclu.org/community/community.html

Center for Lesbian and Gay Civil Rights

www.center4civilrights.org
1315 Spruce Street, Suite 301
Philadelphia, PA 19107
Phone: (215) 731-1447
Fax: (215) 731-1544

Gay and Lesbian Advocates and Defenders

www.glad.org
294 Washington Street, Suite 740
Boston, MA 02108
Phone: (617) 426-1350
Fax: (617) 426-3594

Gay, Lesbian, and Straight Education Network

www.glsen.org
121 West 27th Street, Suite 804
New York, NY 10001
Phone: (212) 727-0135
Fax: (212) 727-0254
State chapters—see Web site

Gender PAC

www.gpac.org
1743 Connecticut Ave. NW 4th floor
Washington, DC 20009
Phone: (202) 462-6610
Fax: (202) 462-6744

Human Rights Campaign

www.hrc.org
919 18th Street, NW Suite 8000
Washington, DC 20006
Phone: (202) 628-4160
Fax: (202) 347-5323

Lambda Legal Defense and Education Fund

www.lambdalegal.org
120 Wall Street, Suite 1500
New York, NY 10005-3904
Phone: (212) 809-8585
Fax: (212) 809-0055
Regional offices—see Web site

Lesbian and Gay Immigration Rights Task Force

www.lgirtf.org
350 West 31st Street, #505
New York, NY 10001
Phone: (212) 714-2904
Fax: (212) 714-2973

National Center for Lesbian Rights

www.nclrights.org
870 Market Street, Suite 570
San Francisco, CA 94102
Phone: (415) 392-6257
Fax: (415) 392-8442

National Gay and Lesbian Task Force

www.ngltf.org
2320 17th Street, NW

Washington, DC 20009
Phone: (202) 332-6483
Fax: (202) 332-0207
Policy Institute—see Web site

Servicemembers Legal Defense Network

www.sldn.org
P.O. Box 65301
Washington, DC 20035-5301
Phone: (202) 328-FAIR or (202) 328-3244
Fax: (202) 797-1635

Transgender Law and Policy

www.transgenderlaw.org
(Web site only)

APPENDIX B

An Introduction to Law and the Legal System

Readers will come to this book with many different degrees of experience in, and knowledge about, the legal system. We hope that it will be useful for all readers, including those who have never studied law. The purpose of this appendix is to explain certain basic concepts and to clear up questions that might make it difficult to understand the meaning of what you will read in the main text.

What sources in law provide a basis for saying that I have a "right" to something?

The primary sources of law are constitutions (both the U.S. Constitution and the constitutions of each state) and statutes (federal and state), as they are interpreted and elaborated in judicial decisions.

The U.S. Constitution, of course, is our fundamental charter of government. For our purposes in this book, the most important provisions lie in certain amendments that address the rights of individuals as against the government. Because the Constitution limits the ways in which the government may encroach upon individual liberty, it does not apply at all unless there is state action. This means that the Constitution protects you only against the government, not against purely private organizations or corporations, no matter how large, unless they literally take on the functions of government (e.g., privately run prisons). Merely accepting federal funds does not turn a private organization into a state actor. This concept applies as well to the protections offered by a state constitution.

Statutes are the laws passed by Congress, a state legislature, or a local legislative body. They are much more detailed and specific than the broad general statements in the Constitution. Also, because Congress has the authority (granted to it by the Constitution, of course) to regulate in areas such as commerce and to implement the broad commands contained in the Constitution, its statutes are not restricted to state action. Congress and state legislatures enact innumerable laws that apply to private organizations, employers, landlords, and so forth.

Judicial decisions are the written opinions issued by judges in cases brought by the party who initiates a lawsuit (the plaintiff) against another party (the defendant). Judicial decisions interpret and apply "the law" as contained in previous cases and in constitutional and statutory provisions. As judicial decisions build up over time, they become part of the law (often called "case law") and thus are also subject to interpretation in future cases. Decisions by appellate courts control the decisions of trial-level courts because every judge is bound by the *precedent* of the courts at a higher level within the same state or judicial circuit. Of course, very often the precedent cited by lawyers in a particular case is not clear or directly on point, and thus new decisions with additional interpretations are generated.

Other sources of law include administrative regulations, which are issued by agencies established to implement acts of the legislature. Statutes regulating the workplace, for example, are usually assigned to the Department of Labor for implementation, and the department issues regulations that address specific questions not fully answered in the text of the statute. Sometimes, those regulations are challenged in court, which produces more case law.

What happens if a statute passed by the legislature is challenged as unconstitutional? Who decides?

The judiciary has the final say, because it is vested with the authority and responsibility of applying the Constitution, and the Constitution governs every branch of government. Thus, some court decisions declare statutes to be unconstitutional and, therefore, unenforceable even if they remain on the books.

Can the legislature change the decision of a court?

That depends. If the court decision was an interpretation of a statute or another nonconstitutional principle of law, the legislature can amend the statute to make clear that it wants the provision to be interpreted to mean something different than how the court understood it. In that case, the court decision will be overridden by subsequent legislative action. However, if the court ruled that an act of Congress was unconstitutional, the only way that the outcome of the case can be changed is if the Constitution is amended or if the court decision is overruled.

What are the names of the different courts?

There are two parallel court systems: federal and state. In each, there are trial-level and appellate-level courts. The federal system has three levels. U.S. District Courts are the trial level courts; almost all cases are tried by a single judge at that level. U.S. Courts of Appeal are the intermediate level; these courts are organized by region of the country (which are called *circuits,* as in "the Sixth Circuit"), and arguments on appeal are heard by a three-judge panel. Sometimes, all the judges of a particular circuit will vote to hear an especially important case, which will lead to an *en banc* decision. The highest level, of course, is the U.S. Supreme Court.

There are various configurations of state court systems. Every state system has a trial court level, but they have different names: "Superior Court," or "District Court," or even, in New York, "Supreme Court." Every state system has a final level of appeal, known as the "Supreme Court" in most states but sometimes called "the Court of Appeals." Many states, but not all, also have an intermediate level of appellate court, again with wide variations in the names.

May the U.S. Supreme Court strike down state as well as federal statutes? If so, why?

The U.S. Supreme Court may invalidate a state law only when that law contradicts federal law, ranging from the U.S. Constitution to a federal statute to an administrative regulation. This power is based on the "supremacy clause" of the Constitution, which declares that federal law shall prevail over state law. However, if a state supreme court interprets a state statute to give it a particular meaning, the U.S. Supreme Court will hear the case only if there is some issue of federal law involved. Thus, the state supreme court is the final and highest authority in cases involving only that state's law.

Is the U.S. Constitution my strongest source of rights?

Yes and no. As we have seen, the U.S. Constitution trumps all other law, state and federal, statutory or case law. However, the fact that it applies only to governmental action means that its scope is actually quite limited.

Does the phrase *civil rights laws* have a specific meaning? Does that include the Constitution?

The term *civil rights laws* usually refers to antidiscrimination statutes enacted by a legislature at some level of government: the Congress, a state legislature, or a city or county council. In general, and in this book, that term does not include the Constitution.

What is the difference between a constitutional equality claim and a civil rights law claim?

A constitutional equality claim, or equal protection claim, arises under the clause in the Fourteenth Amendment that forbids any state from "deny[ing] to any person within its jurisdiction the equal protection of the laws."

The body of precedent interpreting the equal protection clause has led to three tiers of review. If a law explicitly discriminates against what the courts have identified as a "suspect class," it will be extremely difficult for the government to defend its validity. Race, religion, and national origin are the primary examples of suspect classes. Any law that classifies on one of those bases must survive *strict scrutiny:*

the government must prove that the law is "necessary" to achieve a "compelling state interest."

The courts have used a less stringent test, *intermediate scrutiny,* when evaluating laws that discriminate on other bases that the courts have found to be usually, but not always, illegitimate. Sex or gender is the primary classification that receives intermediate scrutiny. In those cases, the government must prove that the classification is "substantially related" to an "important governmental interest" to have the law upheld.

The least stringent test is *rational basis review.* Laws that contain the thousands of routine classifications used by the government (in different rules for landlords and tenants, for example) will be found unconstitutional only if they lack a "rational relationship" to a "legitimate state interest." So far, laws that classify on the basis of sexual orientation have been subjected to rational basis review under the U.S. Constitution. (Some state courts, however, have interpreted state constitutions to require intermediate or strict scrutiny in sexual orientation cases.)

Civil rights statutes are structured differently. Most such statutes prohibit discrimination based on a list of characteristics, all of which are equally protected. As stated above, statutes reach private as well as governmental action. Furthermore, many statutes also allow plaintiffs to recover without having to prove that the discrimination was intentional, unlike the U.S. Constitution. In this context, *intentional* means that the legislature or other governmental actor set out specifically to penalize a particular group, which is also called *disparate treatment.* Under most civil rights laws, plaintiffs can also prevail if they show that certain actions had a discriminatory effect, regardless of the explicit purpose behind them, known also as *disparate impact.*

What is my right to privacy based on?

The Supreme Court has recognized a right to privacy based on another clause in the Fourteenth Amendment, which forbids states from "depriv[ing] any person of life, liberty or property, without due process of law." The Court has interpreted that to mean that any law (state or federal) that controls or criminalizes certain aspects of intimate life, depriving an individual of the liberty to control the most personal life decisions, is presumptively unconstitutional, unless the government can show a "compelling" need to impose that regulation.

How can I find copies of the cases and statutes cited in this book?

There are two electronic databases for the retrieval of legal materials (Westlaw and Lexis), but they are expensive and usually accessible only to lawyers and law students. However, the actual books containing these texts are available in any law library and sometimes in other libraries as well. In addition, many are now available on the Web. Professor Dan Pinello has put an "Internet casebook" containing the texts of more than 100 LGBT cases on his web site: www.danpinello.com.

All citations to cases follow the same format: number-abbreviation-number (specific subdivision of a court and date), for example, 92 F.3d 446 (7th Cir. 1996).

The abbreviation tells you which court the decision is from. For example, in the federal system, "U.S." cites are from the Supreme Court, "F.2d" or "F.3d" cites are from courts of appeal, and "F. Supp." or "F. Supp.2d" cites are from district courts.

The first number tells you the volume number of the book in that series, and the second number tells you the page. References within the parenthesis such as "7th Cir." or "3d Dist." tell you the particular division of that level of the court system. The date is the year of decision.

Thus, the citation 92 F.3d 446 (7th Cir. 1996) would send you to the F.3d reporters for U.S. Courts of Appeal (third series), volume 92, and page 446.

In addition, many court systems have posted their decisions on the Web so that they are accessible to the general public for free. Those postings do not usually use the abbreviation format just described but instead require that you search by parties' names and/or dates. The example that we just used is the citation to a real case: *Nabozny v. Podlesny* (involving a gay high school student). You can find it on the Web by going to the Seventh Circuit Web page <http://www.ca7. uscourts.gov>. You may see an occasional citation in this book that uses the abbreviation "WL" or "Lexis." That indicates a case or other source for which we had only a Westlaw or Lexis citation.

Citations to statutes do not follow one format. Some state statutes are retrievable by the name of the particular statute, and others by a variation on the volume-abbreviation-page format used for cases. Federal statutes use the case-like format: 42 U.S.C. § 1234 means volume 42 of the United States Code, at section (not page) 1234. All federal statutes are available for free on the Web <http://uscode.house.gov/usc.htm>. State governments also often have a Web page that links to that state's statutory code.

If I am sure that a legal principle protects me, why do I need a lawyer?

You are, of course, always free to represent yourself. But it is usually a bad idea. Very few cases are open and shut, even if they appear to be at the outset. Uninformed decisions made before you even go to court can return to haunt you, because they carry consequences of which you were unaware. Furthermore, the law constantly changes, in no field more rapidly than this one.

INDEX